"*Jornalero* is a power-packed ethnography of the everyday lives and everyday violence faced by Mexican and Central American undocumented day laborers in a privileged West Coast city. On the street, the men try in vain to turn one-off underpaid jobs into patron-client relationships. Off the strip, they live in solitude, poverty, and chastity while longing for their loves ones. They fear 'la migra' and deportation as much as they fear going home to find that the 'Sancho' has seduced their wife and squandered their remittance money. Ordóñez's nuanced narrative is sympathetic but also frank about the rigid racial and sexual hierarchies held by these men, both among themselves and toward their patrons. *Jornalero* breaks a code of silence about the political and moral economies that shape relations among employers and their casual undocumented day laborers. It is sure to provoke debate among social researchers, activists, and citizens concerned with immigration, inequality, and social justice."

—Nancy Scheper-Hughes, author of *Death without Weeping: The Violence of Everyday Life in Brazil* and coeditor of *Violence at the Urban Margin*

"Ordóñez has written a timely and compelling book about this invisible workforce. Using his razor-sharp ethnographic skills, he takes a close-up look at the lived experiences of these vulnerable, yet determined, hardy men."

—Beatriz Manz, author of *Paradise in Ashes: A Guatemalan Journey of Courage, Terror, and Hope*

"Read this. Carefully documented, superbly argued, and crisply written, this book avoids the celebratory tones of many an account of urban marginality and dissects *la parada* (the corners where day laborers wait for work) as sites of deep-seated vulnerability, racialized exclusion, and abuse—veritable traps where men, while seeking to survive and send much-needed money back home, look for respect and recognition. An indispensable and polemic light on the omnipresent, yet invisibilized, busy lives of day laborers in urban America."

—Javier Auyero, coauthor of *In Harm's Way: The Dynamics of Urban Violence*

"Ordóñez takes us beyond the stereotyped images of lowly unskilled workers and reveals the quiet dignity of these men by sharing the story of their lives pre- and post-migration, as well as the everyday negotiations they engage in to make it in America."

—James Quesada, Professor of Anthropology, San Francisco State University

Jornalero

CALIFORNIA SERIES IN PUBLIC ANTHROPOLOGY

The California Series in Public Anthropology emphasizes the anthropologist's role as an engaged intellectual. It continues anthropology's commitment to being an ethnographic witness, to describing, in human terms, how life is lived beyond the borders of many readers' experiences. But it also adds a commitment, through ethnography, to reframing the terms of public debate—transforming received, accepted understandings of social issues with new insights, new framings.

Jornalero

BEING A DAY LABORER IN THE USA

Juan Thomas Ordóñez

UNIVERSITY OF CALIFORNIA PRESS

University of California Press, one of the most distinguished university presses in the United States, enriches lives around the world by advancing scholarship in the humanities, social sciences, and natural sciences. Its activities are supported by the UC Press Foundation and by philanthropic contributions from individuals and institutions. For more information, visit www.ucpress.edu.

University of California Press
Oakland, California

Library of Congress Cataloging-in-Publication Data

Ordóñez, Juan Thomas, 1976– author.
Jornalero : being a day laborer in the USA / Juan Thomas Ordóñez.
pages cm
Includes bibliographical references and index.
ISBN 978-0-520-27785-4 (cloth : alk. paper)
ISBN 978-0-520-27786-1 (pbk. : alk. paper)
ISBN 978-0-520-95996-5 (ebook)
1. Day laborers—California—Berkeley. 2. Foreign workers, Latin American—California—Berkeley. 3. Illegal aliens—Employment—California—Berkeley. I. Title.
HD5854.2.U6O73 2015
331—dc23 2014041592

Manufactured in the United States of America

24 23 22 21 20 19 18 17 16 15
10 9 8 7 6 5 4 3 2 1

The paper used in this publication meets the minimum requirements of ANSI/NISO Z39.48–1992 (R 2002) (*Permanence of Paper*).

For Mechas, who was there always,
Jacobo, who came along halfway through,
and Elías, who appeared toward the end.
May we never suffer such separation.

No nation is so unfortunate as to think itself inferior to the rest of mankind: few are even willing to put up with the claim to equality.

Adam Ferguson, *An Essay on the History of Civil Society*

Contents

Preface

I sometimes wonder how I ended up spending almost two years of my life sitting on a corner a few minutes away from the place I lived as a graduate student at the University of California, Berkeley. Weary of course work in my second year and pining for an anthropology as I had known it in Colombia—where we were in a sense always "in the field" as students—I started working as a Spanish/English interpreter for the East Bay Sanctuary Covenant. My intent was to work with refugees, using my experience as a strong base for later research on internally displaced persons back home. El Santuario, as it was known to the Central American undocumented migrants I met, is a nonprofit organization that helps people make asylum claims in the Bay Area. I spent a year as an interpreter for Guatemalan, Salvadoran, and, to a lesser degree, Nicaraguan migrants who had "discovered" they were eligible for asylum after entering the United States without inspection; that is, as "illegal" immigrants looking for work (Ordóñez 2014). Because the Sanctuary dealt with people who had few resources, I ended up translating during interviews for many Guatemalan indigenous men for whom Spanish was a second language, a nerve-wracking experience where even well-meaning asylum officers seemed to badger migrants who really could not understand what I was telling them and whose confusion seemed to me to replicate the violence they had already suffered (Ordóñez 2008).

I became fascinated and disturbed by the banality of the interviews I witnessed, where genocide and death were relived by the applicants but also scripted and shaped by bureaucracy. Ultimately I found that those most in need of help seemed at a disadvantage because of the very nature of the experiences that made them eligible for asylum. The absurdities involved in filling out paperwork, appearing like an ideal victim, and even understanding the implications of the results of the process shaped many of the ideas about documentation and rumor that follow. By July 2007, I had decided to study the strange relationship that these migrants established with the state through their asylum applications and the violence the process reproduced. Yet the truth is that I was never at ease with the fact that most asylum seekers I met seemed to associate me with "fixing" their papers, *arreglar papeles* (see also Coutin 2000), and always agreed to share things I thought they should be less forthcoming about.

The morning I officially started my fieldwork, I remember dreading the walk to the Sanctuary and another year of leaching off people's stories in this ambiguous power relationship. Although it sounds apocryphal, I walked out the door that day and, instead of crossing the university campus, took the bus to the informal day labor site where many of the men I had met worked. I had never seen *la parada,* as the Guatemalans called it, but it was not hard to find—down University Avenue and toward the marina, a few blocks to the north, on Hearst Avenue. To my surprise I found several blocks of men standing on the curbs chatting and laughing as they waited for work and, almost immediately, decided to shift my research to this site, not really knowing what I would study but preferring to attempt being just another guy from Latin America on the street and not someone with unreal power over the people I was interested in—and yes, this sounds problematic, but no asylum seeker ever turned his back on me, played cruel jokes at my expense, or picked on me like the day laborers did. Although I continued working with the Sanctuary off and on while I was on the corner, as time went by I realized I had to change most of my original research objectives. In the first place, once I was stripped of my role as interpreter, Guatemalan indigenous men were not apt to engage me in any type of conversation because my own ethnicity—a strange ensemble of class and racial perceptions related to my being the only Colombian, a Spanish-speaking *ladino* or *mestizo,* but also a tall native English speaker—made me suspect in their eyes. A second reason was that upon reviewing the existing research on informal day labor, I found little ethnographic data about what goes on in this now almost ubiquitous part of the contemporary US urban landscape.

The main problem I faced was deciding how to look at the men I met on the corner. The obvious theoretical and thematic turn was to frame them within studies of migrant workers, in a sense to set the labor site within the greater contexts that have made migration a keystone of twenty-first-century academic and political debate. However, as I got to know the men on the corner of Hearst Avenue and Fifth Street better, I became suspicious of many aspects of migrant studies in the United States today. The first was the notion of community as it has come to synthesize much of the "immigrant experience," which tends to be set up as a re-articulation of social networks and has come to include local, global, and transnational arenas of political and social organization (Chavez 1994; Glick-Schiller, Basch, and Blanc 1995; Rosaldo and Flores 1997; Guarnizo and Díaz 1999; Stephen 2007). The men I met had few interactions with each other outside the labor site, had very little contact with people from their own hometowns (many, in fact, were from complex urban areas as it was), and did not have strong ties of friendship and reciprocity in the United States. Typical life in the Bay Area for these men meant being on the corner or staying at home alone—even when they lived in overcrowded dwellings—with little else happening.

At the same time, I could not see myself engaging the problem from a perspective of labor alone because, in the midst of the greatest economic crisis the United States had faced in decades, working conditions were only a part of the world I discovered at *la parada.* The men in these pages are not politically organized, had very little work during the time I was on the corner, and seemed to be increasingly dissociated from their social networks back home. I thus spent two years simply trying to answer the first thing that popped into my mind when I saw the men standing on the curbs: What does it mean to be a migrant day laborer—a *jornalero*—on the streets of Northern California? In trying to answer that question I became a fixture on one particular corner—the Fifth Street corner—where my own experience became etched into the social relations that unfolded there.

People who have a multicultural upbringing—I grew up in Colombia speaking English at home with an American mother and Colombian father, attended a German school, and spent summers in Utah and California—suffer from a kind of cultural schizophrenia (and I mean this in the most unacademic, unscientific, and colloquial way) that makes us good candidates for anthropology but leaves us bereft of a clear-cut identity and very uncomfortable about people's assumptions of how and where we come from. Until the age of twenty-five, when I moved to the United States for graduate school, I had never felt like a stranger in Colombia, where I was simply considered a little weird because I had a *mamá gringa;* or in the United States, where I could, at least as a child, blend in with the "natives" in my mother's world. But as an adult, first in Washington, DC, and then in the Bay Area, I found it hard to understand or relate to the world around me; both the "Anglo American," white United States and the "Hispanic" or "Latino" United States were unrecognizable and somewhat foreign to me. I could not use either as a referent for my own identity and thus truly became "Colombian" in my own mind.

On the corner, this unsettling relationship became an asset for both understanding the migrants I met in the social context we were in and for navigating the strange networks that the men used to get by. Because the jornaleros—mainly Mexican, Guatemalan, and Salvadoran—had few referents to Colombia and thus could not sense my strangeness or completely read me through their own class and ethnic hierarchies, I could at some level be simply another character on the street, *el colombiano,* where my fluency in English and education could not completely alienate me from them because I could effectively argue that no matter the difference, I was closer to them than to *gabachos*—that is, to white folk. Furthermore, both aspects of my own history and personality precluded any association of me with US-born Hispanics, *los pochos,* with whom many of these men have conflictive relationships. In other words, and to play off old truisms, I was neither familiar nor strange to the men I got to know but rather strangely familiar. I think this is one of the guiding forces of what I will account for in the pages to follow, where I am inevitably and intrinsically involved as a participant and witness who spent two years, not only trying to understand everyday life for migrant day laborers, but also learning to joke *a la mexicana* and trying to recognize the vernaculars of so many different regions of Mexico and Central America—places I knew nothing or very little about until I came down from the university and sat on the corner.

Acknowledgments

This book is the product of my relationships with many people and institutions. It could have never been written without the help and interest of the day laborers that appear in these pages and who let me in on their conversations, shared their anxieties, and made fun of me for two years. Three jornaleros were especially important during the time I was a fixture on *la parada.* I have changed their names and muddled their lives out of unease and lack of control over what might be done with this study, but to the people I have called Luis, Eduardo, and Lorenzo I am greatly indebted. They took me in on the corner, introduced me to people and issues that are central to what I have written, and always treated me openly and disinterestedly for reasons I cannot quite explain. To Luis especially, I would like to extend my thanks for teaching me to joke *a la mexicana,* for inviting me into his home, for keeping in touch, and in general, for being the best friend I made in eight years in the United States.

In a similar vein I would like to thank my own family, since their presence and support gave me a home to come back to in the evenings and made fieldwork and graduate school worthwhile. My wife, Mechas—to whom the book is dedicated—not only survived my graduate studies relatively unscathed but also made them fun and exciting. She is my biggest supporter, strongest critic, and partner in every sense of the word. My son, Jacobo, will never be able to imagine how much easier he made it for me on and off the street, both because he provided new challenges and entertainment that anthropology cannot and because his birth allowed me to talk with my friends on the corner about fatherhood and children. Elías, who came along afterward, kept me company and brought me books to read when everything else seemed topsy-turvy. Annie, Daniël, later on Sarah, my uncles Juan and Tom, and everyone else in the Ordóñez and Roth clans are all hidden in between these lines. Annie, especially, deserves recognition for surviving her older brother for so many years and shaping his outlook on life in ways he will never again own up to publicly. My parents, Julia Anna Roth and Jaime Iván Ordóñez, set the stage for my time in Berkeley about forty years ago when they met there as graduate students. Their influence is present in every aspect of my life. Hugo, Elfi, Barbara Lynch, and Art Flores, you mean "Berkeley" in my mind and heart.

Two NGOs provided incalculable help during my time in the Bay Area, which started with an exploration of Central American asylum seekers and finally led me to the street corner. To the East Bay Sanctuary Covenant, its directors, and staff, I am infinitely grateful for the crash course in asylum policies, the realities of the asylum application, and their effects on various populations living in Northern California. My work with the day laborers in Berkeley also would not have been possible without the help, friendship, and guidance of the Multicultural Institute that accompanies the jornaleros on a daily basis and relentlessly looks out for them. Father Rigoberto Caloca-Rivas, Paula Worby, Rudy Lara, David Cobián, and all the people who work with them truly make a difference in the lives of these day laborers. Ever present in my mind is their preoccupation that I have overemphasized the negative aspects of the lives of men they see struggling every day to find a place in the United States and a better life; all I can say in my defense is this is what they talked about when I was there. I am especially indebted to Paula Worby, whose own work on the *esquina* paved the way for my research and whose interest and feedback I always welcome.

I am greatly indebted to Nancy Scheper-Hughes, my advisor and mentor. Her guidance helped me through the gray areas of contemporary anthropology and truly provided a sense of home that is lacking in many great academic institutions. Her diligence and interest in my work has always been my greatest encouragement. Philippe Bourgois also played a key role in my academic development and I cannot thank him enough for the straightforward—sometimes even violently funny—advice and comments on my work. At different stages of my research I also had the opportunity of working with Beatriz Manz and Loïc Wacquant, whose mentorship and interest were essential in the ways that I came to engage the field. I am also grateful to Mariane Ferme for introducing me to the anthropology of the political. Before Berkeley, Barbara Miller, Catherine Allen, Stephen Lubkemann, and Richard Grinker at the George Washington University introduced me to writing anthropology in English and gave me my first taste of medical anthropology, migration studies, and Andean ethnography. I am happy to say I have returned to the last subject in a roundabout way.

My graduate studies and fieldwork were funded by various fellowships from the graduate division of the University of California, Berkeley. I am also grateful to UC Berkeley's Human Rights Center for a Human Rights Fellowship (2006) that funded the preliminary research that led me to the corner. I would also like to acknowledge the hard work and friendship of my fellow graduate students Shana Harris, Alfred Montoya, Marc Goodwin, Stephan Kloos, Dan Husman, Erin Mahaffey, and Emily Wilcox. Their feedback on early versions of some of the material herein helped me get a sense of what I was trying to achieve. It was Alfred, after all, who suggested as a joke that I use "street corner cosmopolitanism" as a category.

Back in Colombia I have received further feedback from my colleagues and friends Diana Bocarejo, Maria José Alvarez, Bastien Bosa, Esteban Rozo, Laura Ordóñez, and Nadia Rodriguez. In truth, their commentaries in our Social Sciences Colloquium at the Universidad del Rosario greatly influenced the structure the book took as I wrote. The Universidad del Rosario also provided ample institutional support and I am greatly indebted to the dean of the School of Human Sciences—Escuela de Ciencias Humanas—Stéphanie Lavaux, for time to work on the manuscript, her encouragement, and sound advice. For four years I have also had "victims" of sorts; students who have patiently listened to too many of my stories, read some of what I have written, and, like my friends on the corner would appreciate, showed me the need of great *humildad* in what

I do. I am sure none of them would believe me. To Fabio Colmenares, Michelle Gracia, Andres Vargas, and Ana Bolena Pedroza I am especially indebted in this sense, and I look forward to seeing what they make of their own experiences in the field. I would also like to thank friends past and present, especially my brothers in arms Santiago Rohenes and Luis Cayón, for everything that cannot be said or written.

Finally, I cannot thank Naomi Schneider and her team at the University of California Press enough for their patience, encouragement, and hard work on the manuscript. I am also grateful to the anonymous reviewers who commented on different stages of the book and those who reviewed two articles that I have meshed into various chapters. Part of chapter 5 was originally published in *Culture Health and Sexuality* as "'Boots for My Sancho': Structural Vulnerability among Latin American Day Labourers in Berkeley, California" (Ordóñez 2012), and some of the last section appeared in a much earlier form in the *Revista de Antropología Social* as "Documentos e indocumentados: Antropología urbana, inmigración y ciudadanía" (Ordóñez 2013). My aunt Claudia was, as she always has been, the first filter for both these articles and many of the chapters herein. Much of the material was presented in various conferences, where I received feedback and suggestions from many people. I would especially like to thank Jim Quesada and Robert Desjarlais who commented on drafts as "discussants" on AAA panels. Jim has also been a great source of support when we have crossed paths since my move back to Colombia. All photographs herein are my own.

A Brief Note on Language

Day laborers of different backgrounds refer to the labor site in distinctive ways. I came to the Berkeley site knowing it as *la parada,* the term the Guatemalan men used when they told me about their work as we waited in the asylum office. After almost four months of hanging out at the Berkeley *parada,* I realized that the unexplained snickers the word aroused among my Mexican and Salvadoran friends were the product of the play on words that also makes *parada* an erection. The verb *parar* in Spanish means "to stop" but can also mean "to stand," as in *estar parado.* Many vernaculars play on this second meaning to connote an erection. *"¿Parada? Más bien esquina. ¿O la tienes parada?"* my friends joked, even as I corrected myself with exasperation. I was never able to completely avoid the mistake and instead use the more neutral term *esquina,* literally "corner," which does not describe the entirety of the situation. Day laborers, after all, stand along the curb of a long stretch of roadway, not only on a "corner." I allow the sexual connotation of the labor site to stand in my work, for as I discuss later, sexual word plays, sexuality, and gender are an integral part of these day laborers' lives. The terms "the corner," "the site," *la esquina,* and *la parada* all refer to the same physical space and I use them interchangeably.

Day laborers use different terms to describe themselves and their work. The closest translation to "day laborer" is the Spanish *jornalero,* which is the most common word used on the street. *Jornalero* shares the same etymology as "journey" and "journeyman," but the central connotation that matters here is the term "day," which in terms of labor in Spanish can be *jornal,* used both to describe "a day's labor" and "a day's wage." *Jornalero* is also the official translation of "day laborer" used by the Cities of Berkeley and Oakland on the signs they post to direct the men and their employers to the appropriate parts of the street where they should interact. People also use *esquinero,* meaning "the man who stands on the corner." This term was not as common at the Berkeley site, and only men who had been jornaleros quite a long time used it. *Jornalero* more clearly denotes the link between Latin American labor relations in both rural and urban landscapes, while *esquinero* is particular to day labor in cities. Finally, many refer to themselves as *un leibor,* meaning "a day laborer," in a way that ties them to the English term but also suggests their commodification. In this vague Anglicization, jornaleros seem to bypass the connotation of person and focus on themselves as a unit of labor. In general, readers will find that I latinize English colloquially following the ways any Spanish speaker with no knowledge of English would try to make it sound and based on their own orthography. This, I find, closely represents the way the men I met use English words when speaking Spanish.

Employers are as ubiquitous in street parlance as the corner and its inhabitants. Here everyone agrees on the term *patrón* or its feminized version *patrona.* These derive from the same Latin root as "patron" in English and in Latin America denote more than just your boss, actually something closer to the person who owns your labor and to whom you owe allegiance and depend on for sustenance. Latin American day laborers of all nationalities refer to their employers as *mi patrón,* which makes the relationship sound exclusive when in reality no man has only one employer, because by definition a jornalero sells his labor to different people on a daily basis.

Finally, there is the term "migrant" itself. Contemporary academic literature likes to call attention to the implications of using the terms "migrant" or "immigrant" to denote people like the jornaleros I studied. De Genova (2005) suggests that "immigrant" and "immigration" have a unidirectional connotation, where population movement is skewed from the viewpoint of the receiving state and understood as the arrival of outsiders. The term "migrant," he argues, does away with the directionality and finality of "immigration." This in fact is my take on the issue as well, since other middle-ground attempts to use terms like "im/migrant" (e.g., Worby and Organista 2007) seem less effective in doing away with the problems they attempt to correct. Like De Genova and others, I think the term "migrant" more clearly denotes the multiple sides of migration and, especially, the notion of movement, which for the men I studied was greatly hindered but central to how they understood themselves. I thus use "migrant" except when referring to "immigration" from the standpoint of the US government, its laws, and policies. That said, the term "migrant" is to some degree ethnographically inaccurate, because on the street, jornaleros used the Spanish *inmigrante,* or "immigrant," to refer to themselves. I would rather not obsess over the tensions in word choice, then, in part because it was as common in everyday speech to hear people talk about *mojados*—wetbacks—or *ilegales*—illegals—terms that no academic would seriously use to refer to these men. I retain some such references, with their ambiguous relationship to the politics of representation, in order to leave intact these men's "in your face" responses to their own marginalization.

Introduction

The last two decades have seen a dramatic rise in the number of informal day labor sites throughout the continental United States, to the point that they have become a ubiquitous presence in most of the country's urban areas. These *paradas* or *esquinas*—as day laborers call them in Spanish—are usually inhabited by migrant Latin American men, mostly recent "undocumented" migrants, who stand on the curbside of outlying traffic corridors or in the parking lots of mega retail stores, waiting for someone to stop and hire them. In California, which has one of the highest number of undocumented migrants in the country (Valenzuela 2003; Hoefer, Rytina, and Campbell 2006), day laborers work on construction sites, paint or work on houses and offices, maintain gardens, move furniture, and do other odd jobs. Although historically grounded in much older socioeconomic processes and labor relations, both in the United States and in Latin America (e.g., Vanackere 1988; Townsend 1997; Ngai 2004; De Genova 2005), day labor today is embedded in the post-9/11 political and social climate and shaped by increasing control over the criminalized status of "illegal immigrants" (Andreas 2003; Inda 2006; De Genova and Peutz 2010). Because day laborers literally stand in plain view—unlike other undocumented migrants who work behind the scenes in factories, restaurants, or in domestic capacities—they have come to embody popular stereotypes of the "undesirable immigrant" who has entered the country illegally from Mexico, is unassimilated, and publicly engages in the shadow labor market in a way that is detrimental to the national economy (Esbenshade 2000; Chavez 2001). And while new sites seem to appear everywhere overnight and even make the news once in a while, day laborers are relatively absent from most studies on migration in this country.

This absence might have to do with a politics of representation in the social sciences, not only of migrants, but also of the poor in general. In an effort to demonstrate the social value of marginalized populations, researchers and activists alike tend to emphasize the organization and structure of these groups and to focus on their cultural, ethnic, and political links to social movements striving for inclusion. This, in part, is a response to earlier sociological approaches to poverty that centered on the idea of "aberrance" as a key factor of marginalization, effectively blaming the disenfranchised—usually racialized minorities—for their lot and politically constructing poverty as a product of chaos to be acted upon and ordered. Edward Banfield (1958), for example, addressed poverty in southern Italy as the effect of "amoral familism," which, in conjunction with the particular form of the Italian state, rendered people unable to have economic and community-oriented behavior that would enable the development of financially progressive practices. Poverty, in this perspective, was a function of aberrant cultural practices that affected the social, psychological, and political development of the region.

The now classical "street corner" ethnographies like William Foote Whyte's *Street Corner Society* (1993 [1943]), Elijah Anderson's *A Place on the Corner* (2003 [1976]), and Elliot Liebow's *Tally's Corner* (2003 [1967]) all set out, in part, to argue against notions related to "aberrance" and to demonstrate that there were internal rationalities that structured social interactions behind the behavior of the people—all members of the "underclass"—that they studied. Rationality as opposed to chaos was also the intent of Oscar Lewis's (1966, 1961) concept of the "culture of poverty," which suggested that the poor's responses and attitudes toward the structures of inequality to which they were subjected were perpetuated through the socialization of children, thus constituting the development of particular subcultural traits. Tragically, perspectives like Lewis's were also used "against" the poor in policies that—like in the infamous Moynihan Report—took the disorganization of African American life as the result of self-perpetuating cultural practices, disputing the idea that they were only the effect of discrimination, unemployment, or poor living conditions. This meant that policy had to address the psychosocial conditions of individuals and not the structural constraints to which they were subjected (Parker and Kleiner 1970: 516–517). Many reactions to these blame-the-victim approaches tend to overdetermine the effectiveness of responses to poverty in daily life, thus centering on friendship, alternative ways of understanding family, political articulation, social movements, and participation in illegal activities as a form of subsistence and empowerment.

Paradas, on the other hand, are messy places frequented by men who are usually strangers to each other and who many times live in distant neighborhoods and only congregate where their labor might be needed. Informal day labor sites are, in other words, complex settings where it is hard to find processes of social organization that could result, for example, in political mobilization or even strong support networks among peers. The nature of day labor makes such processes virtually impossible because there is a constant tension between individual gain and peer support that, at least in Berkeley, destined all association between jornaleros to disintegration. It is thus hard to make arguments about social mobilization and political organization among the men, whose visibility on the street—dark, many times dirty and destitute men—also makes them somewhat shady characters.

Jornaleros' inability to develop steady working conditions that provide economic and emotional stability and increase agency to act in the worlds they inhabit make them more likely than other migrants to end up on the street without any form of protection and at the mercy of "the whole domain of infelicities and excuses on the part of the state" (Das 2004: 227). Yet some of the few ethnographic texts on day laborers spend a great deal of time and energy linking the sites to social organization (Malpica 2002), community formation (Pinedo Turnovsky 2006), and resistance to externally managed labor centers (Purser 2009). That these insipient forms of association lack any political or social clout explains why elsewhere in the literature on migration, day laborers seem to appear only tangentially, as members of a more general category of migrant—the undocumented Hispanic or Latino migrant, for example—in more community- or even neighborhood-oriented studies (e.g., Dohan 2003).

This book takes a very different perspective. By choosing—rather finding—a site where migrants were not closely related and where national and regional origins varied, I offer a scenario that is closer to most contemporary urban settings; that is, an array of people living and working in a world they inhabit as individuals and whose understanding of the social, political, and economic conditions that affect them is compartmentalized and fractured (Ferguson 1999: 21). I follow the daily lives of two dozen Latin American day laborers working on the streets of Berkeley and present a more disjointed picture of what it means to live as an undocumented migrant, one in which social and political organization, and even friendship, are trumped by the very intense structures of exclusion to which jornaleros in Northern California—not the worst place to be undocumented in the United States—are subordinate. In doing so, I explore various spheres of experience—labor, exploitation, urban living, family life, gender, sexuality, and the ambiguous nature of being undocumented—linking them to debates about immigration, poverty, violence, and citizenship.

This ethnography offers a glimpse into the experience and daily lives of migrant Latin American men in the shifting political and social arena of immigration in the United States. I explore the ways in which this particular population can effectively live and work in Northern California without having access—or even the interest or will to gain access—to forms of organization that might help improve their lot. It is not too often that anthropologists and other academics stop to look at the mechanism through which people are unable to come together in any recognizable form. Harsh competition among peers, real and imagined state persecution, and the structural constraints implied in being *solo un mojado,* or "just a wetback," come together, collude even, to shape the experience of men whose efforts to sustain themselves and their families inevitably fracture their relations to loved ones and disarticulate their self-image. With this I hope to push migration studies to consider the darker sides of some of the issues they tend to focus on. To wit: interconnection, resilience, agency, contestation, even social organization. To redeem the image of "migrants" we produce through our studies can hide the fact that not all social groups are offered redemption, even in liberal Northern California where "everyone is welcome," as well as in other less cosmopolitan regions of the United States and elsewhere. In the bastions of democracy and enlightenment that so often like to preach to others about the right way to do things, there are very effective, violently efficient in fact, articulations of labor, law, and social sanction of inequality (often hidden as tolerance of diversity) that generate an expendable labor force that is easily kept on the margins of inclusion, in part through its own agency.

Jornaleros must compete with each other. No matter how supportive they appear, they are, by the nature of their labor and living conditions, always at odds with one another, or at least trying to maintain some fiction of stability in a tense and fragile system of social relations that can shatter easily. The environment in which they live and work is one where even men with enough interest in and sense of justice find themselves drowning in the dangerous waters of bureaucracy, where the banality of the "runaround" they get comes together with the fears of making themselves too visible. Finally, there is an argument about the role of rumor in the governance of this population that emerges toward the end of this account but that is latent throughout the chapters. Living the situations I describe—what the men in fact refer to as their *situación*—implies making decisions, some banal, others life changing, based on information that travels strange paths of uncertainty and shape-shifts constantly, to the point that the "reality" of an event can become so distorted that it loses its original content. This is made worse by the fact that such realities—shaped by rumors—seem to find validation in the men's interpretations of their own experiences and in the feedback and confirmation they receive from others' interpretation of similar events.

Rumors are set aside by immigration agents, the police, and other institutions as the product of misinformation: "We were looking for a particular person we knew was in the building, it's not our fault people thought we were coming for them and their children," to succinctly paraphrase some reactions to the *migra* panic I describe in chapter 7. But it is actually the very real certainty that immigration officers can appear anywhere, even potentially come into schools and take minors—"disappear them" as jornaleros used to refer to it on the corner—that keeps people in place and ultimately enables the relations and discrimination I describe. After all, undocumented migrants continue to be seen as transgressors—*they* came here uninvited, *they* crossed the border, *they* broke the law—in a way that ignores the greater context within which these men come to and live in this country.

For me, while on the street, it became absurd to hear immigration debates on the news or to discuss the issue with people who engaged me in conversation off the corner. I saw no reason to address the "What should we do about immigration?" or "How should we control it?" questions that were, and still are, central to much of US politics. A week on the corner would show anyone that immigration is perfectly under control. What is being done is effective in keeping a needed and very cheap labor force on the margins of US society.

IMMIGRATION USA

Immigration, both as a national narrative and as part of the juridical political order, has always been central to the production of notions of US citizenship and has defined the parameters that distinguish "legal" and "illegal" aliens (Rosaldo 1994; Flores 1997; De Genova 2005; Inda 2006). Such distinctions are—not surprisingly—also tied to the country's distribution of labor and production as they are inscribed through foreign and domestic policy into the greater context of global capitalism. Migrant fluctuations in the twentieth century have thus been linked to the distribution of low-wage and high-wage jobs. The two world wars, the Great Depression, and other political and economic junctures can all be linked to shifting tendencies in migration patterns; both legal and illegal, depending on the need for different types labor (Heyman 1990; Ngai 2004). These events can also, of course, be tied to particular immigration laws and politics that fluctuate in an ongoing dance off between migrant-friendly policies—including guest worker programs—and political environments that mobilize anti-immigration sentiments and encourage the stigmatization of migrants as social pariahs (Sacks 1994; Esbenshade 2000; Sayad 2004).

From the 1950s to early 1960s, the United States saw a shift from a predominantly European and high-wage-earning legal migrant population to low-wage-earning migrants from countries of the so called Third World. Sassen (1988: 83–96) ties this change to fluctuations in global capitalism and a US labor market depleted by the reduction of domestic rural to urban migration within the country and the politicization of traditional low-wage workers such as African Americans, Puerto Ricans, Chicanos, and the like. During the same period, Latin America and other regions went through a process of proletarianization, which led a great number of people into wage labor in ways that reconfigured structures of production and social organization—like feminizing the workforce in many settings—that also set the stage for migration to the United States.

Globalization has rearticulated the relations of production, the flow of capital, and migration patterns throughout the world, outsourcing certain types of unskilled labor from the industrialized centers of the North Atlantic (Sassen 1988; Trouillot 2003; Ong 2006), while at the same time concentrating vast populations of service sector and informal workers in its urban centers (Sassen 1999; Zlolniski 2006). Thus, along with the concentration of financial, management, and service sector industries in some of the world's main urban areas, these global cities attract an increasing number of unskilled and marginalized laborers—many times migrants—who enter the labor market through the subsequent process of urban expansion and gentrification. The building industry, specialty markets and restaurants, and cleaning and servicing sectors all expand and require vast amounts of workers whose language skills and know-how need not be elaborate (Sassen 1988: 145). Zlolniski (2006) has analyzed this phenomenon in the links between Silicon Valley and the expanding informal labor market that must inevitably sustain its infrastructure. In his rendering, low-skilled service sector jobs tied to the technology industry—those that cannot be exported, such as janitorial work—open up work settings for unskilled migrant populations, which in Northern California have been mainly Mexicans and other Latin Americans. He looks at the various aspects of this articulation of labor and the political and social mobilizations it makes possible. Globalization and its flows of capital and technology have thus restructured labor relations at a local level, where migrants and their descendants emerge as a particular version of the labor force that to some degree goes hand in hand with the lumpenization of other parts of the region's one-time proletarian African American and white laborers (Bourgois and Schonberg 2009).

The effects of the rise of urban centers of finance and power, however, are diverse and contradictory. While global cities have provided spaces of political mobilization for the disenfranchised and marginal, they have also reshaped the structural reproduction of inequality in ways that ultimately tie social exclusion back into the world economy (De Genova 2005). Migration studies, again, seems to counterweigh poverty and exclusion with emergent political organization and the restructuring of traditional household, gender, and kinship ties that enable the inscription of migrants into an increasingly multicultural configuration of politics and culture (Hondagneu-Sotelo 1994; González-López 2005; Smith 2005). While I acknowledge the importance of these perspectives, my own experience on the street led me to wonder about much of the optimism, sometimes overt, many times tacit, that can be read between the lines of these studies, even in light of their critical perspectives. During the financial crisis of 2007–2008, within which this ethnography is set, many of the migrants I met "looked" different from what other scholars have described. Jornaleros were part of a particularly gendered cohort of migrants, all men among men; "households" were not common and were limited to a few brothers or cousins living together; and political organization was not only nonexistent but talked about as undesirable. Furthermore, this gendered cohort of workers was not concentrated geographically in bounded labor camps that would explain such characteristics (e.g., Ramphele 1993; Benson 2008). The men, in fact, were "free" to choose their places of residence, the corners they stood on, and neighborhoods they lived in, and they had access—theoretically—to certain services. While labor centers, legal aid, and medical and other services were available to jornaleros, the very conditions of these men's lives structured the impossibility of effectively using them in most cases.

THE SANCTITY OF SANCTUARY IN THE POST-9/11 ERA

That I see jornaleros as inherently devoid of political or social recognition does not mean they exist within a social vacuum. The configurations of urban living described above, in the United States, have given rise to social movements for migrant recognition and protection that affect some aspects of everyday life for the men I studied. The Bay Area's generally liberal outlook on most political issues set it at the heart of the sanctuary movement that in the 1980s sought to counteract the federal government's reticence to grant asylum or other protected status to Guatemalan and Salvadoran migrants fleeing US-sponsored civil wars (Coutin 1993; Loescher 1993; Bilke 2009). Cities like San Francisco and Berkeley passed local resolutions explicitly aimed at providing safe haven for people who otherwise might be deported back to a war zone. These resolutions grew into citywide policies that generally dissuaded local law enforcement and government officials from asking any person about immigration status, thus guaranteeing, to some extent, that migrants would feel confident about reporting crime to the police and, in general, feel free from persecution based on their degree of documentation. Sanctuary cities have also promoted policies that destabilize the social exclusion of undocumented migrants. Some US cities have proposed issuing the undocumented municipal IDs, including driver's licenses in some places, like New York City (Bilke 2009); more recently, California passed laws to help integrate foreign nationals of all kinds (Medina 2013), including providing an as yet undefined driving permit for undocumented migrants (Hurtado and Shoiche 2013). Under the argument that formally identifying this population regularizes their activities, facilitating their life—like allowing them to open bank accounts, as I discus in chapter 6—these IDs contest the general move in the country to disallow the use of official IDs to people who are "illegal."

While these practices fit into arguments about how rights, citizenship, and the political representation of marginalized minorities have become rearranged, especially within cities (Holston and Appadurai 1999; Sassen 2000; Holston 2008), they also serve to "confuse" the situation. In the Bay Area, sanctuary policies lead some people to believe that "undocumented" migrants are not harassed or sought by the US Immigration and Customs Enforcement agency (ICE), the enforcement branch of the US Department of Homeland Security that for the most part Latin American migrants call *la migra*. The assumption that migrants are free from ICE or any other federal agencies aiming to control immigration, however, is not true in any sense. For *la migra* conducts targeted raids in factories, restaurants, and other places, even within the boundaries of sanctuary cities where police officers are still required by law to inform any warrant-issuing institutions if they come across somebody whose name is in the system (Bilke 2009: 177). It is not surprising, then, that in the May 2006, 2007, and 2008 immigration marches in Oakland and San Francisco, both sanctuary cities, one of the most common chants was *"La migra, la policía, la misma porquería,"* that is, "*La migra* and the police are the same filth."

This conflation of federal and local institutions into one hegemonic entity of surveillance and control is not simply a perception migrants have, but rather the effect of the hypercriminalization of migrants in the last decades. Especially in the aftermath of the September 11, 2001, terrorist attacks, "illegal" immigration mutated in political discourse from a problem of labor and social resources to one of national security. The 9/11 Commission Report concluded, among other things, that to keep the country safe, control over the borders had to be achieved, and the report thus summoned local authorities to aid in the enforcement of immigration law (National Commission on Terrorist Attacks upon the United States 2004). Enforcement and surveillance were stepped up almost immediately after the attacks, and in 2002 the Department of Homeland Security made internal control of "undocumented immigrants" a priority (Aldana 2008: 1084). New policies effectively increased the problematization of the United States/Mexico and United States/Canada borders and generated an unprecedented increase in border policing. Since 9/11 the geography of the border has effectively shifted from relatively safe passages to dangerous dessert crossings ruled by drug- and migrant-smuggling mafias. Death on the border due to harsh conditions and violence thus increased dramatically (Inda 2006; Andreas 2003). People not only die abandoned in the dessert, or in the crossfire of gang and drug violence; they are now the victims of more elaborate crimes, like kidnapping and being held for ransom—usually demanded of family in the United States (Lacey 2009). Finally, as any middle-aged jornalero can attest, the price of crossing has increased exponentially, making the investment of migrating—with money borrowed from family, friends, loan sharks, or banks—an uncertain endeavor with no guarantee of returns and many possibilities of economic and personal loss.

But within the country, this new era of migrant surveillance has had the confounding effect of destabilizing the role and activities of different institutions that come into contact with migrant populations. Calling the police when in need might land a person in jail, some people say, and they can never be sure if the officers in the particular place are "racist" or not. This is in fact the rationale many men use to navigate the puzzling geography in the Bay Area, where they might not notice a change in the urban landscape while crossing from a sanctuary-rich environment to one without any such policies. In this brave new world of uncertainty, migrants come to doubt any and every institution they encounter, from the police to NGO staff, social workers, banks, pro bono legal aid, and—at least on the streets of Berkeley—even university students who take pictures or interview people. All such encounters can potentially result in a visit from *la migra,* because people on the corner explain unwarranted interactions with police and ICE as the results of giving out personal information of any kind. "Reality" on the corner thrives on rumor, and multiple stories about arrest, deportation, and disappearance abound on the street. These perceptions set the stage for how jornaleros understand their experience. *La situación*—the situation or the current state of things—is a function of how these men's conditions of labor become inscribed in ambiguous practices of doubt and fear.

LA SITUACIÓN: EVERYDAY VIOLENCE ON THE CORNER

Jornaleros are thus integrated into the labor system in that they respond to market demands as a cheap alternative to legal and responsibly hired manual labor. They are, in other words, cost effective from the perspective of a society that has done little to train or provide them with social, economic, and political rights (Burawoy 1976; De Genova 2005). Their marginality assures their inability to access legalization processes and/or to effectively contest the effects of changing perceptions about migrant workers in times of economic stagnation. As will become clear in these pages, jornaleros also find themselves "on the edge," so to speak, closer in many ways to becoming lumpenized (Bourgois and Schonberg 2009), as the destitute alcoholic *borrachitos* they share the street with can attest.

On the corner a person can have a good month and make quite a bit of money—enough to send some home and still buy clothes and pay cell phone and other bills—and then, only a few weeks later, literally be out on the street. This precariousness is a function not only of the economy but of the ways the men handle money, their inability to effectively counter employer abuse, their state of mind—all elements that come under the sphere of experience jornaleros refer to as *la situación.* Although this term literally means "the [economic, labor] situation" in most cases, it is used ambiguously to describe the current state of a person's life—the accumulated result of all the things he must deal with. *La situación* points to the combination of structural and intimate constraints that day laborers must navigate in day-to-day life, the petty violence of everyday existence as marginal subjects in US society. Day laborers' *situación* can include the lack of work opportunities, low wages, employer abuse, health problems, family life, and political aspects like police control over public space and the proximity of the state's repression machinery, embodied in *la migra.* *La situación* is a naturalized condition, to a certain degree external to the men's ideas about the reach of their own agency, and thus paradoxically constitutes an internalized expression of their social exclusion, what Pierre Bourdieu has called symbolic violence (Bourdieu 2000; Bourdieu and Wacquant 2004). For jornaleros in the Bay Area, symbolic violence articulates the reproduction of greater societal structures of exclusion through the men's own agency in ways that relate to the racialization of the poor and their relation to state and local social services (Quesada 2011).

The central theme of my work follows the *everyday violence* that life on the corner entails. Philippe Bourgois and Nancy Scheper-Hughes have attempted to distinguish types of violence—political, structural, symbolic, and everyday violence—to discern the nuance and complexity inherent in any approach to marginalization and oppression, and to avoid "blaming the victim" and grand-scale assumptions about their structural production (Scheper-Hughes 1997; Bourgois 2004; Bourgois and Scheper-Hughes 2004). Political violence is set up as physical violence and terror administered by official (state) authorities and those opposing them (Bourgois 2004: 426). Structural violence relates to the structural effects of poverty; it constitutes political-economic oppression and inequality as they are deployed in historical contexts (Scheper-Hughes 1992; Bourgois 2003). Symbolic violence is taken from Bourdieu as internalized legitimations of inequality related to class power; it is coercion and oppression that are not recognized as such but are actually consented to by the dominated (Bourdieu 2000: 170). This stems from the fact that dominated and dominating groups are incorporated forms of the general structure of relations of power and hence use the same framework of understandings in order to perceive and evaluate life. Symbolic violence is the internalization of gender, ethnic, and class differences that become "natural." Finally, everyday violence is an elaboration of how the other three types interrelate in the day-to-day, intimate experience of marginalization (Scheper-Hughes 1992, 1996). For the day laborers in these pages, labor problems, employer abuse, state repression, and estrangement and isolation from friends and family come together in a single sphere of experience and give rise to a particular version of reality where exaggeration, fear, rumor, hearsay, and threats set the pace for everyday life.

I thus draw on jornaleros' conditions of poverty and exclusion to provide an account of what it means to be a migrant Latin American man working on the streets in Northern California. I address the ways in which the labor site, and the work with which it is associated, determine the social relations that jornaleros establish with one another, their employers, and other people with whom they share the same urban space. The above forms of violence interrelate, blend into each other, and ultimately shape the experience of the people I studied. And yet jornaleros' experiences do not seem violent enough to warrant such a framework, unless we consider the links between day laborers and what Taussig (1986) has called the "culture of terror." Here the normative mediums of experience lie in the precarious condition in which day labor is embedded, where at any given moment life can come crumbling down, where reality and illusion are mediated by rumors that make hearsay fact and vice versa. Representations and experience are the vehicles of an indirect form of domination from which migrants cannot escape. Within this landscape lie their personal relations, work, health, masculinity, and sense of belonging—both in the United States and at home with the families they have left behind. Everyday life for the jornaleros is embedded in activities that threaten their health, emotional stability, and ability to survive and support their families. This vulnerability, coupled with the tensions inherent in long-term separation from loved ones, inevitably results in the fracture of identity for men who must provide for people that depend on their absence.

WHY NOT TRANSNATIONALISM?

Over the last thirty years or so, studies of migration to the United States and elsewhere have emphasized the transnational links that migrants maintain with their countries and regions of origin (Glick-Schiller, Basch, and Blanc 1995; Kearney 1995; Levitt 2001; Levitt and Glick-Schiller 2004; Fog Olwig 2007; Stephen 2007). These studies have provided nuanced analyses of the multiple and variegated ways in which people's movements across national, regional, and also social and ethnic boundaries come to shape both the experience of migrant communities and the physical and social space they inhabit. My objective here is not to question the degree to which transnational, transborder, and other such categories exist, but rather to offer a scenario where the flows in these relations have become stagnant. For the jornaleros I studied, the transnational has in many ways become a fiction of relations they can no longer sustain. Post-9/11 immigration policies, border surveillance, and the border's effective conversion into a war zone, along with the economic downturn of the first decade of the twenty-first century, have made the back and forth that "transnational" physically implies in terms of movement very dangerous, expensive, and almost impossible from the perspectives of the people migrating. When I met them on the corner in Berkeley, men who used to travel seasonally or for short periods of time to work in the Bay Area—what others have called "sojourn immigrants" (Massey 1986; Hondagneu-Sotelo 1994)—were entering their fourth to seventh year without returning to their home countries. Interconnectedness for them was limited to timed phone calls, bimonthly remittances, and the highly problematic perceptions held by all those involved of what life in the United States really entailed. While these relations to the men's home countries make the men part of something "transnational," the feeling on the street was one of loss and increasing estrangement. Globalization, for the jornaleros, has consolidated them into cosmopolitan subjects of sorts, transnational migrants in theory, while it has simultaneously trapped them within the boundaries of the United States and subjected them to both real and imagined practices of state repression and social isolation.

RACE ON THE CORNER

Some readers of early drafts of this book commented on the problematic portrayal of race relations in it. They feel I have not done enough to address the fact that the jornaleros in these pages are openly and vocally biased in their assessment of the racial hierarchy of employers they use to measure risk and in their general racism toward *morenos* (African Americans and anyone considered black), *chinos* (anyone considered Asian), and *árabes* (anyone considered Middle Eastern). I hope even a cursory reading will illustrate the structural position these men find themselves in, where their own notions about race and ethnicity become entangled with the violent and many times incomprehensible racialization all migrants undergo when they cross the border into the United States (see also De Genova 2005). Maybe the most difficult thing for me personally, at least half a US citizen but raised abroad, was coming to terms with being equated—as a Hispanic or Latino—to a variety of people whose history, national origin, ethnicity, social class, and education were so different from my own that I could not even imagine the worlds they came from. Readers will notice I do not use the terms "Hispanic" or "Latino" except in reference to someone who actually speaks these words; for the most part, these terms are not how I and the people I studied speak about ourselves.

Racialization, for the mostly recent migrants in these pages, is furthermore exacerbated by the fact that these migrants share echelons of US society with inner-city African Americans and other migrant and ethnic groups that inevitably compete with them for resources and labor. US racial politics thus become a central frame of reference in relation to which Latin Americans must learn to position themselves. The term *moreno,* which in most Latin American countries is generally used ambiguously to describe a great part of the ethnically diverse mestizo population (De Genova 2005), thus becomes anathema to their own identity and encompasses an archetypical opposite; that is, anyone considered black. Migrants quickly learn to differentiate themselves in these ways and learn the programmatic stereotypes that have marked US racial politics: African Americans are lazy, *they* abuse the system, *they* want everything for free (Quesada 2011). *Morenos* moreover are also perceived as "out to get" the jornaleros; *they* are the worst employers; *they* are the most dangerous people on the streets. In the worldview of the men in these pages, *morenos* are, overall, the bad guys they encounter the most. Only *tongas*—a vague ascription relating to Tongans, other Pacific Islanders, but also heavyset, foreign-sounding blacks—come close to competing with *morenos* as the worst employers, but in Berkeley they were not as prevalent as in Oakland and other parts of the Bay Area.

I do not think that African American employers are all that much worse than white employers, but many African American employers in Berkeley differed greatly from the upper middle-class white *patrones* who came to the corner. While contractors and subcontractors from both groups (as well as other ethnicities) were common on the street and had been more present before the economic crisis, white homeowners were more prevalent than any others during the crisis. These men and women, well educated and politically liberal, were more likely to pay better wages and offer tips. So the reason for a preference for white employers—*patrones*—is pretty clear to me. Whereas all African Americans had to compete with the representations of *morenos* as inner-city thugs that almost all the jornaleros had been victims of at some point, white *patrones* had no ethnic equivalents in the neighborhoods where the men lived.

Whatever the reasons, I choose to let the reader assess these issues as part of the exercise of ethnographic reading. Antipathy toward *morenos* was prevalent on the street, but so were exceptions, as with the person I have called Luis, who openly referred to African Americans as "damned pieces of coal" and yet in a visit I made to him in 2012 said he had left the street and gotten two jobs thanks to a *moreno* friend he made washing dishes in a restaurant in San Francisco. All in all, I do not think the day laborers are any more racist than other people in the United States, but rather their world is not informed by US cultural politics and the essentialized political correctness that leads most middle-class cosmopolitan

"Americans"—and here is another problematic term I use sparingly—to think they are colorblind. On the street, color is part of the game and learning to be racist "American style" is essential for survival.

ON FIELDWORK AND WRITING

In rewriting some of the material for this book, I have tried think through the effects ethnography should have on readers, academics, and the general public alike. I have thus attempted to avoid weighing the text down with too much theoretical analysis, instead framing my interactions on the street so that most informed readers can follow along. I have divided the book into three parts that I think constitute specific elements of daily life that can be addressed under the same heading. Each of these sections is preceded by a brief introduction where I contextualize the chapters theoretically or thematically. My hope is that the material in the chapters speaks for itself as much as possible.

My rather synchronic approach to the labor site is probably the most questionable aspect here. Readers will not find a typical "historical context" chapter, where I attempt to account for why the men I studied migrate, or a chapter that tries to set contemporary migration in the United States and other industrialized nations into a political and social framework. Readers interested in a more historical or politically informed analysis of Latin American migration to the United States can turn to scholars such as Ngai (2004), Coutin (1993, 2000), Smith (2005), and many others. This is also not a "multisited" ethnography where the anthropologist—as omnipresent narrator—can jump from one place to another, talk to wives and children back in the countries of origin, and then masterfully weave their stories together. On the street, I encountered a world of isolation and estrangement from families and social networks, and the day laborers I came to know as friends had mixed feelings and diffused images about the people they left behind and supported. I thus leave these families, especially wives and children, as faceless characters—distant images of people whose very nature, feelings, and intent shift in the obscure realm of jornaleros' experience.

In a similar vein, I have done little to contextualize the characters on the street whom I present throughout the book. I suppose I risk painting a stereotypical picture of the undocumented day laborer by creating faceless individuals that seem like ideal types of migrants. However, on the corner people do not know each other well, and it was only after many months that I became familiar with some of the day laborers and their personal histories. In fact, by the end of the first year I think I knew some men, and they me, better than they knew their peers on the corner. To stop and give brief outlines of them would seem artificial, and I have opted to let them appear on the corner as I saw them and, in many ways, as they see each other, diffuse and distant. As the chapters progress, the men I considered my friends, about six of the main group, will come into better focus. One thing that can be noted, though, is that most of the jornaleros in my "inner" circle were over thirty years old and had established homes in their countries of origin, which they supported with the little money they made. There were a few younger guys, such as Chucho, Hernado, and Iván, all in their twenties and single, whom I got to know well, but my closest friends—Luis, Francisco, Sindi, and Eduardo—were men nearer to my own age (early thirties). I also became very close to two men in their fifties, Lorenzo and Adolfo, who were not really part of the Fifth Street crowd but stood there and other places every once in a while.

I spent almost every day between June 2007 and August 2008 on the Berkeley *esquina,* diminishing my visits to two or three times a week until August 2009, when I effectively managed to pull myself out of the field, at least to a geographical extent. Until the day I returned to Colombia in June 2010, I continued to talk to my friends from the corner, go out for drinks, and visit some of them in their homes. Fieldwork among jornaleros is both easy and difficult in the sense that the men are apt to talk extensively about everything they are experiencing—they do it among themselves every day—and yet they obsessively mistrust all strangers to the corner and assume them to be trouble. Once I became a fixture on a particular street corner, my presence was mostly acknowledged, even welcomed as novelty by many people along the strip. However, mistrust and misinformation ruled the site, and I mostly refrained from using cameras and recorders on the street. Using either while among friends who had no problem with the devices simultaneously caused distress and panic up and down the corridor, where other jornaleros immediately assumed the worst no matter how many times they had seen me. This was in part an effect of the many college students from up the hill who liked to come down to talk to people and take pictures for class projects and who many times inadvertently became associated with rumors about immigration raids, Minutemen—*los minut*—and other such misfortunes.

The information herein is thus the product of extensive field notes I took after every visit to the corner. My little notebook became well known among the men, who took to pulling it out of my pocket to write down slang or expressions they used to tease me and others in an effort to "teach" me to speak in *albures*—double entendres—and different vernaculars of Spanish. I also took walks around the nearby shops and recorded notes and reconstructed snippets of conversation during the normal comings and goings of the men at the site. I conducted semistructured interviews with some of my close acquaintances, usually in their homes or in coffee shops. These interviews never seemed as rich as my field notes, though, and with few exceptions I came to rely on what I could obtain on the corner. One exception consists of a few conversations I taped in the afternoons during the second shift with outliers Eduardo, William, and Bicho, who played around with phones, a Discman, and later an iPod. These three loved to take my digital recorder out of its case, turn it on, and, speaking loudly, start long discussions with, "Man have I got a story for you," or "Listen to this, this is something to tell the people at the university." After they grew tired of speaking into the machine, they would lay it down beside them, with the result that I have a few spontaneous focus groups directed by Eduardo and William that appear in chapter 4.

I was also invited by a few of my close acquaintances to their homes, and I went out drinking with Lorenzo and a few others every once in a while. The man I have called Luis lived with two brothers and two uncles, and he invited me home at least once a month. I also joined him for building parties and other get-togethers in Oakland. While the lack of community seemed prevalent on the street, at least in Luis's case life with his male relatives was stable. Most of the other men lived in crowded dwellings with strangers—I also visited several of these—and invitations were less forthcoming, since cohorts of roommates were often at odds with each other and people preferred to drink in their rooms with a few friends.

For the most part, the main characters in this book represent real people I met and talked with during my time at *la parada*. I have changed names, countries of origin, and home states in Mexico in some cases, a somewhat programmatic effort to jumble the identifying information, even though I consider these men's identities protected by way of the structural violence I describe herein. After all, finding any of these jornaleros after only a few years would prove difficult even for me or other men from the corner. In certain cases, composites of several men form ancillary characters, in order to maintain some of the narratives and reduce the "noise" of too many secondary characters making onetime appearances. I have done nothing to hide the fact that this research was undertaken in Berkeley or to hide the labor site itself. This is not only because *la parada* is well known to its residents, the police force, and so on, and so hiding it would be somewhat absurd, but also because the location should speak to the politically correct smokescreen I lived in for six years. The fact that the state and society in general know where the action in these pages takes place is part of the point I am trying to make.

Working on the Street

Some of the owner men were kind because they hated what they had to do, and some of them were angry because they hated to be cruel, and some of them were cold because they had long ago found that one could not be an owner unless one were cold. And all of them were caught up in something larger than themselves.

John Steinbeck, *The Grapes of Wrath*

The three chapters that follow comprise the central aspects of day labor as a form of employment in Berkeley. I describe the labor site and the people that transect it, address the ways in which labor works through weak ties of solidarity, and show the difficulties inherent in contesting employer abuse and other problems. This is a snapshot of what takes place in a small liberal city and does not necessarily reflect a typical corner in the United States. If anything, what I describe is a benevolent reflection of very harsh realities, which at the time of my fieldwork (2007–2009) were even worse, because like the rest of the country, the economic crisis was running rampant on the street and there was little work to be had. This notwithstanding, the informal labor site is part of a nationwide phenomenon. Valenzuela (2001, 2003) has categorized labor sites according to specialization of activities there and the degree to which the sites are regulated: the Berkeley *esquina* is an "unconnected" site, not associated to any specific industry or trade and also partially openly regulated in that it is associated with a nonprofit organization, the Multicultural Institute, which offers various labor programs and social services the men can choose to be part of or not. Most of the men follow independent labor practices that shape and are shaped by their relationships on the street.

The most comprehensive and cited survey on day laborers in the United States is the National Day Labor Survey (NDLS) undertaken by Valenzuela and colleagues (2006), which includes information from 2,660 day laborers at 264 sites nationwide. The NDLS estimates that on any given day there are more than 117,000 jornaleros on US streets waiting to be hired, 98 percent of them men. Undocumented migrants comprise 75 percent of the sample, although of this, 11 percent had pending applications for adjustment of immigrant status. The survey was not able to determine how many people were actually eligible for temporary or permanent immigration status. Recent migrants, furthermore, were the most common on the street in the survey, of which 60 percent had been in the country fewer than six years (Valenzuela et al. 2006: 18). In the sample, 59 percent of the jornaleros surveyed were born in Mexico, 14 percent in Guatemala, 8 percent in Honduras, and only 7 percent in the United States. This reflects the general national tendency of undocumented migrants to the United States (Hoefer, Rytina, and Campbell 2006), although the Berkeley site had almost as many Guatemalans as Mexicans between 2007 and 2009. I never met any US-born jornaleros during the time I spent on the corner.

Some day labor studies call attention to the fact that it is hard to gauge the degree to which successful jornaleros work because, by definition, these men will not be on the street (i.e., they will always be working), and thus they are difficult to interview, count, and so on (Worby 2002). The rationale is that successful day laborers will have extended networks of repeat employers, *patrones*, who hire them on a somewhat regular basis. However, the assumption that there are day laborers that are so effective in maintaining labor relations obscures the reality of what it really means to work on the corner. To be a jornalero, as Lorenzo liked to remind me, is simply to *"vivir del jornal,"* in other words, to "live by the day wage." That no jornalero I met actually worked every day, all day, underlines that day labor requires one's presence on the street almost on a permanent basis in order to be economically viable. A man ceases to be a day laborer when he can avoid the street altogether. On the corner where I did my fieldwork, there were a couple of men who were in between jobs or complementing their income on the weekends; the rest spent most of the year on the street, some getting longer stints of work that lasted no more than a couple of months but usually just a couple of weeks. I doubt I missed any men who frequented my corner at some point in the year that I was there almost every day. An average week for the jornaleros was made up of only two or three days of work, many times only a few hours a day. Furthermore, only with construction could day laborers gain regular or long-term employment—*trabajo regular*—directly from the site. During my time on the corner, the downturn in the economy erased these possibilities.

Another question often addressed is why these men chose this form of work, which entails unstable income and great risks to their health. That jornaleros are predominantly recent arrivals and foreign-born Latin American men who cannot easily access more regular employment because they lack documents, specialized skills or training, and/or proficiency in English points to the structural position they occupy in US society (Esbenshade 2000; Malpica 2002; Organista and Kubo 2005; Quesada 2011). Valenzuela and others have also called attention to how this structural position makes an unregulated, tax-free work environment desirable (Valenzuela 2001; Worby 2007), since the men can to some degree choose the jobs they take and their employers. There is, among many jornaleros, a sense of independence and agency in the reasons they give for turning to the street, something Gill (2001) has also noted among day laborers across the Pacific in Japan.

Yet almost all jornaleros prefer to work for *patrones* they know. Only recently arrived men with no labor networks depend uniquely on ad hoc jobs from the street, and most men quickly establish some continuous relationship with a couple of repeat employers. These relationships are short-lived at best, and few if any of the men I met in Berkeley actually make a living working solely with this type of *patrón*. That jornaleros have two basic options when it comes to employment—either getting into the car of a stranger (which entails a great amount of risk) or working with repeat employers—has led researchers to argue that labor sites are highly structured, with rules that dictate who works with a first-time employer, under what conditions, and who has access to repeat employers. Malpica (2002), for example, identifies significant differences in status and earning between jornaleros working with "regular employers" and those working with "unclaimed employers." In Los Angeles in the 1990s, he described people without regular *patrones* as new on the street and in the process of learning the ropes. Those with seniority and established employers, he says, were granted deference and "preferential treatment in the job hiring process" (Malpica 2002: 140). He goes as far as arguing that effective jornaleros with regular employers managed to attain a status of "unsubstitutability" that structured the labor site he studied. This is not the case in Berkeley. There is no preferential treatment of experienced men there, but rather a complex web of weak relations among the jornaleros, their acquaintances on the site, and the employers. In this sense, employers and acquaintances constitute a fragile social network that regiments labor and is complemented with other relations, such as the men's dealings with NGOs like the Multicultural Institute.

ON SOCIABILITY AND FRIENDSHIP

Classical sociological and anthropological ethnographies of "street-corner societies" and marginalized populations have shaped the ease with which ethnographers latch onto sociability as a key response to poverty and exclusion expressed in transient spaces of the urban landscape. Ties of friendship, fictive kinship, and so on have been put forth by authors such as Anderson (2003 [1976]) and Liebow (2003 [1967]), in part, to illustrate the rules and rationales that the poor develop in order to deal with their situation. Liebow, for example, recognizes the weakness of the ties of friendship he studied among African American men who, like jornaleros, lived and socialized on street corners where they sought informal employment. Yet friendship, for him, structured the brittle balance of personal worth, identity, and sociability among his informants, in a way that strove to explain the importance and centrality of these relationships: "the resources in the street corner world are almost entirely given over to the construction and maintenance of personal relationships" (Liebow 2003 [1967]: 105). For the jornaleros in Berkeley, however, friendship is costly and marked by the difficult realities of labor, which require a high degree of individuality and pragmatism in order to make ends meet. Personal relationships in Liebow's case are also valued in as much as the men are interacting within the general urban space where they live, while these jornaleros usually do not share spatial proximity outside the labor site. In fact, all of the classical street-corner ethnographies, and most works I cite on jornaleros, deal with street corners located in the neighborhoods where informants live. In contrast, the Berkeley site is located, for most men, miles away from their place of residence, which in turn is not necessarily the same neighborhood that their coworkers inhabit.

Pinedo Turnovsky (2006) underlines the importance of the street corner as a social sphere where men interact with each other while waiting for work. The corner is, in her perspective, the closest space in which men can develop a sense of community; a place where they can talk with each other and share the anxieties of separation from home, their absent position within the family, and other aspects of their experience. In many ways, some of the chapters in this book mirror her argument. Yet, as I will show, solidarity on the corner is fickle at best, and "community" is precluded by individual necessity. Solidarity and friendship are articulated in a complex arena of competition, distrust, and misinformation. This seems contradictory, in a sense, to my own—almost interactionist—rendering of social relations, where the men joke around and socialize quite a lot. What I suggest is that ties of solidarity and work relations among jornaleros—the intersection between labor networks and personal acquaintances, for the most part—are frail and unpredictable. That they are effective plays in to what Granovetter (1973: 1371) suggested in the 1970s, wherein weak ties do not preclude effective networks but rather make them more efficient in providing exposure to different work scenarios, because they enable access to a more ample universe of relations. Weak ties are what permit the establishment and rapid dissolution of work teams and cohorts of men that share physical space on the corner. Such ties also play into the moral economy of perception required to maintain the networks while undertaking practices that threaten them.

A MORAL ECONOMY OF PERCEPTION

Historians and anthropologists have used the term "moral economy" to refer to small-scale communal subsistence economies where reciprocity and a sense of the common good take prevalence over market-driven rationales. In his analysis of eighteenth-century England, E. P. Thompson (1971) explained the British food riots as specific reactions to the change of economic system from peasant exchange systems (inscribed in a paternalistic state structure) to capitalism. His work opened the doors for the reframing of peasant economies facing capitalist cooption, not as remnants of past systems, but rather as culturally and politically productive forms of peasant resistance (e.g., Scott 1977). Thus the term has come to integrate the study of social norms and economic practice in "traditional" societies assailed by global forces. In this arena, the notions of what constitutes just distribution and pricing vis-à-vis capitalist expansion are what regiments how the economy is interpreted. What is considered just or unfair in these particular power relationships becomes central to understanding people's behavior, not the rationality or irrationality of their economic practice (Larson 1988). "Moral economy" has also become an elegant synonym to explain notions of reciprocity in unequal systems of exchange where power relationships are "governed primarily by morality . . . or by ethics governing particular version of the good life" (Ong 2006: 199). For Bourgois and Schonberg (2009), the moral economy of sharing among drug addicts in San Francisco was central to how these researchers came to understand the intimate realm of addiction and abuse of people who depend on pooling resources such as money, drug paraphernalia, and drugs themselves, for their survival.

On *la parada* I came to see the problems of organization that NGOs find when they try to regulate work or provide legal and medical protection as an effect of a moral economy of perception. In this case it is not a sense of justice inherent in the action of exchange that is central to the system, but how those involved managed others' perceptions of the action of exchange. In a system of harsh competition where even close acquaintances can come to blows over who said or did what to some employer, hindering others' chances, the jornaleros are forced to maximize their own exposure to work and labor networks while at the same time maintaining a semblance of spreading wealth and job opportunities. The moral economy of perception I observed and inevitably participated in is almost always destined for crisis, and it explains why groups come together and then dissolve so rapidly and why no day laborer in his "right mind," at least at the time of my fieldwork, would trust a labor center. The sense of outrage that Thompson used to explain revolt and resistance is here turned inward, against peers suddenly deemed not *humilde*—humble—enough and thus excluded in such a way that cooperation, organization, and mutual support are hindered.

INFORMAL LABOR

Working informally on the street is a hazardous endeavor, in which those so engaged are in constant danger on many fronts. Most studies on the subject call attention to the problems involved in unregulated manual work, which many times results in injuries. The most usual injuries are minor scrapes and twisted joints, the result of carrying heavy burdens while moving furniture or doing construction work. More spectacular accidents are expensive and life threatening, and on the corner we all heard of people falling off roofs or ladders and being permanently disabled or even dying. Most day labor studies report a high rate of injury on the job (e.g., Esbenshade 2000; Walter et al. 2002; Walter, Bourgois, and Loinaz 2004; Valenzuela et al. 2006; Quesada, Hart, and Bourgois 2011). More than half the day laborers surveyed by Valenzuela and colleagues (2006) in the NDLS did not receive adequate medical attention for their injuries, mainly because they lacked any form of health insurance. Although injury was a very real possibility we sometimes discussed in Berkeley, there were no cases of grave injury in the immediate cohort I studied, and hence the possibility appears here only tangentially. This by no means implies that the subject has been exaggerated elsewhere, but rather points to how an ethnographic approach distances itself from problems addressed through surveys and interviews. The everyday lives of the men in these pages are precarious at a different level.

At the site I studied, the most common and discussed danger of day labor was related to employer abuse. Here my work coincides with the studies cited above. Jornaleros are frequent victims of a variety of abuse by employers, who find it easy to withhold the promised wage and/or fail to provide basic necessities such as food, water, and protective gear to employees who have little or no access to the legal means to report such maltreatment. In fact, there is no study where employer abuse is not mentioned by the laborers themselves as one of the key risk factors of working on the street (Valenzuela 2003; Theodore, Valenzuela, and Meléndez 2006; Valenzuela et al. 2006; Purser 2009; Quesada 2011). As I will show, the ubiquitous theme of employer abuse is related to the absurd and virtually impossible means that jornaleros have to contest exploitation and mistreatment.

THE STREET-CORNER BIAS

Part 1 of this book thus follows the dire circumstances of work and survival related to what goes on at the corner. That I saw little in terms of community formation on the corner points to the conditions of labor that jornaleros face but not necessarily for all the jornaleros in their private lives. As I have already mentioned, some of the men—like Luis, Eduardo, or the *trillizos,* who will appear in short—shared living expenses with close, usually male relatives. These men had strong social relations outside *la esquina,* which offered social interactions and ties that would seem more robust than what I describe, and I may have missed other elements of social organization present in the men's neighborhoods by concentrating my attention on the street corner. Yet most of the people in these pages were in the United States without their close relatives, wives, partners, and children, and they lived with other men whom they usually did not know well. Luis and the others, in fact, were anomalies, and most of the jornaleros shared living quarters with strangers.

My take on the absence of solidarity, then, is both biased by the street corner but also informed by the general demographics I encountered. Even the jornaleros who had stronger support networks like Luis and Eduardo were "in the same boat," more or less; none of these external relations had radically different effects on these men's daily lives while I was with them. Eduardo is the best case in point, since his inability to understand gender norms, the moral economy of the street, and general male behavior was not ameliorated by living with cousins who treated him fairly. Eduardo was the first of all these men to disappear outright, tired of his *situación,* which ultimately included the generalized ostracism he eventually felt on the street. I thus offer a snapshot of what the Berkeley *parada* looked like to these men, part of a worldview that did not necessarily include their whole experience in the United States but that, at least, determined a great many of the events upon which this experience was rationalized and understood.

1 *La Parada de* Berkeley

The Berkeley informal labor site is a seven-block corridor in the western part of the city, near the freeway and marina. All along Hearst Avenue, from Ninth Street to Second Street, men stand on the curbs in small groups waiting for potential employers to drive up and offer them work. The site is only a block to the north of University Avenue, one of the city's main streets. *La parada* begins to suggest itself several blocks east of the site itself, on San Pablo Avenue, the main thoroughfare that brings the men to work from Oakland. Mixed into the diversity of the street, which is full of ethnic markets and visited by a diverse population, the jornaleros only really stand out when they walk into the residential areas to the north of University Avenue. Yet on Hearst Avenue toward Ninth Street, they materialize suddenly as a group, standing or sitting on the curbs, chatting, drinking coffee, and eating breakfast from microwavable noodle cups and ready-made wraps bought at local gas stations or from one of the informal food sources that cater to the corner. Day laborers spread out, mostly along the south side of Hearst. Some men seem barely teenagers, while others are much older, even beyond middle age. The odd man out might even look like he is well into his sixties, and I have heard rumors at other sites of seventy- and eighty-year-old men standing along with everyone else.

La parada transects a popular commercial district that has grown through it in the last decade or so (Worby 2007). Between Fourth and Sixth Streets, the jornaleros who stand on the curb are constantly passed by motor and foot traffic directed to and from the upscale shops and businesses. The physical space here is thus not isolated from everyday, mainstream passersby (as is the case with many other sites in the Bay Area and other parts of the country) but is rather smack in the middle of one of the city's main commercial streets: West Berkeley's "Forth Street Shops" that include stores, a bank, and several offices. Few jornaleros venture into the commercial district, which comprises about three blocks along Fourth Street. Thus, patrons of the shops and restaurants a block away from the labor site are unlikely to see the dark, short bodies clad in jeans and sweatshirts that predominate on Hearst Avenue.

Between Sixth and Ninth Streets, *la parada* enters a residential area with parked cars, leading most groups of men to concentrate on the corners where employers can easily see them. Their presence here is more recent and contested by neighbors who feel intimidated by the dark, apparently grungy bodies of men whom residents claim watch them, urinate in the street, litter, and supposedly drink alcohol and consume drugs. The general consensus among the jornaleros, however, is that these activities usually happen *en las vías*—at the train tracks—between Third and Fourth Streets, where one can find homeless alcoholic men who either have ceased working or work only when they are moderately sober. Many of these *borrachitos*—little drunks—live under the freeway underpass nearby and in empty lots on San Pablo Avenue. In fact, this area (specifically from Second to Fourth Streets) was the only part of *la parada* officially designated "white zones," where soliciting work was allowed by the City of Berkeley.

The labor site is also a product of the time of day, its social topography dwindling as the morning advances. *La parada* proper only exists between sunup and about three in the afternoon. Anyone passing later might not even notice the stragglers who remain down toward *las vías* and who, in most cases, look like dirty men loitering on the street, a scene not uncommon in many areas of the city. The men thus refer to the corner in terms of shifts—*turnos*—the first lasting until about one in the afternoon, when most "serious" day laborers have been hired or have gone home, followed by the *segundo turno*—second shift—that lasts the rest of the afternoon

Sign posted at the Berkeley labor site.

and sees a few men slowly giving up hopes of work and just hanging out and sometimes drinking beer or liquor in paper bags.

Jornaleros usually come to the site every day, weekends and holidays included, but Saturdays and Sundays see less men hanging out in the afternoon. As Michel de Certeau (1984) has masterfully shown us, space and time are intrinsically linked to the comings and goings of urban living, generating and then dissolving the social spaces where jornaleros spend their time in apparent destitution, talking, telling each other stories, giving each other advice, and waiting long hours for work. This space is unbounded and expands and contracts during the day, and from one day to another, depending on a wide rage of factors that can include weather, perceived harassment by *la migra* and the police, or the downward spiral of the country's economy.

The proximity to the freeway, along with the commerce associated with nearby businesses, also makes *la parada* an incredibly noisy place; trucks come and go, stopping for deliveries, and for some reason big rigs coming off the freeway drive by constantly. This noise becomes deafening at times, and a casual conversation is likely to end abruptly or turn into a screaming match as huge trucks attempt to make complex maneuvers in the small streets, often resulting in fender benders with parked cars. Thus, to stand on the corner is to stand amid the constant hum of motors that becomes so ingrained in conversations that you forget how loud it is until you strain to hear recordings made there.

The Berkeley *esquina* is a place of convergence that jornaleros travel to from distant parts of the vast metropolitan area in which it is located. Few men on the street actually live in the city of Berkeley, or even near it. They usually live in distant parts of Oakland, some even two hours away by bus, although most men spend between thirty and sixty minutes on public transportation each way. I even met jornaleros who live in Richmond, El Cerrito, and Orinda and some who come across the bay from San Francisco. These other places have their own informal labor sites, so coming to Berkeley is a conscious choice—one that entails a monetary investment in transportation. Jornaleros have chosen the site because word on the street is that wages there are higher and there are fewer people to compete with, better employers, and less police harassment. That the *esquina* is in a sanctuary city, however, does not seem to play into the decision. In the first place, few men actually know what a sanctuary city is, and, as I will show later, jornaleros generally feel that no place is exempt from the influence and surveillance of *la migra*.

Most men wear old and stained clothes, usually jeans, sweatshirts with hoods, and baseball caps. No matter the season, the early passerby will see jornaleros standing or sitting with their hands in the front pockets of their pants or sweatshirts, hunched over with their faces covered by hoods or caps. The faceless, thug-like effect of this pose makes the men look "shady" and distinguishes them from the scantily clad joggers who use the street in the morning, as well as the elegantly dressed business people who work in the offices and stores nearby. Although most men look like they are wearing work clothes, some look quite disheveled, as if they had slept on the street. Among some of the younger crowd, US inner-city youth culture has influenced their style, and one might see what at first seem to be teenagers in baggy pants, tennis shoes, and even flashy jewelry.

Early in the morning, between the railroads and Fourth Street, a food truck known as La Lonchera stops and raises its side panels to sell coffee, sodas, tacos, chicken dishes, and sandwiches. There are actually several *loncheras,* whose occupants are usually other Latin Americans, but in the case of the lunch *lonchera* also Asians—invariably referred to as *chinos*—speaking Spanish with heavy accents. Coffee is taken with milk and lots of sugar, and at fifty cents is more than a dollar cheaper than anything else nearby. By 8:30 or 9:00 A.M., the morning *lonchera* is gone, leaving food provision to several individuals who drive by in their cars selling tamales and assorted tidbits for a dollar. When the *loncheras* are absent, most jornaleros go to either of two gas stations on University Avenue and Sixth Street, where they can buy soft drinks, coffee, junk food, phone cards, and other items.

There are also weekly food rituals like the *monjitas,* Catholic nuns of the Missionaries of Charity order founded by Mother Teresa of Calcutta, who come every Wednesday and hand out pastries, hotdogs, and coffee in exchange for a few moments of prayer and Catholic doctrine. "Praying for hotdogs," as I referred to it on the street, attracts jornaleros from all along the strip. Saturdays sometimes see Jehovah's Witnesses do the same, but, unlike the soggy hotdogs of their Catholic counterparts, their fried chicken is excellent and highly regarded. On hot days the *paletera*—the popsicle lady (from the Spanish for "popsicle," *paleta*)—might walk up and down the street before going to the local school. The jornaleros are good clients and take turns treating each other in the small groups. Other people come by every so often and hand out food, water, gifts, and even money (especially around the holidays).

While I was on the corner there were free lunches, English classes, and sometimes, vocational training at the Anglican church on Hearst and Ninth Street on Fridays. All of these were organized by the Multicultural Institute,

Jornalero in a UC Berkeley sweatshirt on the Fifth Street corner.

an NGO contracted by the City of Berkeley as a liaison between the jornaleros and the community, which also provides help with access to health services, *mercados*—groceries—and sometimes second-hand clothes. Watching the men shuffle through the boxes of donations, it became clear why so many of them seem to wear clothes that are too big and why UC Berkeley sweatshirts are as prevalent as on the campus a few blocks up University Avenue.

Like NGOs at other Bay Area sites, the Multicultural Institute (MI) mediates between the ever-increasing number of jornaleros and the area's residents and businesses. During my fieldwork, the MI outreach programs were tied to the county health services, which included a health truck that delivered general checkups once a month and referrals to the family clinic across the street from the gas station. Along with these county programs, members of the institute also helped people file claims at the California Labor Commission, contacted problem employers, and referred special cases to other NGOs, notably El Centro Legal de la Raza in Oakland.[1] The MI also advertised day labor work on its website and in the community, making referrals to employers who called. The onsite members of the outreach program were on the street every weekday and organized the referrals, volunteers, donations, and Friday lunches. For special events like Thanksgiving and Christmas dinner, the MI joined forces with a variety of community and religious organizations. Every jornalero that came to the Berkeley site regularly knew the people at the MI and had some idea that the organization might be able to help with information or solving problems. From time to time, other members of the MI visited the site, most notably Paula Worby, whose thesis in public health dealt with alcoholism among the men there (Worby 2007), and Father Rigo, the group's director.

Finishing her research a year before I arrived, Worby (2007: 67) calculated that there were between 80 and 100 men on the street most days at peak hiring times. During the three-year period of her study, the MI registered about 1,000 men that came to *la parada*. The MI calculated that only a third of those registered in a given year were present the next year and that only 75 men were there for the three years. Worby also found that while the site was predominantly Mexican in 2001 (see Worby 2002; Organista and Kubo 2005), by 2006 half the day laborers were Mexican and the other half were primarily Guatemalan, with a few Salvadorans and Hondurans (Worby 2007: 7). Although the dynamics of the site imply a constantly changing population, this distribution reflects the demographics of my own field site, which comprised about 25 men I interacted with closely and another 25 or 30 with whom I had intermittent contact.

Unlike other informal labor sites, the West Berkeley one does not have an inherent distribution of trades mapped onto the corridor. There is no part of

1. El Centro Legal de la Raza was widely known and mentioned by the migrants I worked with. However, I never had any direct contact with the organization or anyone working there. All my references to this organization, then, are based on what I was told by the jornaleros, that is, on their perceptions and understanding of what goes on there.

the street where painters or masons hang out, for example. In 2008, the Berkeley *esquina* had a highly regulated minimum wage of ten dollars an hour. Although a few men might agree to work for less, they did so at the risk of heavy criticism from their peers, who came to Berkeley because wages were supposed to be better. Among my friends on the corner of Fifth Street, I never saw anybody go to work for less than ten dollars an hour. This wage was in fact considered low and only appropriate for easy tasks, like taking out the garbage or sweeping. In a few cases employers tried to offer people seven, eight, or nine dollars an hour. In every instance, my friends shook their heads and watched the potential employer drive up the street to the next group of men. Most of the people I know assume that only the Guatemalan indigenous jornaleros—*los guatemalas*—east of Sixth Street would even consider such a low wage, but in truth, I doubt any jornaleros in Berkeley worked for less then ten dollars an hour on a regular basis.

It is hard to describe the variety of day laborers that came to the Berkeley site. I cannot say I know exactly where each jornalero came from, where he had been, and what brought him there. Although some of the men were related to each other or came from the same place, most groups consisted of migrants from different countries and regions, where some were acquaintances but where most were strangers. On the corner where I was a regular, a small contingent of people from the Mexican state of Veracruz were kin or knew one another in passing. There were smaller groups from Guadalajara and a few from the state of Mexico and Mexico City. There were many Guatemalans at the Berkeley site, roughly divided into two groups who hardly spoke to each other, namely indigenous people from various parts of the country's rural areas and ladinos—nonindigenous "whites"[2]—from the urban centers. Some of the latter had attended

2. Grandin (2000) elaborately addresses the particularities of ethnicity in Guatemalan history. The term "ladino," in his rendering, originally denoted indigenous people who had been baptized or Hispanicized throughout the Spanish colonies. After independence the term became increasingly used in Guatemala to denote all nonindigenous people. To other Latin Americans, myself included, the use of "ladino" by Guatemalans sounds and feels very similar to our use of "mestizo," which points to the intermixing of indigenous European and, nowadays, several other ethnic groups depending on the country. Grandin (2000: 239), however, suggests that "ladino" is not synonymous with "mestizo" but rather has historically "suggested a Hispanicized or European cultural identity." Other references to the difference between ladinos and indigenous people can be found in Manz (2004).

Jornaleros on the Fifth Street corner.

institutions of higher education and universities and worked white-collar jobs back home. Salvadorans were also present but to a lesser degree. They tended to have work permits, legal residency, Temporary Protected Status (TPS),[3] or asylum and were in their thirties and forties, which sets them in the context of the war that scourged their country in the 1980s (Danner 1993; Loescher 1993; Coutin 2000).

I spent a great deal of time on the only corner that has a good place to sit, a small wall that is also a bus stop on the south side of Fifth Street. I came to this place after several failed attempts at talking with people along the strip; the men I approached seemed weary of strangers or simply not interested in speaking to yet another student from the nearby university. So I decided to simply appear on the street before the jornaleros

3. Temporary Protected Status is a specific immigration status for people from countries experiencing armed conflict, environmental disasters, and other disturbances that might hinder returning or deported migrants. It is a status that must be renewed periodically and does not automatically lead to legal residence, although it allows recipients to work. I do not go into the particularities of TPS because I did not directly deal with migrants with this status on the corner. Several analyses of Salvadoran migration to the United States and the specific circumstances of TPS for this population show the interplay between US-funded violence in El Salvador, political and religious activism in the United States, and natural disasters that make this status more common among these migrants (Coutin 1993, 2000; Baker-Cristales 1999, 2004; Mountz et al. 2002).

and let them form around me. The wall was the least conspicuous place I could be—shortly before sunrise—when people started to arrive. The men who gathered there constitute the main characters in this account, although I discuss people from all along the street. The four corners at the intersection of Hearst Avenue and Fifth Street were the immediate work and social environment. Although we—the men usually at the bus stop—did not know the people on the western two corners or those who stood with us or directly across the street from us, we saw them every day. Thus, when we measured the number of day laborers present on a particular morning, our calculations started with the four corners. After I stopped visiting the site regularly, Luis, for example, would tell me how many people he had counted there in order to illustrate the vast increase of jornaleros since I had left.

Every now and then some men—like Clemente, who constantly kept an eye on the traffic coming his way—would step into the street with a raised arm trying to hail down a car or truck, calling out "Leibor! Leibor!" If someone stopped, the closest man to the car leaned into the widow and briefly talked with the potential *patrón,* quickly deciding if he would take the job or not. Many times, he shook his head and turned to the others, saying, "He only pays ten dollars"—*Sólo paga de a diez*—or "It's only for two hours." In these cases there was a brief exchange among the men on his corner, who usually all shook their heads, forcing the driver to continue up the street. The men, however, kept a close eye on the next group the driver approached and laughed if they too shook their heads, or complained if someone got into the car. Unlike the Oakland sites, as many jornaleros pointed out, in Berkeley one was unlikely to see people swarming around cars and fighting to get in. I have witnessed such scenes, however, on mornings when *la situación*—usually toward the end of the month—has everyone worried about paying their bills. In fact, a common occurrence at the end of the month was that people failed to pay their cell phone bills and lost access to this precious commodity necessary for both work and social life.

The men I befriended and came to know well do not constitute a "group" in any sense of the term. With the exception of Beto, Carlos, and Pablo, *los trillizos* from Veracruz, none of the regulars were related. These day laborers coincided in time and space enough to usually know each other's first names, and in some cases they worked together. They came from different parts of Mexico, El Salvador, Guatemala, and to a lesser degree, Honduras. During the years I spent on the corner, some of us became friends, while others remained simply casual acquaintances. In two particular cases, there was friction and fission among some characters I initially saw as very close to each other. I was also chastised by my closest friends for talking to men on the western corners of Hearst Avenue, who they believed to be drunks, drug addicts, and bums. East of Sixth Street, a few groups of men from the same town in Guatemala were at odds with the city and the MI because of their slow but continual expansion up the street.

It was in this setting that I arrived early one morning in June 2007. Over the two years that followed, I came to understand labor on the corner as a complex set of relations, all based on weak social ties in unstable networks, where the people involved were always measuring what they did in relation to different idealized perceptions. Among these, the most important were what others on the corner would think, what constituted fair and unfair labor practices, and what people back home might think of how these men made a living. At the crux of the labor situation was always the myth of *trabajo regular*, that is, "regular work" consisting of an extended period of time, regular paychecks, and a schedule. For most men—but there were also exceptions—regular and formalized work was the main mold by which they measured other jobs. Regular work also provided the representations of the street corner as the "workplace," where men talked about the first and second shifts or, like Luis, referred to the corner as their *oficina*—office—or pulled down imaginary metallic doors to "close up shop" before leaving. At least in the case of the day laborers I came to know well, *trabajo regular* was what they had come to the United States for, and almost all of them had held such jobs back home. I thus start my exploration of labor on the corner by looking at why the jornaleros were not working anywhere else, a problem they were very conscious of themselves.

THE MYTH OF *TRABAJO REGULAR*

Early on a cold February morning, Luis, Clemente, Hernando, and I sat shivering on the Fifth Street corner when Esteban stopped to greet us on his way to work. With subtle briskness and constantly looking down the street toward the shops and restaurants where his new job awaited, he shook hands with each of us and then handed Luis a folder with a copy of the CV he had used to land the job. "You better hurry," he said in an offhand way. "They're moving a lot of people and are going to have openings." He walked down the street in his sharp black outfit as Luis, who was wearing a dirty bright yellow jacket, worn jeans, and work boots, put away the folder.

For the past few days, Esteban's appearances had become brief because he needed to make a good impression at work. *Trabajo regular* did not come easy to most men on the street, and he felt lucky that one of his contacts had managed to get him an interview at the Italian restaurant where he now worked. Straight off the corner, he had started out as *un bus*—a busboy—but in only a few weeks he managed to work himself up to drink server and claimed to be making between 40 and 60 dollars on weekdays and almost 120 a day on weekends. These wages, even after tax deductions—he was using a pretty good fake Social Security number, or *social chueco*—were unheard of on the street. Trying to get his friend a job was his way of "returning the favor" in a world where labor and friendship do not always complement each other. Luis, on the other hand, was pessimistic and skeptical, and he reminded me that Esteban had no real power to convince his bosses, who preferred *gabachos*—white Americans—anyway.

The next day, Luis tried to copy the format of Esteban's CV on my laptop and fill it with his work history while we waited for work that never materialized. Over the last twenty years, Luis—a Mexico City native—entered the United States illegally five times and accumulated ample job experience, working in restaurants and hotels. His current trip, however, had lasted more than twice as long as any of the others, and after five years he had failed to land a long-standing job. *La situación,* this time around, was dire. With his old pay stubs on our laps, we now tried to write a good résumé that would simultaneously hide his return trips to Mexico and erase his life as a day laborer. Like remnants of a better time past, Luis always carried these pay stubs as proof of employment in case one of his *patrones* offered more stable work. Now we realized that none of the names and phone numbers, kept over the years on multiple business cards in his wallet, were still in use by the people he had worked for. "Do you

"Three jobs for the entire city!" Joking around on the corner.

think they'll really call these people?" he asked me with a nervous face. "This might be a bad idea." Luis, whom I had come to consider one of the most streetwise and competent men on the street, never took his application to the restaurant. Even though he and Esteban were close as day laborers and had even spent some time walking the streets of San Francisco looking for regular jobs, Luis doubted the intentions of his friend and seemed to think of them more as empty reciprocity than true help. He was probably right about this, for in the end Esteban lost his job after two months and returned to the corner.

Nonetheless, it surprised me that Luis was so worried about the CV, since he complained constantly about the lack of work and spent every morning looking through the want ads of the newspapers he found on his way to the corner, where he would then sit and make remarks like *"¡Va tocar robar!"*—We're going to have steal!—and *"¡Tres trabajos para toda la pinche ciudad!"*—Three jobs for the entire damned city! He jokingly pushed the other men to apply for the few jobs he thought might accept undocumented migrants and even convinced Clemente, who had just become a legal resident by way of asylum, to apply for a UPS entry-level position. Around the same time that Esteban was hired at the restaurant, Clemente finally gave in and asked the UPS man who delivered to the office behind us how he got his job, only to learn that it was by way of an online application. Luis immediately offered my services as an Internet-savvy English speaker and convinced Clemente to spend an afternoon with me in front of a computer he did not understand, filling in information for a job that was offered to able-bodied people who owned a car and were willing to start out half-time working nights. Having been injured in his youth by a mortar shell in the Salvadoran Army, Clemente, whom everyone called "limpy" in Spanish because of his awkward gait, fulfilled none of these requisites.

During the two years I spent at the informal labor site, other men found stable jobs of sorts. There was Fernando, *el panadero*—the baker—who only came on weekends to chat and maybe make a few extra bucks until he lost his job. El Sindi, or just Sindi—short for *el sin dientes* because he was missing his front teeth—and Francisco, both regulars at the site, also disappeared for a few weeks every once in a while to work with contractors they knew (one even took Francisco to Washington State to work on a contract cutting trees). There was also Iván, a young kid from Puebla who, having come to the United States in his early teens, spoke excellent English and had managed to get into community college, paying his way by day labor on the corner and weekend work at a local social club where he was a waiter. None of these jobs were permanent and the men always returned to *la esquina,* either to complement their income or for another stint of work.

The same month that Luis tried to write his CV, I was asked to help three friends fill out a different type of application, one for a factory job.

Hernando, Chucho, and Toño had gone to Hayward, where a friend was working, and brought the application back to the corner. They were stumped as to what to write and joked around, waving the papers in the cold morning air, asking each other what they were writing in the empty boxes. The first problem was that Chucho's work history was almost exclusively at day labor sites, in Berkeley and Los Angeles. He had held regular jobs briefly with contractors of different sorts, which I helped him translate to "construction" and "carpenter," but he could not recall the names of any of his employers. His references, then, were the other two guys he was applying with and the uncle of another friend. None spoke English. Chucho furthermore could not explain his "reasons for leaving" the other jobs, since none were actually formal. Finally, he had no education in the United States and jotted down the name of his *secundaria*—middle school—in Mexico, wondering if that was enough. As he looked at the wrinkled and almost empty application, he turned to me, smiled mischievously, and mumbled, "May God repay you"—*Que Dios se lo pague, Tomás.* We had hardly written a word on the paper. Finally, he ran to his car and came back with a wrinkled certificate he had obtained in LA, telling me why he thought it might help. "It's a welding certificate from [when I worked in] Los Angeles," he explained. "Sometimes the places where you work give you certificates if you learn to do something."

For about two weeks the three friends went around the Bay Area filling out similar applications in places they had heard were hiring. They all had fake Social Security cards that were registered, somehow stating they were two years older than they actually were, since they had got them as minors when they first came to the United States. They had used these papers before and told me they had paid taxes and had even been returned money—*"así que son de los buenos"*—in other words, the papers were good fakes. Yet no matter how good they were, when Chucho and his two friends finally landed a regular job, it was at a place that obviously did not even check their papers, paid them the minimum wage ($7.50 in 2007), and required working through the night, on demand, from two to four nights a week. When they returned to the corner shortly thereafter, the men—all Mexicans in their early twenties—were in dire need of money, since, after taxes, their wages did not cover their room and board, phones, and travel expenses.

Trabajo regular, in other words, seemed within the grasp of some of the men I knew, even though none of these jobs lasted more than a few months, most only a few weeks at best. In July 2007, when I started fieldwork, many men still talked of construction work lasting a few days or even weeks, and some jornaleros had employers who called them regularly to organize other men and work on a house that was being remodeled or, in one case, on refurbishing a motel in San Francisco. These jobs were not regular in the same way as Esteban's was, but they entailed bigger payments and a continuous amount of work while the jobs lasted. These types of work diminished throughout 2007 and all but disappeared in 2008.

In general, even when talking of better times when the economy was up and immigration control down—one Guatemalan veteran even talked about *la era Clinton* as a golden age—the men usually agreed that getting *trabajo regular* required inside contacts. Clemente had several regular jobs before he came to the corner, the most exciting of which was working as a guard at the Oakland airport. He told me over the years we knew each other that these *trabajillos* were offered to him through acquaintances—"It never works out if you don't have someone on the other side." For the previous five years, however, he had been on the corner because he had lost contact with people who could get him work. By 2012, when I returned after a two-year absence, he was the only one of my friends still on the corner.

Trabajo regular, however, is not an ideal for some of the more experienced men, such as Lorenzo, who after getting hired as a janitor by a subcontractor realized that he made substantially less money earning minimum wage and paying taxes than working as a day laborer. Like the three guys I helped, he discovered that hourly wages were significantly reduced in relation to the street-corner minimum wage of ten dollars an hour that everyone more or less enforced. Coupled with less money, Lorenzo and these men also found that *trabajo regular* meant working at night and thus entailed a wide array of transportation and personal safety problems.

Day labor, it seems, was the only viable form of employment for the jornaleros I met on the streets of Berkeley, one with no security and many risks. Day labor comes in many forms and depends on variables that the men cannot control, resulting in problems like not being paid, being left in unknown places by subcontractors who never return, hardship for little money, and injury due to dangerous and unregulated work. That almost every man I met talked about not getting paid the agreed-upon wage at some time, or being left on a job with no payment at all, contradicts what many jornaleros like Lorenzo described as the upside of their work—namely, choosing their employers and turning down poor wages or suspicious characters.

DAY LABOR IN BERKELEY

The most immediate type of work available on the street is employment with an unknown *patrón* who stops by to hire a laborer. A car, truck, or van pulls up to a jornalero, who talks to the driver, learns about the work and wage offered, and decides whether to get in. Usually other men will walk up behind him to see if more than one man is needed or to take the job, should the man in question refuse. In some cases, a stranger might try stepping in front of the first jornalero and getting in the car, but this is looked down upon and thought of as something that happens at the Oakland sites. If more men are needed, the first jornalero will turn to his friends and either chose one or two or nod so they can decide. When a jornalero has a good experience with first-time employers, he tries to keep in touch by giving them his phone number, and, in a few instances, a business card, hoping to be called later on. Ideally, the relationship will lead to more work in the future.

The men on the street measure employers first and foremost in terms of risk. Unknown employers pose several problems, and jornaleros must rapidly assess the situation and decide what to do. The most common problem is not getting paid at the end of the day or being paid less then the agreed-upon wage. Clemente and I sat on the corner one morning when a gray pickup truck came by with a tall, white-haired man calling out loudly. I did not understand what he was saying, but Clemente lifted up his hand in greeting. I asked who he was. "I've worked with him before," said Clemente. "He is from Iraq." The *árabe* backed up to the corner of Sixth Street where three men stood. We watched as one of the men went up to the window and talked with the man briefly, finally shaking his head and sitting down. The truck then drove in front of us and the man stuck out his head, making a sign of two fingers, which he moved back and forth. This meant he needed two jornaleros, but Clemente did not move. "Shouldn't you go see what he wants?" I asked. Clemente shook his head and the man finally drove down the street. "Why didn't you go?"

"I don't know," he answered cryptically.

"And the other guys?" I insisted.

"They don't know him, they don't know what he's like, and they don't trust *árabes [no confían en los árabes].*"

La situación was pretty bad at the time, and in the first days of September, people were short on money. But to Clemente it was obvious that people should be wary. Trying to explain, he told me another story. "About a year ago a Tongan *[un tonga]* hired us to break up and carry concrete *[echar pica y cargar concreto]*, so we worked hard, for twelve hours." He explained that the *tonga* left them working in front of a house and never came back. When Clemente and his partner rang the doorbell to collect payment, the owner of the house said he had already paid the contractor and it was not his problem. Contractors and subcontractors come to the corner for cheap labor and then simply leave people at the work site, or house in this case. If the house is empty, the men loiter until they get tired and then try to walk home. In some instances they do not know where they are, and more than a few jornaleros spoke of spending the night alongside freeways and major thoroughfares they reached after hours of walking, afraid to ask for help in middle- and upper-class neighborhoods, where their lack of English and immigration status made them weary of *gabachos*.

Clemente, however, had a work permit at this stage—as an ex-child combatant in the Salvadoran conflict he had obtained asylum early on—so he called the police. With great pride he pulled out his wallet and showed me the business cards of the police officers he had spoken to. The first was an Emeryville officer who had also written the Berkeley police department number on the back.[4] Leafing through all the cards, Clemente also pulled out a Richmond officer's card. Clemente pointed to each card and said

4. Emeryville is the town immediately south of Berkeley, within the same county and indistinguishable from Berkeley to most of the jornaleros.

something personal about the officer, as if they were friends. He told me that the police went to talk to the owner of the house and finally located the contractor. The police found the contractor at another site and took Clemente there. They were harsh with the *tonga,* he told me proudly. Months later I would hear this story include a spectacular arrest that involved ten patrol cars—*patrullas*—and ended with the *tonga* in handcuffs, but the first time, alone with Clemente, he simply said the police gave him the *tonga*'s information so he could file a claim in court. "*Este es el fregado,*" Clemente concluded, showing me yet another card with the employer's phone number and address. He did not file a complaint and the man never paid him.

Another common problem is agreeing on a wage for work that sounds easy but that turns out to be difficult and taxing. Here, language plays an important role, for most of the men do not speak English fluently, but eagerly take on work that "sounds" good. Thus, when Beto agreed to carry some boxes for ten dollars an hour, he was enraged to discover that the job actually involved breaking up a driveway. "For that," he explained later, "one charges twelve or fifteen dollars." Having settled on the lower price, he was unable to justify charging more. Another version of this is to get hired for a specific task that entails a day wage, say 80 to 100 dollars, and finishing in a few hours. Most *patrones* would then try to recalculate an hourly wage. Claudio, a young indigenous Guatemalan who worked at one of the Oakland corners, said that employers sometimes promised these amounts, but after hours and hours of work they would only pay 40 or 50 dollars. "They know we won't tell anyone so they do what they want."

New employers many times do not offer work for the whole day, and in many cases the jobs are short menial engagements that last one or two hours. For some men these engagements are a waste of time and money, and they turn them down because they hope to be offered something better. But others like these short stints, which can be highly paid if the employer is a *gabacho.* People can earn between 25 and 40 dollars for two hours of work, for example, which in the worst-case scenario is five dollars above the minimum of ten dollars an hour and, at best, double the amount. These short stints of work include a wide range of activities. Jornaleros get hired to maintain gardens—*trabajar una yarda*—paint rooms, work on decks, help people move furniture, and in a few instances clean a garage

Clearing a garden, or *trabajando una yarda.*

or something of the sort. Longer-lasting jobs are usually related to home improvement, breaking concrete—*romper concreto*—to fix the garage entrance or other more elaborate remodeling.

Employment with first-time *patrones* is thus regimented by the desirability of the work, the wages offered, and the visibility a jornalero can attain on the corner. First-time employers like to see and assess the men they hire. This I experienced first-hand, since I was never offered work until I shaved my beard and left a mustache, which to the jornaleros made me look less "degenerate" and to employers made me better fit the stereotype of a day laborer. Until then, my height, glasses, and beard earned me a variety of nicknames among the day laborers, like Che Guevara, El Italiano, or El Judio Errante, all of which pointed to my "strangeness" on the corner. After I shaved, however, I was addressed directly many times, the employer even getting out of the car and pointing at me, because at more than six feet, I looked like a jornalero but appeared much bigger and stronger than most of the people around me. Racial and age typing plays an important role here. My friend Lorenzo, who is in his midfifties, clean shaven, and light skinned, got many jobs with older white women who hired him for work inside the house, in part, I think, because he looked less threatening than the rest of us.

Jornaleros also need to evaluate their employers and follow highly racialized and, to a lesser degree, gendered assumptions in how they judge potential *patrones*. These notions of how to measure an employer are based on past experience and on conversations among peers. My first notes about *la parada* are riddled with allusions and direct references to a discrete categorization of employers along racial/ethnic lines. *Morenos*—African Americans and anyone perceived as black—are the worst employers. The men consider *morenos* to be stingy and say they offer very little money and are likely to give you less than promised or simply leave you on a job and never come back. *Morenos* are followed by Tongans—*tongas, tongos*—who can be Pacific Islanders or any type of contractor perceived to be both ethnic and foreign. I heard complaints about Tongans in Berkeley, Oakland, and Palo Alto. As Clemente put it, everyone knows that *tongas* are the most likely to leave you on a job and never come back to pay you. After these almost archetypical bad guys come *árabes*—anyone Middle Eastern looking or sounding—and *chinos*—Asians. Both groups are said to be lousy *patrones* for several reasons; mainly, they pay low wages and demand the hardest work, usually denying jornaleros food and water or telling them to buy it on their own time. Although the men consider these employers to be stingy, they are not as likely to leave a man stranded or pay less than promised. *La raza*—that is, other Latin Americans—is only slightly higher in the hierarchy than the previous groups. "They don't see you as a brother, they see you like something to take advantage of, they treat you as a lesser person," explained Lorenzo, who preferred older *gabachos*, men or women. For him and others, the inequality that characterizes employment in their countries is transposed to the United States, and Latin American *patrones* do not change when they migrate. "Why would he come here and be different? You must take advantage of that here also," explained Lorenzo. It is thus common for jornaleros to judge and suspect "ethnic"-looking employers, who often get frustrated when nobody wants to get into their car.

Going up the hierarchy, women of any ethnicity emerge as less likely to abuse the day laborers. *Gabachos*—white folk—are the best employers, those who value a person's work, pay well, and in general treat jornaleros fairly. Lorenzo told me several times that *gabachos* like it when you speak English: "Here they value that you want to get ahead *[que tú te superes]*, that you do something with your life." *Gabachos* also tend to give tips, something that would not cross the mind of most other *patrones*. Although these stereotypes are riddled with exceptions and many jornaleros have good relations with employers considered *chinos, árabes,* and *morenos,* every man in Berkeley assesses a job along these lines.

THE NETWORK ESTABLISHED

Less that a month into my fieldwork, I was trying to chat with Clemente one morning, when a gray van stopped in front of us. Three men standing nearby walked up and got in without a word to the driver, who was a *chino.* One of the men who had already buckled his seatbelt leaned forward and called out to us, the tension in his voice apparent from the speed of his comment: *"¡Falta Luis, falta Luis!"* They were missing a member of the work team. As Clemente stood up and grabbed his backpack to get into the front seat, Luis appeared, jumped into the van, and they drove off. "They've been working with him for some time," Clemente said, sitting back down next to me with no particular expression on his face and no comment about his attempt to replace Luis. "That *chino* has a lot of work, but he doesn't like it when you're late. He'll just take someone else," he explained. The "team," in fact, consisted of four men who did not know each other well but who had been hired one morning to work on the employer's home-renovation project. For the days they were on the job together, they hung out before work and discussed what they were going to do. The rest of us just sat on the wall, watched the passersby, and listened.

Most work on the street starts with a jornalero getting a job with someone he does not know. Once he establishes a closer relationship with the *patrón*, it is possible that more work will materialize. There are also occasions when a man works with friends or acquaintances who take him on a job with someone they know. These *patrones* can also potentially become part of a network of employers. The *chino*—actually a Korean—came to *la esquina* off and on for the two years I was a regular there, favoring Luis because he understood and spoke English quite well.

Networking, in theory, is more profitable than simply waiting for a *patrón* on the street, since repeat employers are more likely to hire someone on longer-term jobs, either because they are subcontractors or own small construction or gardening businesses, or because individuals fixing up their homes are more likely to hire someone they know for a more complex endeavor. Network employers are also more trustworthy, since the jornaleros never go to work twice for someone who they feel has cheated them. Developing an effective network is up to each man. For a network to be successful, day laborers depend both on their ability to establish a relationship with repeat employers and on getting along with the other jornaleros they know. They also need to be able to keep up with cell phone payments, since in almost every case networks are articulated and set in motion through this precious commodity, which is usually the first to go in a bad month.

In truth, it is hard to assess why some men are better at establishing network *patrones* than others. I know men who were able to handle an effective network a few weeks after arriving on the corner, while others, like Clemente, after years still did not have regular contacts. Managing a network entails being reliable but also has to do with a man's cultural capital, his ability to do specific jobs, and ultimately his willingness to accommodate particular employers. When these elements come together, the men find themselves not only making ends meet but also doing more interesting work. Sindi and Don Raúl, for example, spent a weekend in Nevada, helping a woman they had met in Berkeley clean out her vacation home. They came back with pictures of themselves playing in the snow with mountains in the background. Similarly, Carlos and Pablo—Beto's cousins—were hired to paint another vacation home in Lake Tahoe. Francisco also had an employer who took him to Washington State to cut trees in what he thought to be a "private reserve," a job that one of my asylum-seeker friends was also hired to do in Oregon. However, even in these cases, the men did not consider the work particularly profitable after they returned and they all complained that such jobs really did not produce more money than regular day labor. In Francisco's case, he was paid eight hundred dollars for a week, and his *patrón* covered meals and hotel expenses, but Francisco still considered it a bad deal because after he got back he did not get a job for almost two weeks. It might have been smarter, he argued, to stay and take the few local jobs he had been called for, which he had had to decline, risking loosing contact with employers who hired him regularly.

Even when a man has a well-established network, its effectiveness is not guaranteed, since it is common to spend weeks without work and then get hired for a couple of days during which you then get called by some of your other *patrones* for jobs you cannot agree to, as in Francisco's case. This common occurrence weakens jornaleros' networks, since the employer will simply go to the corner and hire someone else who might then become the person they call later on. Furthermore, homeowners have only so many things they need done and people to recommend a jornalero to, and it is unlikely that they will keep a phone number from one year to another, although Lorenzo has *patrones* who call him every spring to help with the garden and then in the fall to clean up. As Luis aptly put it, "No one here is essential"—*Nadie es indispensable aquí*—and if a man cannot work for his *patrones,* these employers will go back to the corner and find someone else, who in turn might gain the upper hand. This also makes referring a friend to a known *patrón* somewhat dangerous, because a jornalero risks losing the contact. The fact that long-term employment can weaken a man's network undermines ties among jornaleros, who are always implicitly competing with one another.

Networks, at best, are ephemeral. A good repeat employer might contact Luis two or three times after his first job, but then either stop calling because the work was finished or turn to another jornalero because Luis was busy on a given day. A few things do make a jornalero more effective. A cell phone is essential, given the "on-demand" nature of day labor. A car and tools are also useful, since a repeat employer might keep contacting a jornalero because he saves them money in transportation and maintenance. Yet of the men I came to know well, only three had cars that were all, at one point or another, out of service for extended periods of time, impounded, or stolen. Finally, all the day laborers I knew who had established network *patrones* were also somewhat proficient in English and followed instructions well, something many jornaleros do not do, especially those like Jaime—a stubborn Honduran in his fifties—who prefer to subsist by daily work alone. This particular day laborer was apt to complain about most of the work he was hired to do and would walk up and down the street talking to acquaintances and explaining, "I am no machine"—*No soy máquina*—when telling people he had been, once again, exploited.

There is a final version of *trabajo regular* that is highly desired on the street and is the most unlikely to happen. This is when day labor becomes regular work through a jornalero's own agency. Most men I spoke to daydreamed about buying a *troca*—pickup truck—getting some tools, and doing contract work on their own. A few men on *la parada* had something close to a "business," although they hung out with the rest of us because they never had enough work to avoid the street altogether; in fact, they were on the corner almost every day. One of these men—owner of a truck with "Professional Gardening" and a phone number printed on its doors—tried to hire me to sue a man who owed him thousands of dollars. The others were two brothers who hung out *en las vías* and owned a truck, with which, they claimed, they made a lot of money moving furniture. In both cases the other jornaleros resented the men, whom they considered "bossy," conceited, and not humble enough. Most other jornaleros felt they put on airs unnecessarily, since they too spent most of their time on the corner taking any job.

In part, cultural capital and the contingencies of living by a day wage make it difficult to learn the ropes. After returning to the street, Chucho came to me one morning, nudged on by Luis, to ask if I could help him. He was confused as to what he wanted to ask and explained that a woman wanted to hire him to fix her driveway, like a contractor. After a few attempts, he managed to tell me that the lady said "that she wanted me to write down how much I would charge on a piece of paper." He was not quite sure what that meant. We talked about this a while. Luis said it was a *presupuesto* and I said it was like the card of Luis's uncle, which said "estimates." Chucho did not understand why she wanted it on paper and explained he had already agreed to do the work for six hundred dollars, after the woman told him his initial offer of eight hundred was too much, even though this was almost half what a contractor would charge. The final outcome was a wrinkled and scribbled piece of paper on which he wrote exactly what he had told the woman verbally: *son seiscientos dólares.* He never got the job.

During the years I came to *la esquina* regularly, most men were thus undertaking short-term jobs, interspersed with some longer stints they usually found through their labor networks. Labor networks and friendships were personal relationships that emerged and were cultivated while we waited for *patrones* to appear. Jornaleros and anthropologist alike had little more to do than sit around and talk to each other as we passively watched the goings-on of the world around us. The corner, if nothing else, was about waiting expectantly in hopes of getting lucky, while appearing considerate of others' *situación.*

2 Friendship and the Inner Workings of Day Labor

Standing on the corner for long hours, waiting for work at *la parada,* but also waiting for a phone call from a *patrón,* the men can spend days on end without getting a job. The street corner is a place of socialization where the men have a lot of contact with peers and where the relationships that arise are central to their lives. Yet, as with all other relations on the street, friendship is highly unstable. On the corner, jornaleros establish important personal and labor contacts and interact with one another at different levels, some very intimate. It took me months to realize that these relationships are not as strong as they seem at a given moment. At first the men on Fifth Street appeared to cherish their time on the corner. "There is no work here but we come to have fun," Luis liked to say after a good session of joking, to which Don Raúl was wont to reply, with a chuckle, "No work, but we come to keep our spirits up"—*venimos para no agüitarnos.* Before I began to understand the dynamics of labor at the site, these uplifting comments seemed to point toward an implicit comradeship among the day laborers. But solidarity and camaraderie are much thinner, weaker in every sense of the term, than anybody lets on. And while the sentiment about keeping spirits up is common, most men feel threatened by the others, who can have a negative impact on their ability to sustain themselves and their families. To see men commiserate, help each other out, and advise each other on issues from the intimate to the practical leads one to somewhat cherish the resilience they have in the face of adversity. Strife, intrigue, and outright conflict, however, are just as common on the street.

SPREADING THE WORK

To work on the street entails practices and relationships that come together in a tenuous balance, where what one does and what people think about what one does come into conflict. On the street, friendships are easily forged and dissolved, work teams become consolidated and disintegrate just as quickly, and status among peers can turn to antipathy and ostracism from one moment to the next; these circumstances are all a function of the perceptions the men develop about what other jornaleros think and do in relation to work and collaboration. In this sense, it is impossible to talk about a "community" of day laborers or even just a cohort of friends and acquaintances, because the realities of their work allow only fickle relationships to develop in passing. It is perception that counts. Jornaleros thus become inscribed in personal and labor relationships that require getting work, ensuring the agreed-upon payment, being treated with respect by *patrones,* and ultimately appearing to act for the benefit of others in their cohort. Through these relationships a jornalero enters into a moral economy of sorts, where it is the perception of his fair and just behavior toward others that becomes central to his status on the corner. In this moral economy of perception, day laborers must try to maximize their access to work—directly, by being chosen over others on the street; and indirectly, by managing labor networks in which one man will call upon acquaintances when offered work for several others. At the same time, jornaleros must appear unpretentious, humble, and active participants in the relations of reciprocity that seek to maintain a fair balance of available work. A day laborer must thus ensure that people do not think he is hording jobs at the expense of others and simultaneously manage to make ends meet in a system of harsh competition.

The perception the men have of their peers' behavior entails creating an image of "spreading the work" and being conscious of other men's *situación*. This is the first thing an external observer notices when he or she arrives on the corner. When I started fieldwork, for example, I was always surprised when a car stopped on the curb to offer work and the group apparently decided whose turn it was to get in. The men seemed to organize around the corner with an implicit understanding that whomever the employer addressed had first dibs on the job offered but was also obliged to consider *la situación* of the people around him. Luis was particularly careful about passing on jobs to others, and it took me a while to realize that he usually did so only with shorter work stints lasting a few hours or when someone had explicitly mentioned being short on money and Luis had worked the day before. Other men acted in similar ways, especially when they had hung out with the people involved. When Luis stood up to talk to a man in a van one morning, for example, he turned to Beto and said, "The job is only for three hours, lets send Campeche, who hasn't worked yet." Campeche was new on the corner and for two weeks had sat next to us without getting any work. The three guys standing next to him all nodded and encouraged him to go. It was the first job he got in Berkeley.

This form of solidarity was presented to me as one of the reasons for choosing Berkeley over other sites in the region and investing in the transportation costs involved, especially over the two sites in Oakland and Richmond, which were closer to where the men lived. "In Oakland," Beto explained, "people run in front of each other, they elbow you to get ahead. Some *patrones* see the horde of men coming and pushing and take off. Here it's different." Beto put his hand on Eduardo's shoulder and continued, "For example, I know he hasn't worked lately, so if they tell me to bring someone else I'll tell him." Beto then pointed to Luis, Clemente, and Don Raúl: "They know that also, so we all agree he should be the one." This was put into practice around me in my first weeks of fieldwork, especially in relation to the newcomers Eduardo, a Mexico City native who had left his variety shop to improve his lot in El Norte, and Campeche, the son of indigenous Guatemalans, born and raised in the Mexican state that gave him his nickname. While Campeche—barely twenty years old and quiet—quickly became close to Beto, sharing jobs and referring each other to employers, Eduardo failed from the start.

EDUARDO'S DOWNFALL

The ease with which a falling-out between jornaleros can change the social composition on a given corner was surprising, and over a period of two years I learned that no group of friends or workmates lasted very long. I also learned to be careful with the men's perceptions of me, always offering help to anyone who asked—I was mainly a source of information, asked to look things up on the Internet or translate a variety of documents—but never appearing to favor anyone more than others. Eventually, my friendship with some of the men aligned me with them over others, and I was teased for being *el achichincle de Luis*—his sidekick or assistant. I managed, however, never to antagonize anyone explicitly.

It was Eduardo, in fact, who helped me become close to the various men who came to the Fifth Street corner. At thirty-two, he was close to my age and we got along from the beginning, although he made it difficult at times. When I arrived, he was a relative stranger to the other regulars, which was the reason Beto chose him to illustrate that they had to lend a hand so he could get started—*hay que tenderle la mano*. Eduardo, in turn, tried to learn to "talk the talk and walk the walk" with other men who, over a period of about ten months, became convinced that he was not the guy to work with.

I think Eduardo considered me a cosmopolitan kindred spirit with whom he could discuss science and his poetry. Unlike the others, he never seemed suspicious of me when I first appeared—Luis, in fact, would initially greet me each morning with a grin and a friendly "Who the hell is this guy and when is he leaving." Before coming to the United States, Eduardo owned a store on the outskirts of Mexico City where he sold *peluches*—stuffed animals—and had a computer with which he surfed the Internet, favoring museum webpages from around the world and various documentaries. He also liked talking with friends and customers and made a point of telling us how he loved to *platicar con las morras*—chat with the girls—who came into his store. His work as a shopkeeper set Eduardo apart from many of the other Mexicans, who were mostly unskilled manual laborers back home, but many of the men shared his passion for knowledge. On the corner, we talked for long hours about science, history, and when joined by Luis—whose family had nicknamed him *el animalitos* because of his appetite for nature documentaries—tested one another's knowledge about common and obscure endangered species. I was never a contender in these conversations—both Eduardo and Luis had encyclopedic knowledge about these subjects, and I lost bets over the exact speed of light and the differences between Asian and African elephants.

Eduardo lived in Orinda with cousins who had come to the United States eighteen years before him and whom he had not seen since childhood. Their relationship was good, although Eduardo was not really considered part of the family. He rented a small room from them, joining in family activities like flying kites at the marina and going out to eat. He also seemed to be proactive about work. The first time I met him he gave me his business card, which he said made it easy for *patrones* to get in touch with him if they ever required his services again. Eduardo considered himself an excellent painter and worked on weeklong jobs painting hotels in San Francisco and Sacramento during the time he was on the corner. He also had an incipient network of *patrones* who were beginning to call him for jobs around the house. When I met Eduardo in August 2007, he would spend most of the morning on the Fifth Street corner and then walk down to *las vías* to hang out with another group on Fourth Street. He seemed to be well known by the men on both corners and partook of the daily revelry and joking, went on some jobs with others, and helped the Multicultural Institute prepare the Friday lunches.

In truth, Eduardo was also a strange character at the site. Hyperconscious about my own behavior among the jornaleros, I wondered why he made himself an easy target for jokes and cruel teasing. When we talked about women, he told outrageous stories about sexual exploits that none of us believed, tried to act "macho" about always having a water bottle next to his bed so he could hydrate while having sex, and then separated himself from the others by making a big deal about liking older women. When he was not participating in our conversations, he put on the headphones of a cheap CD player and sang along to sappy love songs in a high-pitch and out of tune voice that anyone mildly acquainted with male behavior in most of the Western world would avoid. Finally, he was very loose with his feelings around relative strangers and talked about his intimate sexual experiences—including being propositioned by men—to people he did not know. Eduardo also set himself apart from the others by bringing stories and love poems he wrote and reading them to the men on the corner, ignoring their jokes and scorn.

Eduardo's behavior also made him an easy target for *albures*—double entendres—about his masculinity, and I was not always able to avoid jumping on his childish or "touchy-feely" remarks as I learned to joke *a la mexicana* and became part of the scene. The truth is that I always got along with Eduardo better when we were alone and not subject to the scrutiny and approval of others, who did not see me as "soft" as they saw him. All I can say is that as anthropologists we are not exempt from taking sides in our fieldwork, just as we cannot "act" in ways that do not coincide with our own personalities. I never bullied Eduardo, but I never aligned myself with him publicly either. Both options would have been equally artificial, since in the first instance I could not ignore his friendship, but in the second I simply could not understand why he made himself so vulnerable to the criticism and joking of his peers. Eduardo's background as a shopkeeper as opposed to a manual laborer is not sufficient explanation, since in private he got along better with other men besides me too. I think he simply could not manage group dynamics and sought to position himself in a system of relations he did not really understand.

It was not Eduardo's "weirdness" alone that got him in trouble, however, but his inability to learn to manage the moral economy of perception at play on the corner and his tendency to trust people he really did not know. A few months into his sojourn on the street, Eduardo sat on the wall one morning telling us that while he was painting in San Francisco one of the women who had been hiring him around the house in Berkeley had called him for work. Matter-of-factly, he mentioned that he had turned down the offer because the San Francisco stint was supposed to last a couple of weeks. Now he was frustrated because the job had fallen through, he had not been paid, and he could not reach the woman who probably had hired someone else to do the work. Luis, who was listening, turned and sharply scolded Eduardo for waiting a week to contact her again: "You have to do it immediately or they'll get someone else, no one is essential here *[acá nadie es indispensable]*." Then he turned to me and repeated, "*¿No crees Tomás? Nadie es indispensable en la esquina.*" Luis meant that Eduardo should have held onto the contact by either offering to work at some other time or telling the woman he would send a friend. Eduardo tried to argue that there was nothing he could have done, but Luis was unrelenting: Eduardo should have sent someone he knew to do the work if he could not. That way, he could have kept the contact.

Two days later, Eduardo got a call from a *filipina* who sometimes hired him to work around the house. He stepped aside for privacy to talk to her, which inevitably caught our attention. We watched him intently, and after hanging up he was forced to explain that he had declined the work she offered because he already had something else the next day. The guys around him all let out angry and exasperated sighs. Luis said he should have told her that one of them could go. Then, lecturing Eduardo, Luis told him that in these situations he should always tell the person he would send a friend, always. These were not empty words, since I had seen Luis do this with other men he trusted several times. Eduardo defended himself, explaining that he could not recommend anyone now because she said she was leaving the house and he did not have her cell phone number. Luis told him to call quickly and tell her that one of them would go the next day. Eduardo agreed but refused to call back because he thought that was too aggressive, instead promising to mention it if she called again. Then, dumbfounded, he asked which one of us he should send. There was an uncomfortable silence and they all made circular motions to indicate that he should take anyone. Eventually, the group decided it should be Clemente, and he and Eduardo went off together so Eduardo could show him where the house was (only a few blocks away), just in case. They came back shortly, and Luis told Clemente that if he could not make it, he should tell one of the others.

The next day I asked Clemente if he had gone to the job that Eduardo was supposed to set up for him. He made an exasperated face and, ticking his temple with his forefinger, said that Eduardo was wrong in the head. Luis seemed to agree. Clemente explained: "He told me sometimes they pay fifteen, sometimes twelve, and sometimes ten dollars but that he didn't know how much [the woman was paying this time]—he said she didn't tell him." Clement and Luis both shook their heads. Eduardo had made himself suspect because he did not effectively handle networking with his peers, and he lost their respect because he seemed unable to hold on to his *patrones*. His isolation was also becoming apparent because he did not even know who to send in his stead, a decision that was, in fact, usually made quietly between men, lest the others think two or three men were monopolizing referrals and boasting about it.

Four months later, things continued to get worse. Eduardo was part of the "regulars" on Fifth Street and often participated in the joking but still made himself suspect by how he managed networks. One morning he appeared late on the corner and told us he did not want to do anything because he had worked hard the day before. Eduardo was trying to boast about his hard work, something everyone did at times, but he chose to do it out of context. The other men smiled, shaking their heads in mock disbelief. Eager to talk, Eduardo told us that on the weekend he had turned down a *patrón* who called to offer work because he only paid twelve dollars an hour. "There are many of us here who want to work, why didn't you call?" asked Clemente angrily. Feeling attacked, Eduardo answered. "I don't work for twelve dollars, only for more than thirteen, and I did call you but you didn't answer." Since Clemente had recently changed his cell phone and had a new number, it was hard to challenge this, even though we all suspected it was a lie. In an effort to make amends, Eduardo pulled out his phone and asked Clemente for the new number. Even though they had been on the corner together every day for several months, the exchange made it clear that neither of the men knew each other's last name.

Shortly after this event, Eduardo began to loose his patience with the Fifth Street crowd, who laughed at his singing, doubted his stories about women, scolded him for not referring others, and had begun to openly exclude him from communal jobs. He thus took to coming only for the second shift—*el segundo turno*—appearing briefly to say hello at around eleven or twelve o'clock, when most of the Fifth Street jornaleros were thinking of going home, and then walking down to Fourth Street. The men on Fifth Street concluded that Eduardo must be doing drugs and drinking down *en las vías,* and they nicknamed him Cocoliso, an allusion to snorting cocaine—*coca*—after he appeared one morning with something that looked like white powder under his nose (which he tried to explain, to no avail, was just sunblock).[1]

1. *Cocoliso* is also the Spanish translation of Swee'Pea, the adoptive son of Popeye in the cartoons created by E. C. Segar. Although the men knew this and I initially thought the nickname was an allusion to Eduardo's childlike nature, the men all mentioned snorting cocaine when I asked where the name came from.

I started following Eduardo down to the other corner where, alone, we discussed his problems. He was tired of the street, he said. The others were saying he was always stoned because his beady eyes watered constantly (he had a congenital malformation of the cornea and used contact lenses). He missed talking with women, and the men on the corner said he was too ugly and dark to meet anything better than a *gorda*—a fatty. By this time he had the greatest number of nicknames of anyone I knew. These included *el espantapájaros* (the scarecrow), *la tortuga ninja* (the ninja turtle), and Freddy Kruger, all referring to his looks. I asked if the men were not just joking—after all, I had a few nicknames myself—and Eduardo became even more serious: "Well yes, but at the same time no, and you know that when you aren't around they say even worse things. You come and talk to them and joke around, but I have come to the conclusion that here one is alone."

Originally, Eduardo explained, he thought he had *compañeros*—mates—on the corner, but even the new people he had befriended on Fourth Street always called other guys when *patrones* needed more hands, "even guys they don't know as well as they know me." He complained about Luis, his main tormentor, whom he thought only looked out for himself but still managed to keep on everyone's good side. He reacted to my disbelief with a curt, "Here people would rather lose a job that refer someone else." He could not understand why no one called to refer him when he was clearly good at everything he had been asked to do, and he kept repeating, *"Aquí no hay amigos, Tomás"*—There are no friends here. He actually said there was no "reciprocity" on the street. It was a moment of frustration, and I could not bear telling him that I thought he had brought these problems on himself with his failed bragging. What was worse, except for contact with his family, which were distant relations at best, his only social outings were with men on the street, younger jornaleros I never really spoke to but who stopped by every once in a while to make fun of Eduardo's behavior in bars. "Music is all I have," Eduardo said sadly, fidgeting with his CD player.

By April 2008 Eduardo was hanging out on Fourth and Fifth Streets only in the afternoons and had new friends, *el bicho* or just Bicho—which roughly translates to "critter"—a twenty-four-year-old alcoholic Guatemalan who looked like a teenager, and William, a Salvadoran in his midforties who had recently arrived, was always in high spirits, was an outspoken adherent of Alcoholics Anonymous, and was a proud member of an evangelical church. Eduardo had also managed to get paid for his work in San Francisco and bought a 350-dollar iPod, which, with his cousin's computer, he had filled with songs downloaded from the Internet. The morning crowd scoffed at Eduardo's attempt to move to the afternoon shift and jeered about me becoming an alcoholic by following him to Fourth Street. Luis, in particular, thought that I was mixing with the wrong crowd and disbelievingly asked almost every morning if those people actually got any work in the afternoons. They did, and along with William, Bicho, and others, Eduardo was scrapping out a living just like his onetime companions in the mornings.

Nonetheless, Eduardo was also the brunt of cruel jokes and nicknames among the new crowd, and, as before, did little to avoid it. For example, he insisted on keeping his work clothes in his backpack, wearing always new and fashionable clothes and a pair of transparent work goggles he found on the bus that protected his eyes from dust and wind but that also gave him a distinctively 1980s look, which provided ample opportunity for smartass remarks from the other men. He also continued his singing—poem and story writing now included his own songs—and, finally, his absurd boasting about women had now earned him the nickname *el padrote,* which roughly translates to "pimp" but also has a "well-dressed" connotation that makes it sound more like "sugar daddy." Furthermore, as Eduardo had mentioned before, William and Bicho seemed to go on more jobs together than they did with him, and they socialized on the weekends without calling him. Nonetheless, Eduardo was more at ease with his new group, especially because he had aligned himself with two characters who were also outliers and considered a bit "weird." Bicho was always drunk and close to becoming a *borrachito,* and William constantly proclaimed the advent of Jesus Christ and acted too happy for most people. They shared the corner of Fourth Street with the two brothers who supposedly had a "business" with their pickup truck and who were considered snobs by almost everyone. Eduardo managed to ingratiate himself with his two newfound friends by contesting the brothers' ill treatment with a song he composed on the street. Titled "El Jornalero Rucanrolero," the song made fun of one of the brother's advanced age, physical appearance, and boastful attitude toward work, something I will address later.

But the song, which I discuss in chapter 4, did little for Eduardo's problems and by June, Bicho had stolen his iPod and William had gone on to other corners and made friends. When word about the iPod got around up on Fifth Street, no one was surprised. Eduardo was simply stupid to lend the thing out, explained Luis, who once in a while had handled the music player. In one of our final conversations, Eduardo was almost in tears as he told me he wanted to go back to Mexico: "You don't understand, Tomás, you come here to have fun, to talk with people you like, but I have met murderers here, people who boast about killing their girlfriends, people who steal. In Mexico I had a store, I had a house I built, I myself hired the people to work on it, like they hire me here. There are no friends on the street." Two months later, after a few weeks on vacation with my wife, I returned to a *parada* without Eduardo. Some people said he had gone to Los Angeles; others claimed he had gone home. His phone was disconnected and I never heard from him again.

Eduardo failed to understand many of the underlying principles of the moral economy of perception at play on the corner as well as the tenuous balance between joining in manly banter and exaggerating his own status and masculinity. He used the general rhetoric about fair wages incorrectly, boasting he would not even work for twelve dollars around men who had not been picked up in days. He did not appear to "spread the work" and seemed to forget the importance of maintaining this perception, proudly claiming that he turned down jobs he could have easily passed on to others. He apparently did the same thing on the other corner, since William and Bicho also excluded him from joint ventures. The ostracism Eduardo felt was not explicit at first, for every group included him in conversations and he even got along with Luis when they were alone. But the others learned not to count on him and grew tired of his exaggerated tales. The fact that he would not wear his work clothes while at the site was perceived as putting on airs, as was the purchase of an expensive MP3 player that cost more than what most men sent home every two weeks or so.

Studies of masculinity have called attention to the tensions inherent in managing perceptions about gender and social position (Brandes 1980; Gutmann 2007). On the corner, bragging about being macho was combined with intimate accounts of married life and childcare in ways that Eduardo could not replicate. He either went to far in his exaggerations or became intimate in his accounts too easily and at the wrong moments. In reference to masculinity in Andalucía, Spain, Brandes (1980: 37) has argued that "a man's identity depends in large measure upon his estimation of his social rank, including his overall notion of both the social hierarchy in which he finds himself and of his place within the scheme." In a way, Eduardo was unable to enter the game of identity and rank among his peers; he simply could not understand or identify the appropriate behaviors and boundaries as they shifted in different situations, which basically made him always suspect. Gomberg-Muñoz (2011: 88–100) identifies hazing and humorous banter as a mechanism of cohesion among busboy work teams in Chicago. In her rendering, these serve to get newcomers in line, maintain the group's efficiency, and also to ameliorate the tedium of long hours of work. On the street corner, however, there were no set work teams, and humor and hazing centered on perceptions that affected temporary relations. Masculinity, know-how, knowledge, sexual prowess, and humility—including spreading the wealth—became articulated into the men's interactions as jokes and back-and-forth conversations that resulted in perceptions about solidarity and ethics on the corner, as well as maintaining their status as men. Eduardo failed phenomenally in this arena, but all the jornaleros were inevitably positioned precariously in relation to their peers, and falling out with acquaintances they had worked and shared much time on the corner with was an everyday occurrence.

WORKING ALONE, WORKING TOGETHER

Jornaleros make their living from a combination of individual and joint undertakings. Working alone can entail social ties, when friends who already have work "recommend" another jornalero to a known *patrón,* as is clear from the events described above. Joint ventures can involve ad hoc groups of men who were standing together when the employer appeared or groups formed when one jornalero is asked by a regular *patrón* to bring others for a particular job. Yet because not all people on the corner hit it off well, and because not all jornaleros accommodate their employers, it is

Work team.

common that in a group of men some will be rehired for the rest of the job, and some will not. Those excluded inevitably blame their workmates, and tension among acquaintances is common.

The Fifth Street corner of the Berkeley site was exceptional in that it included a great many jornaleros who liked joking around. *La esquina de los albures*—roughly, "the corner of double entendres"—as others referred to it, seemed to be a place of great personalities and great friendships. Yet within six months of my being there, these relationships changed radically. Don Raúl left in December, around the time that Beto and his two cousins *(los trillizos)* began to be ostracized by the rest of the men. This led Sindi to hang out on other corners, because he had a falling-out with the three men, who were from a community near his hometown in Mexico and who, he thought, should have behaved better. The *trillizos,* who initially seemed to be everyone's friends, became distanced from the others because, as Sindi told me, "They only [work] with each other and mistreat the rest. They don't work with anyone else and treat us all like if we were lesser men." They had landed some good jobs that lasted several weeks and never included anyone else. That most of these jobs only included Carlos and Pablo (the two brothers) and not Beto (their cousin) seemed irrelevant, and no one spoke to Beto when he came to the corner, because they felt it was inappropriate for him to compete for work if his cousins had gotten such good jobs.

This falling-out was subtle and it was only in going back through my field notes that I began to recognize some of the symptoms. A few months before, Luis, Campeche, Iván, Beto, and I were on the same corner one morning when an old pickup truck drove up and parked next to us. A small blonde woman got out and came up to us, saying in native Spanish that she needed a *cerrajero*—a locksmith. She explained she had locked her keys inside her house. Luis, whom she mainly looked at when she spoke, said he did not know a locksmith but that he might be able to take the door off its hinges. We all discussed whether these would be on the inside or outside of the house, and the woman became impatient. Finally Beto hesitantly approached and said, *"Seño, si quiere vamos"*—Ma'am, why don't we go and see. He claimed he had opened a door before and that he had the right tools in his bags. As he spoke he seemed reticent, and he looked at Luis several times to gauge his reaction. Luis never looked back and said nothing. The woman had business in the office behind us and told Beto to wait for her. He eyed Luis as he nodded, finally adding, "Sure, unless you [meaning Luis] want to go." Luis shook his head and mumbled that he had no idea about opening locks. Beto was trying to be diplomatic and show deference to Luis, who was respected by most of the other men. Luis had already decided that Beto and his cousins were monopolizing the work and putting on airs.

Family ties and family solidarity, along with the wrong attitude, seemed to have worked against the three men. Beto took to hanging out on the Sixth Street corner, a block up the street. Even then, the men of Fifth Street mumbled under their breath when they saw him: "Look at him, since his cousins have work, now he comes here to see what he can find." The once close group was divided in two and I seemed to be the only go-between. This also brought me trouble, since Luis and the others became nasty and quiet if I joined them after talking to any of the three men, who in turn took to greeting me without speaking to anyone else. Luis, a master at manipulating such situations and somewhat of a ringleader, fell into the same position as the *trillizos* toward the end of my fieldwork.

Clemente had a similar falling-out with everyone else after I finished fieldwork. I later learned that problems started many months before when

Clement, Luis, Iván, and two other men were hired by a *chino* to do work in his house. The "team" constituted some of my closest acquaintances, the "main" cohort of people I had interacted with and whom I envisioned as a close group of jornaleros who looked out for each other. For two weeks the *chino* came every morning to pick up the guys. Halfway through the job, Clemente was late one day. The men waited a few minutes in the van and seeing that the *patrón* was losing his patience, simply told Campeche to come instead. When Clemente arrived and I told him what had happened, he shook his head knowingly: "That's the way it is, Tomás, that's the way they are. They hate me because I am Salvadoran, because I have papers."

Clemente, in fact, was physically disabled, stubborn, and opinionated. He had trouble holding all his regular jobs and fought constantly with employers on the street. Although the other men were friendly toward him and he seemed to be part of the group, several of them told me in confidence that they did not like working with him. Others complained that Clemente argued with employers and threatened to leave a job half-way done. His failure to arrive on time led to his replacement by a quiet twenty-year-old who was considered hardworking and easygoing. Over the first year I was on the corner, Clemente told me several times that the other men hated him, always after he had been pushed out of a work group. I never heard anyone express outright dislike for him, but it is noteworthy that he felt this when at odds with the others. The fact that he was Salvadoran also never came up when I talked to other people, yet he felt excluded from the primarily Mexican cohort on the corner. That he had papers also never seemed to be a problem, and I saw many men suggest to him that he apply for a wide variety of jobs to which only a documented person would have access.

Like other times, these tensions were not expressed in a face-to-face encounter; Clemente only complained in passing that he had been replaced and stood on the other side of the street for a couple of days, after which everything seemed to go as before. But the problems continued in a roundabout way until he broke all relations with the men of Fifth Street. In February 2009 I returned to the corner a couple of times to catch up on what was happening. One morning, sitting alone with Clemente, he complained to me that he had not worked all month and had only had two little jobs in January. He also asked surreptitiously if I had talked to *el dos*

Working together, a short-term endeavor at best.

cejas—double eyebrows—a nickname he had given Luis in better times. I mentioned that we had spoken a couple of days before. "He must be working because I haven't seen him this week," Clemente said, shaking his head. "That one never speaks to me anymore, he isn't like before, he's changed." His complaint started with a situation similar to the one above: "One day I got work and they needed four [men] and I called him and we went, but later they didn't take me, and I had been the one who got the job." Clemente did not seem mad, just annoyed, and he shrugged his shoulders when I asked why they had not called back. I tried to get him to talk about the problem with Luis, but Clemente cut me off: "*That one* owes me money *[una feria]* and he hasn't paid me back . . . On top of that he gets mad when I say something, *that one* doesn't like to pay people back . . .Well it's my fault for going around lending money."

I was surprised, since I had witnessed the loan and knew Luis often borrowed money to pay the rent, always repaying it when he got work. Clemente went on to complain about Iván: "I also lent money to that guy, the light-skinned one *[el güerillo]*, a hundred bucks *[cien baros]* that he never paid back. It's my fault for lending money, and I know it was because *el dos cejas* told him he should ask me, but he still owes me and hasn't paid." Clemente was a good candidate for a quick loan because unlike the other men who had to send money home, he sent no remittances and hence had more cash on hand than men who got more work.

Later when I asked him about this event, Luis answered with bitterness: "I'll never speak English again when we get picked up." He had been the only one fluent enough to understand the *patrón*, who had said he thought Clemente did not really do any work and told Luis not to bring him the next day. "The *gabacho* decided that he only needed three [people] and didn't take *limpy* [Clemente]," said Luis. "Now he and the other guys are saying that I told the *patrón* not to take him." Luis was suspect because the others could not understand what he said to the employer, and so he was blamed for Clemente's dismissal. "Because they don't understand [English]," Luis complained, "they think I am telling him [the employer] who to call and that he is paying me more." Luis was not happy and repeated several times that on the corner "we are all friends until we have to work together." The moral economy of perception had turned against Luis, who for the most part was a master at managing other people's opinions of him. Not wanting to be accused of excluding a fellow jornalero—even though everyone had their doubts about Clemente—the other men on the team had used Luis's superior knowledge of English against him to argue they had no say—literally—in the matter.

To see only solidarity among jornaleros in their response to *la situación* hides the very real tensions involved in this type of life and the fickle nature of the networks that it can establish and that it depends upon. To assume that work at the site is a function of a communal effort is short-sighted. It is in the notion of *humildad*—humility—that balance is maintained in the moral economy of [illegible] uggestion that a person is putting on airs, manipulating employers, and hording work can result in ostracism by one's peers, something noted in other types of Latin American undocumented labor, such as among restaurant busboys (Gomberg-Muñoz 2011). There is a tenuous scale upon which social and work relationships must be balanced with an individual's need to make ends meet. The precariousness of the system is determined by the conditions of labor and jornaleros' access to work and employers. Each time someone decides to go on a job he is risking conflict with someone else who might feel he is more entitled to the work, or is risking having a falling-out with someone who is not hired back later.

I also fell into this murky practice of risk management when I was hired for a job moving furniture. I had spent months wondering if I should go to work with some of my friends who pushed me to try it—"so you can see how the work is," Eduardo used to say to egg me on. But no one ever actually chose me from among the others when the opportunity arose. The *situación* being as bad as it was, I found it hard to take someone else's place, and the men I interacted with seemed to think that others needed the work more than I did. My friends solved this in their usual—cruel schoolyard—manner by sending me to do the work no one else wanted. In every case this entailed strange *gabachos* that either "looked" like homosexuals searching for cheap sex or simply like people who were a little off and thus probably meant trouble.

One morning, a *gabacho* pulled up in a pickup truck with a *china* in the passenger seat and said he needed one guy who spoke English to help her move furniture. When he asked who spoke English, the five or six men on the corner all said "Me, me," jumping up and down. "If you understand me raise your left arm," said the *gabacho* with a smirk. Everyone continued hopping and calling out "Me, me." Without understanding what was going on, the men realized the employer was being difficult, and Eduardo turned to me and said, "You go, Tomás, since you are the one who understands him." Reluctantly I raised my left arm and spent three hours helping the woman arrange furniture in a storage facility nearby. When the *gabacho* returned to pay me and discovered I was a PhD student, he dryly remarked, "Gee, I guess my test was too complicated if it takes an advanced degree to pass it." He said he had a construction company and usually hired a Guatemalan named Mario who brought trustworthy friends when needed:

"He is very reliable and works hard, I called him this morning but he didn't answer, so I came to the corner but I couldn't find him." I knew exactly who this man was, and two days later I bumped into him on Seventh Street. He was respectful but not happy and wanted to know why the man did not call him the day before. "I came early and was hired to work in a yard," he explained defensively. Mario wanted to know if the *gabacho* had said he would hire me again, and I tried to calm him down by saying that the *patrón* did not even ask for my number. Mario was not convinced and walked away mumbling.

To my surprise, a week later as I was standing in line for Friday lunch, a day laborer I had never spoken with came up to me and said, "There is a *gabacho* that was looking to hire you. He asked at several corners for the student who speaks English, but you weren't around." With dread I scanned the room and saw Mario glaring at me, but when I went up to tell him I had no intention of working with his *patrón* again he patted me on the shoulder and laughed, "Relax friend *[tranquilo, amigo Tomás]*, he called me last night and I told him I couldn't go. What he wanted was me to help the *chinita* again, but I already have work for the next week." I averted a crisis by seeming subservient and respectful in a way few other jornaleros could afford. In most cases these tensions remain unresolved, and had I been a regular jornalero Mario would have likely pigeonholed me as a troublemaker or as someone who had taken his *patrón.*

ON COLLABORATION AND ORGANIZATION

The dynamics addressed above point to the intrinsic difficulty of establishing day labor organizations to regulate work and protect jornaleros from unscrupulous employers and dangerous jobs. Day labor centers exist in the Bay Area, mainly in Oakland and San Francisco, and have established programs to organize the workers with different degrees of success. However, many of the men in Berkeley who are familiar with such centers cite them as a reason for not working there, and criticism and distrust of such operations permeates most labor sites I have seen. Trying to regularize employment on *la parada* would require a complex system of taking turns that would have to both be transparent and appear cost-effective.

The Multicultural Institute discussed labor center initiatives frequently but never followed through with the idea because the staff knew of these dynamics, and knew most men felt their chances would always be better on their own. The MI thus attempted to follow the perceptions of jornaleros more closely and to maintain the men's sense of autonomy via a job referral program on the street.

Yet the referral system the MI developed was riddled with problems and accusations of favoritism. The system involved a sign-in sheet and a few hours of holding an advertisement for the institute's labor program on University Avenue. The idea was that the sign-up sheet would establish the order in which men would be sent to work, and they would take turns standing on the curb advertising the labor service to potential employers, using the MI's phone number. But since men come and go, the sign-up order was not strictly kept and many day laborers got bypassed because they were otherwise working when they got the MI call. When the calls did come in, employers expected the jornaleros to come to their homes, and those who did get a turn often lost their way, since most jornaleros only know how to get from their neighborhood to *la parada* and expect to be picked up there.

I spoke to many jornaleros who felt excluded from the MI program, either because they had not been able to take the jobs offered or because they had failed to arrive at the specified place and had been blacklisted as no-shows. People like Luis or Lorenzo, on the other hand, who had been in the Bay Area longer than most of the others and could find their way around easily, were offered jobs several times. It is not difficult to understand why the precariousness of the labor site led to accusations of unfair treatment and, in turn, to resentment that was vocalized when the MI staff was not around. Those perceived as favorites risked others seeing them as "manipulators" working in their own self-interest. Luis quickly inferred that this would happen and stopped participating before others became outwardly aggressive toward him.

Friction with the MI was always based on accusations of favoritism and discrepancies between the men and the institute's main objectives. One of the main problems day laborers had with city officials and the police, for example, was the slow but constant expansion of *la parada* from the recognized "white zones" near the freeway up toward the residential neighborhoods. The men explained this expansion as a result of the increasing number of jornaleros at the site and the need to spread out to achieve better visibility. On my corner, for example, the men crossed the street when too many people appeared in the mornings. As people got hired, or left, the groups contracted and jornaleros crossed back to sit and chat. Other parts of the labor site expanded and contracted in similar ways.

Mario—whose *patrón* I almost unknowingly stole—and other *guatemalas* insisted on standing on Seventh Street (outside the allowed area). "I can go down there and be bunched up with the others," he told me, "and maybe I'll get something *[tal vez agarre algo]*, but probably not. If I don't come up here I won't be at ease, I'll think that maybe if I came up here where there are less people . . . Crowded like that we will achieve nothing and we are here to work, not because we like it, it is necessary . . . We have to pay rent and none of us has sent money back to Guatemala. Where will we go if we do not make money? Under the bridge?"

Not only was *la parada*'s expansion a product of more people. It also resulted from the idea that the better a jornalero stands out from others, that is, the fewer people in his immediate vicinity to compete for the job, the easier it is to attract employers who might otherwise be intimidated by a horde of men trying to get into their car. Spreading out, becoming highly visible, then, was essential for survival. Jornaleros tried different areas of the site, joining friends here and there until they developed a sense of where the good spots were. The City of Berkeley, however, argued that the NGO should try to keep the men in the allotted areas. One attempt was to exclude men who frequented the upper streets from Friday lunches. This blew up into an open confrontation where the outreach workers were accused of favoring Mexicans. The men felt that it was not the MI's place to limit their job opportunities but to increase them. Following the rationale that the MI's employees made a living off of jornaleros suffering, a few men tried to rally others to "force" the group to "do their job," in this case to magically get the city to allow the men to expand toward Tenth Street and to keep the police from ticketing men who stood outside the white zones.

The issues with the *guatemala* expansion up the street did not get better, and one morning I arrived to find the corner in a panic, men walking down from the upper blocks, cursing and talking rapidly about the end of their way of life. After many complaints from neighborhood residents, Berkeley police had appeared and asked the people between Fifth and Eighth Streets to stand in the allowed area between Second and Fourth. Everyone blamed the *guatemalas* east of Sixth Street—the residential area—for being selfish, stupid, and "thick." In turn, the *guatemalas* blamed the MI for being inefficient and racist (which in this case meant "pro-Mexican"). Both these accusations were unwarranted: the men above Sixth Street had been warned repeatedly that neighbors were complaining about their presence, that the City of Berkeley was not going to expand the allowed area, and that the police would eventually get involved.

Clemente also had a falling-out with the MI outreach workers who got him a job cleaning the church where we ate Friday lunch. "They don't help anymore," he told me. "They kicked me out of the church and hired a woman they knew." He had not been back to lunch either. "That's the way they are, Tomás, they hired her for more time, a friend of theirs, I got mad . . . I went to take my name out of a notebook they have and she was dancing, listening to ranchera music, and she treated me poorly *[me trató mal]*. 'Hey! What's the problem with you?' I said, and crossed out my name." Clemente wanted to cross his name out in the church's notebook because he had no intention of ever speaking to the MI again. During the months he worked at the church, he always referred to the MI as his employer, yet it was the church that paid his wages and ultimately decided to go with someone else.

EFFECTIVE OUTLIERS

In the end, the two most economically effective jornaleros I met in Berkeley were both ladino Guatemalans who had some higher education. In fact, the greatest indicator that solidarity on the street was unstable and ineffective is that these particular men, although quite chatty and acquainted with many of the "regulars," worked almost exclusively alone.

Adolfo was in his late fifties when I met him and on his second trip to the United States. As a young man in Guatemala, he had learned his father's trade, masonry, and had also graduated as an accountant from a vocational high school. Even in Guatemala, Adolfo was able to make more money as a mason than in accounting. In the United States, his skill allowed him to earn higher wages, on average, than other people on the street. In fact, Adolfo was regularly paid twenty-five to thirty dollars an hour between 2007 and 2009, twice as much as a good wage on the street. The second time around, he was hired shortly after arriving on the street, to help a homeowner build a small wall in his backyard. The man came to *la parada* and explicitly asked for someone with experience and, not entirely convinced, took Adolfo. To his surprise, this older Guatemalan's work was more than he expected, so he hired Adolfo for a similar job in the front of his house. The employer was so pleased that he told friends about Adolfo and hired him for a couple of other jobs. He also recommended Adolfo on a local webpage. The day we met, Adolfo came explicitly to ask for help finding that recommendation, which had resulted in several phone calls. I found the review, printed it, and translated it for him few days later. He was fascinated that anyone could find his name like that but also worried that someone might write a negative review, since he had recently had trouble with someone who saw his name online.

Another distinctive feature of Adolfo was that he had a run-down car and owned tools, both of which he managed to buy during the year I was on the street. Yet his living conditions were not different from other jornaleros. He spent little on himself and sent everything he made to Guatemala, where he had built two houses and bought household appliances, and where his wife managed his money in order to support his three adult daughters and his grandchildren. Adolfo lived an ascetic life, sharing an apartment with other men he did not socialize with. Feeling he was getting old, he quit drinking and never went out at night to bars, mainly from fear of *morenos,* who roamed his neighborhood in Oakland, stealing from Latin American migrants, and who had injured people he knew.

Lorenzo and Adolfo grew up in the same town and were roughly the same age. Although they knew each other back home, they were in Berkeley independently and talked with great glee of the day they had bumped into each other on the street. Lorenzo had attended college for a couple of semesters after getting a scholarship to study engineering, but money was scarce and he dropped out, working odd jobs for a couple of years and then becoming a door-to-door software salesman. In 1996 he divorced his wife and came to California. Except for a brief stint as a janitor in Oakland, Lorenzo always worked as a jornalero. He had no special skills except that he spoke English well and was amicable and chatty. Of all the people I met, he had the greatest and most consistent amount of work, and employers who hired him did so repeatedly and many times referred him to friends. Other jornaleros considered Lorenzo a nuisance on the street, and most of my friends quietly walked away when he came to talk to me. This was in part because he dominated any conversation and—since he spent his free time watching the news and reading online newspapers at the public library—was prone to try engaging people in "eternal" conversations. This was probably the reason he befriended me, since I could keep up with talk of European socialized medicine, Latin American literature, and US and Latin American politics. Lorenzo was so intense that after the first time he and I went out drinking, he left twelve messages on my cell phone in one afternoon, scaring my wife a bit and earning the dubious title of "my stalker." That said, he was one of the men I got to know best, a close friend who introduced me to his extensive but somewhat estranged family and who took me to meet "friends" in Oakland.

Of all the men I met, Lorenzo was the closest to his employers. He had been hired to clean people's houses and help them set up parties, and he often did "the whole house," starting with garden work, painting the deck, and then cleaning and painting the interior. One example of his ability to network *patrones* was a job he got a little before we met: "A white lady *[una güera]* picked me up to do her garden, and as I was finishing she started setting up a barbecue and I asked her, 'Do you want me to help?'" Lorenzo helped and the woman suggested he stay for the party she was throwing to help her cook the meat, carry out furniture, and then clean up. Lorenzo stayed and helped out, chatting with the guests and giving them his phone number. Of the twenty or so guests, almost everyone hired him to clean their garden or paint their house.

Lorenzo even had a couple of *patrones* who invited him to share meals with the family when he was working for them. Although I never quite believed how close he was to some of these people, I did "witness" an event, where after several hours of heavy drinking in San Francisco, Lorenzo discovered he would be unable to make it home on the bus. He called "Mister Smith" and spoke in English briefly, telling me later that the man would pick him up at the BART (Bay Area Rapid Transit, the local subway system) station and let him stay in the guest bedroom where he slept when he worked for this person.

I attribute Lorenzo's success to several factors. He was quite light skinned and older that most jornaleros in Berkeley and did not fit the stereotype of the somewhat "shady Hispanic." He was also willing to do any job, no matter how menial, and prided himself in his work. In his own words, whereas some other jornaleros did "just enough to get paid," Lorenzo took every job seriously and usually suggested improvements and other jobs to his employers. Although prone to drinking binges every few months that lasted about a week, Lorenzo was responsible, always on time, and very friendly. He also learned that there were things he could say to *gabachos* that resulted in better wages and tips. He always tried to speak English, for example, and told his employers about the English classes he took at the adult school. When the Multicultural Institute made a failed attempt to teach a gardener certification course that entailed attending classes at the church on five consecutive Fridays—something only one person on the street had the luxury to do, namely me—Lorenzo jumped at the possibility of certification. Although he only went to one class, he kept the photocopies and irrigation instruction manuals they gave us in his backpack to show employers that he was taking a course. He also tried to draft me into his network because I was the only "jornalero" to actually fulfill the course requirements; he called nonstop for a whole weekend because he was trying to convince a woman to pay him for cutting down a tree as a "contractor" instead of by the hour: "I told her we took a course and that you were a teacher—call me, Tomás, it is a business deal in which I need a person I trust, someone responsible." On another occasion, when Lorenzo heard about Adolfo's Internet recommendation, he excitedly tried to convince him to become partners and asked me to help them make a webpage to publicize their labor. "If we get organized," said Lorenzo, "we can make a small business. *¿Vah Tomás?* The only problem is the papers."

Both Adolfo and Lorenzo understood their success as a combination of good luck, hard work, and, in Lorenzo's case, a willingness to take any job. At the height of the financial crisis in 2008, when my other friends were spending weeks without work, both these men had jobs lasting several days. They were called for most of these jobs, pointing to an extensive labor network that was mostly composed of *gabachos*. Both men thought their proficiency in English gave them an edge, not only because they could discuss the work with their *patrones*, but also because they could "chat them up." I saw this firsthand with Lorenzo, who many times received calls while we were together and who always enquired about the *patrón*'s family, the weather, and other things I never heard the other men discuss with employers. On the few occasions when a job required more men, Lorenzo and Adolfo recommended each other. "For example, Tomás, I am painting a house and the employer tells me he needs another guy," said Lorenzo. "I'll say, 'Let me talk to a fiend of mine who does a good job,' and then I call Adolfo because I know he will be trustworthy. If Adolfo can't come, I'll tell the *gabacho*, 'Look, if you want we can go to the corner for someone else, but I don't know him so I can't be held responsible for him.'" Both Lorenzo and Adolfo attributed the failure of others to laziness or poor habits. Neither, however, tried to do anything other than day labor for the whole time we were in contact with one another.

In the end, my perspective on the closeness of the men I met was marked by the constant disarticulation of the people I was drawn to because they looked like a group. Lorenzo and Adolfo were, in this sense, an exception, since they never appeared close to any of the other men. Because my account here is not chronological, many of the "regulars" will appear in subsequent chapters and will seem close to each other. The sadness inherent in these relations will be more evident later on, as the inevitable end of closeness, or rather its nonexistence beyond "passing the time" as my friends put it, shapes the tone with which I address the events to come.

3 Abuse and the Absurd Bureaucracy of Small Things

Understanding the ins and outs of day labor involves more than outlining the inner workings of jornaleros' networks and the mechanisms through which they succeed or fail to make ends meet. For marginalized "legal" and "undocumented" Latin American migrants, employer abuse and unjust treatment are the order of the day and regiment many of the decisions men make in relation to work. Almost everyone on the street has had trouble with a *patrón,* whether in the form of withheld wages, on-the-job accidents, or lack of rest, water, or protective gear for dangerous undertakings. Most jornaleros consider the frequency of abuse to be a function of their immigration status, which is many times thrown in their face as a threat when they try to complain. This vulnerability is embodied and naturalized by men whose sojourn in the United States is marked by skepticism toward the possibility of contesting abuse and whose daily experiences reinforce the certainty that they can do little to oppose unfair and illegal actions once they become victims.

All the jornaleros I met have experienced firsthand some variety of employer abuse, mainly being paid less than the agreed wage or not being paid at all. On the street, however, the men understand exploitation as a continuum that starts with notions about the appropriate way to be treated. Thus people complain as much about employers who do not let them rest, or do not provide food and water, as they complain about *patrones* who trick them out of the promised wage. As I have already mentioned, this regiments notions about which employers to trust and which ones to avoid, a process that roughly follows racial lines.

One morning at around 8:00 A.M., an African American in a pickup truck stopped in front of us. The *patrón* called out to Iván, who looked up and shook his head. Luis asked if that was the guy he had worked for the day before. Iván nodded, adding that he would not work with him again. There was a moment of confusion, since the *patrón* seemed to be waiting for Iván to go over and talk to him. Finally, the young Mexican went up to the window, exchanged a few words with the driver, and then turned to Chucho, who had been complaining about money problems, and said, "You go." Chucho spoke no English, so he got up and stood behind Iván, who translated what the *patrón* wanted. The whole exchange made Chucho nervous, and he shook his head several times, saying, *"No me voy güey, no me voy,"* even though Hernando, Luis, and Toño were egging him on to go. Chucho seemed about to get in, but as he saw Iván move away decided against it, closed the door, and walked back. Exasperated, the *patrón* drove up the street and stopped just before the corner to talk to another jornalero who also refused to get in.

"How much was he paying?" asked Chucho after the man left.

"Ten bucks," answered Iván.

"Ten dollars, man? *[¿Diez, güey?]* You should have told me, for ten I would have gone."

I asked what the problem with the *patrón* was, since the confusion and comings and goings were pretty strange. Then I realized that the main issue was that Chucho could not figure out if Iván refused to go because the man was offering too little—most offers below ten dollars I witnessed, in fact, were made by African Americans—or because the man was a bad employer. As usual, in his know-it-all attitude, Luis stepped up and sorted the whole thing out, for both me and Chucho. "The thing is we don't work for the *morenos*," and turning toward Iván asked, "What happened? Did he treat you poorly?"

Iván nodded and said, "Not poorly, but he was not considerate *[pero no fue atento]*—he didn't even offer me a glass of water." Iván explained that the guy was doing gardening jobs. Luis chimed in: "He charges 250 dollars and then pays you 50—he makes 200 dollars without working, that's wrong. The right thing to do would be to pay you 100 or 150 dollars, that would be more fair." Iván said the man didn't even give him a sandwich or anything to drink, and he would never work for him again: *"Y eso que me dijo que le gustaba mi trabajo,* 'I like your work,' *me dijo."*

Luis continued: "The thing about *morenos*—damned piece of coal *[pinche carbón]* we call them in Mexico—they are not good *patrones.* I hardly ever work for them, maybe with the older ones, yes, the ones that are older may be more considerate. I worked for an older one who was more considerate." I asked what exactly he meant by *considerados* and he said, "They don't pay well, they don't offer anything to drink, or give you lunch, or want you to take a break."

"Then who are the best *patrones?*" Luis shrugged his shoulders and said *gabachos* and repeated himself a little: "They are considerate because they know you are doing a job they don't want to do. The *moreno* doesn't, the *moreno* is inconsiderate and doesn't think like that."

"And why do you think they act like that?" I asked.

"Bah! Because they were slaves and they were forced to work and that's why they want to screw you *[por eso también te quieren chingar]."*

Refusing to get into a car was an everyday occurrence on Fifth Street, and jornaleros warned each other about particular employers. While this might indicate some degree of cooperation in trying to control unscrupulous labor practices, everyone knows the *patrón* will eventually find someone to do the work because need—*necesidad*—will be greater than someone's pride or common sense. There are also always *guatemalas* willing to do the work, many of my friends would add. The key issue for Chucho above was that he suspected something was amiss, because Iván refused to work with the *patrón,* which in turn prompted an open discussion about why *moreno* employers are always suspect. Combined, the two exchanges—Iván with Chucho and then Luis with all of those present—illustrate how a jornalero learns the ropes and comes to understand how to measure risk. That most men eventually have encounters with unscrupulous employers then plays into the exchanges, establishes the speaker as an experienced day laborer, and augments the pool of information about *patrones* that is available on the street.

On Fifth Street, men in dire need of money refused to get into the car of an African American because everyone knew the *morenos* paid less (which was, in fact, what Chucho assumed initially), tried to jip you, and never gave you food or water. *Chinos* were reputed to work you to the bone for little money; *árabes* and other Hispanics had similar reputations. Jornaleros rationalized abuse as an effect of "racism," something they understood both in terms of their ethnic or national background and their relative marginality. In the case of Latin American employers, the discourse turned to a "typical" lack of solidarity among *la raza* that distinguishes Latin Americans from other groups: "There are really bad people around, and we really screw each other *[somos bien culeros entre nosotros mismos]*," Clemente told me, explaining that "we," that is, Latin Americans in the United States, were not like the *chinos* who provided ample support for their own. Most jornaleros agree that *gabachos* are the best employers, not only because they tend to pay a fair wage, but because they acknowledge a man's work and effort, provide food and drink, and sometimes even allow work breaks.

In many parts of the Bay Area, especially Oakland, it was the *tongas* who were supposed to be the worst employers, and "everyone knows" that only recently arrived *guatemalas* are dumb enough to go with them. In fact, many jornaleros told me they kept away from Oakland because the *guatemalas* were so easy to swindle that the *patrones* there expected to pay less than any other place. *Tongas* were said to be very big and heavy, but none of the jornaleros I spoke to knew exactly where they were from. *Tonga* is a racial category that gets scripted onto *patrones* who are either from the Pacific Islands or perceived to be foreign or heavyset and who work as subcontractors. The story is always the same, as my friend Leonel explained: "When I was just starting I went with a *tonga.* He left me in Pleasanton [working on a garden] and didn't come back for me, he didn't pay me, I had to catch a ride to get back, because I had no idea where I was. Later people told me how to recognize them, they said, '*Tongas* are big and fat.' Many people refuse to work for them, but you know how it is, *por necesidad,* especially those who are new, they go with them, they don't know how they really are."

Tongas, word on the street dictates, leave you working in a garden they have been hired to do and never come back. When you talk to the house owners, they say they paid the man who hired you and then slam the door.

In one case, I met a man who spent the night by the freeway after realizing that the *patrón* was not coming back. The jornalero was so disoriented that he could not find a bus stop and was too afraid to ask for directions in the affluent *gabacho* neighborhood where he was. The *tongas* have such ill repute that many men agree they like Berkeley because there are very few of them.

In fact, I never actually saw a *tonga* while I was on *la esquina*. Other sites cannot boast the same—and this is not limited to Oakland—as I discovered when visiting a site in the South Bay, on the fringes of Silicon Valley. In answer to the Multicultural Institute's question, "What is the greatest problem you have here?" came agitated exclamations: "What we have to do is to report the *tongos;* we must do something about the *tongos!*" Several men had been picked up by *tongos*—the pronunciation was different but they were talking about the same people—employers who at the end of the work day promised more work and payment later, never to return. "Out of necessity we say yes and they agree to come back another day, but we end up waiting and they never return."

In order to avoid abuse, day laborers couple assumptions about race with "the word on the street." Employers who hire men regularly, like the *moreno* above, do not always realize they develop reputations among the jornaleros, who warn each other when a bad employer appears. These reputations are in many cases so important that they trump economic need. Men who were about to be evicted, or who had lost their cell phone service because they could not pay the bill, preferred not to work than to risk such an encounter. This was a common event on the street, one I witnessed almost daily with *patrones* who perceived to be *morenos, árabes, chinos,* and *la raza.* Although *gabachos* were supposedly the most honest and desirable employers, many men had problems with them too. Reticence to go with unknown white men was also influenced by the fact that all the cases of homosexual harassment I heard of were allegedly perpetrated by affluent *gabachos,* something I will return to in chapter 5.

CONTESTING AND ATTESTING ABUSE

Problems with employers make the day laborer's marginality and vulnerability evident, especially in their own eyes. When I started asking about abusive employers, most of the men told me stories in which they appeared to have a great amount of agency. They all exaggerated the extent to which they could avoid or control abuse. In one of our first conversations, for example, Sindi explained, "Sometimes you work and they pay you nothing. Other times they say work the concrete for 150 dollars, and if you do it too quickly they say no and only pay you 50." This happened often, and Sindi was proud to say that once he had thrown the money at the *patrón*'s feet, saying he would not take it. The jornaleros on the wall with us that day explained that they always paid attention to where employers took them, writing down the addresses, license plates, and phone numbers of the person who picked them up. They said that if a person refused to pay them, or offered less than the agreed-upon wage, they could call the police or go to the Multicultural Institute for help. Sindi, in fact, made it seem like he always made sure his *patrón* knew he had written down his license plate and that the jornaleros had no trouble going to the police. Yet, of all the men I spoke to, only Clemente—who had papers—had ever called the police to deal with a *patrón*.

The MI and other nonprofit organizations also play an important role in telling the men how to avoid exploitation and what to do when it happens. When Sindi told me he wrote down the addresses of his employers, he was repeating instructions that the MI and another organization had given the men at a recent Friday lunch. The importance of the address is twofold: the men sometimes get the MI to contact employers "off the record" to try to solve a problem quickly, and an address is also required on the California Labor Commission forms and in small-claims court when the men file complaints and lawsuits. This explains why, as we talked that day, many men took out little notebooks or cards given out by NGOs and union organizers, on which the men had written down the name of their *patrón*, the address where they worked, and the amount of time they spent on the job.

Although this practice initially seemed widespread, it was not carried out with every employer. Most jornaleros in Berkeley only kept accounts when the job in question lasted several days and the *patrón* deferred payment to the end of the week, the end of the job, or some other prearranged time. For most, the notes were a personal record of money owed and never included an address. In the end, disputes about work and wages usually resulted in the employer disappearing, making an explicit or tacit threat to call *la migra,* or a simple "take it or leave it," which is what Sindi had faced. I came to realize that the little papers with employer information and hours worked were seldom used, as the men could not openly ask *patrones* for the information without sounding like trouble. Jornaleros thus were usually at a loss when it came to producing this information and usually only had the employer's cell phone number and a phonetically latinized version of his or her name.

Even when day laborers do have the required employer information, filling out Labor Commission or small-claims forms is a daunting experience that usually scares people off before they even try. Leonel, a Guatemalan ladino, had been living and working in an informal arrangement with his *patrón,* another Guatemalan, who gave him a space in his garage as living quarters in exchange for work. Leonel received a monthly wage minus what the *patrón* deducted for rent. At five hundred dollars a month, Leonel's rent was the most expensive I heard about on the street. The first time we met, he explained that he had started work in February 2007 and had had continuous employment with the man—who bought houses, fixed them up, and resold them—until November. But his employer had stopped paying him consistently in August, which forced Leonel to go to the corner to make up the difference so he could buy food and send something home.

Leonel had several little wrinkled papers on which he had noted some of the work he had done, but he was not sure how much of it his *patrón* had already paid for. Many of the papers had no date. When I explained how the Labor Commission worked—Leonel calculated that the employer owed him about two thousand dollars—he insisted on knowing how long I thought the process would take, since, disenchanted with *la situación,* he was planning on going home. Leonel had all the necessary information about his employer to fill out the applications; after all, he had lived in the man's house for several months. However, he became distressed when he heard he needed the addresses and dates of all the places he had worked. We discussed this for a while and with the help of one of the MI's outreach team also determined that Leonel needed to quantify the amount of money the *patrón* owed him in terms of days worked. This, to Leonel, would be a gargantuan undertaking, since he had been paid monthly or for specific jobs, not by the hour or by the day.

Leonel came to realize he was trapped—he had only a month to leave the United States before high season doubled airfare to Guatemala, and he had nothing to take home after a year and a half absence. He sadly told me that he had spent his last bit of money on his passport and that he would contact me if he figured out how to quantify his earnings. Two weeks later he appeared on the corner once again, but not to speak to me, simply to see if he could get work. He had decided to stay the summer and return to Guatemala in the fall but said he thought filing a complaint was useless, since according to his calculations, he could only account for five hundred dollars his *patrón* owed, even though he knew it was much more. Furthermore, all the people on the street who heard his story had advised against going to the Labor Commission, because it would take up a lot of time, might get him in trouble with *la migra,* and would most likely result in nothing.

Luis and others on Fifth Street felt bad for Leonel but thought his problems were his own fault, since he had managed his money based on unrealistic assumptions. He was paying 500 dollars for rent, 50 for his cell phone, and he had bought a run-down car that required insurance. Leonel had borrowed more than 2,000 dollars to cross into the United States, and in a year and a half had just barely managed to repay the loan. The men all agreed that he would return home with nothing to show for his absence. Like most jornaleros I met, Leonel never filed a complaint about his employer but simply gave up, trapped between the need to survive, the certainty that he would never see his money, and the longing for a home he felt he had failed.

Leonel's case is more exemplary of the reality on the street than Sindi's boasting, which initially gave me an artificial impression of the ability of jornaleros to deal with abuse. As with other aspects of a day laborer's life, the impotence inherent in this type of work is expressed in exaggerated narratives about one's ability to deal with the exigencies of migration. Only twice did I ever meet men who actually used their notations to file complaints, and in both cases the problem remained unresolved. Boasting about fighting exploitation was thus the closest many men ever got to obtaining redress. In general, abuse is so rampant that jornaleros respond to it with righteous indignation—empty of valence, since it leads nowhere—like Sindi, or with internalized submission, trying to justify their right to the money by arguing that the employer must not have recognized the amount and quality of their work.

Around the time Leonel was asking me about his case, Eduardo and Iván also had a problem with an employer. Eduardo had worked on a construction site for a few days and, even though the man had not paid him yet, did not think twice when the man said he needed another laborer. By the time Eduardo realized he was not getting paid, the *patrón* owed him six hundred dollars and Iván two hundred. On the last day of work, another employee came to the site to close shop and sent the guys home without their money. Fortunately Eduardo knew where the *patrón* lived (they had picked something up there), so the two jornaleros went to his house and left a written message on the door. A few days later the contactor's girlfriend called Eduardo and told him in broken Spanish that they would give him half the money then and half in two months' time. She also said they would pay Iván his part in full. Angry, Eduardo decided the best course of action would be to talk to the *patrón* directly, so he and Iván stopped by again and rang the doorbell, but nobody answered, even though the lights were on and they could hear voices. After waiting twenty minutes, Iván said they should leave, because someone might call the police.

"Well, I told Iván that *we* should call the police," Eduardo explained with anger, "so we can explain that the man owes us money. We already left a note on Friday saying that we need him to pay us because we also have to pay our debts." Iván said the police would not care about that; instead he suggested asking the Multicultural Institute for the papers they needed make a report. Eduardo still thought he should reason with the contractor: "I want to tell him that it wasn't easy, that job, it was hard, I almost cut my arm carrying that metal." *"Puro metal,"* added Iván for emphasis. I told Eduardo that the complexity of the job was irrelevant and that the guy could not decide out of the blue to pay him part now and the rest in two months. "But maybe he thinks, or is going to argue, that we didn't work, that we were there sitting on the ground or something, when we weren't, it was the opposite, that job was hard and he paid the other guys for it," answered Eduardo.

Luis was optimistic about the report and said they should go to the police themselves: "The law here is the same for everyone." Luis said nothing about the report but nodded and added, "They think that because we are wetbacks *[mojados]* we are ignorant, that we are not going to say anything, that they can do that." Iván agreed: *"Lo creen a uno ignorante"*— They think us ignorant. Convinced he should do something, Eduardo showed me the man's name and address, although he was not sure if they were correctly spelled. I looked at the address and asked what city or town it was, and neither Eduardo or Iván was quite sure.

Eduardo was insecure about why the contractor was reticent. Did the man think they didn't work? Did he think the work was easy? If only he realized, then he might pay. Many men internalize the marginal position inherent in standing on the street and counter abuse by reproducing their own powerlessness, as Quesada (2011) has shown in his study of San Francisco day laborers. Eduardo's apparently meek response was common among many men who felt undervalued by employers and sometimes explained abuse as resulting from the misplaced assumption that their work was easy. There was no sense of rights in how Eduardo talked about the situation, although Iván, who had less to loose, was gung ho about making a claim at the Labor Commission, something neither of them had ever done or knew how to do. With the MI's help, the two men managed to start filling out the papers, but so many people scoffed at the pair's certainty that they would be paid that they decided to compromise with the employer. In the end, Iván got all his money and Eduardo had to settle for two-thirds of what the *patrón,* who claimed he had gone bankrupt, owed him. Eduardo and other people who heard about the problem all agreed that getting something was to some degree a success, which legal action would have hindered. Eduardo was lucky, in other words.

DOING SOMETHING ABOUT IT

Although there is general interest in figuring out how to force employers to pay, few jornaleros attempt to do anything about it. *La parada* is riddled with tales of men failing to get their money, some of which include calling the police or going to NGOs for help. Stories like the ones above not only dissuade jornaleros but also make people think that going to the police is a necessary step in filing these complaints, which is not the case. Police in fact can do little to immediately address such problems, which are legally considered civil matters. Contact with the police, even in a sanctuary city like Berkeley, is something all jornaleros want to avoid.

In truth, the most common way to deal with not getting paid is to avoid unscrupulous employers and to be wary of the types of people who might swindle you. A jornalero must make sure that his *patrón* is good before working for him or her, because once he gets in the car everything depends on the employer. If the *patrón* decides to pay a jornalero less, leaves him stranded, and so on, there is little the jornalero can do. This is also one reason why the men prefer repeat *patrones* and long-term jobs. Yet because an ideal job is one that lasts a couple of weeks or months, many men let themselves get into situations where unknown employers convince them to wait a few days or weeks to get paid. This is what happened to Eduardo. In some cases, employers tell jornaleros to call them at the end of the month, even after the work is done, because they do not have the money on hand. It is thus not uncommon for men to say they are waiting to get paid for work that is long past.

If a jornalero ignores all the tales and warnings about seeking legal action against an employer, he is suddenly faced with a complex bureaucratic procedure that no one around him really understands. Most day laborers rightfully fear that contesting a case of abuse will set in motion a long and tedious process that will cost time and money, all for nothing. For most men, time is something they cannot afford to lose, since life by the day wage entails balancing personal expenses with remittances, always on the threshold of destitution and failure. The immediacy of the need for money, then, works against the development of any formal consciousness of rights and contestation.

In Berkeley, contesting abuse usually starts with talking to the Multicultural Institute. The MI suggests that the day laborer try to work out his problem with the employer. If he cannot, the NGO staff call the *patrón* to say that a complaint has been noted and that if it is not addressed, the day laborer will file an official report. If this fails, in theory, the MI helps the jornalero make a complaint to the Labor Commission or sends him to other NGOs in the area for help. Filing the complaint requires a detailed list of the hours and places where the man has worked and the employer's contact information, which not everyone has. There are innumerable banalities that can leave the case hanging in the air.

I met a man, for example, who managed to make the complaint but then changed houses and missed the letter about how to follow up on the case. It took two years to get to the point where the court—the California Superior Court, he claimed—determined that the *patrón* had to pay him, but even then he was in the dark as to how that was going to happen. The Centro Legal de la Raza in Oakland, the NGO that helped him, said it could do nothing else and sent him to a sister organization in San Francisco, which suggested that he hire a lawyer. The lawyer told him it would be better to insist on help from La Raza, since her commission would be 35 percent if she ever got the man to pay up.

The last time I heard from this jornalero, on the corner the day Eduardo and Iván were discussing their own case of abuse, he still had not been paid the eight thousand dollars the *patrón* owed him. He was trying to decide if it was worth waiting; he wanted to go home, and the *patrón* was now filing for bankruptcy, so perhaps the money would never materialize. This man's claim was exceptionally high, several months' work for an employer he had known and worked for before the economic crisis, which might explain why he went through with it in the first place. Most claims, however, are much smaller. In a good month, a jornalero in Berkeley could earn somewhere between fifteen hundred and two thousand dollars. Yet my sojourn on the street (August 2007 to February 2009) coincided with the greatest economic recession the United States has seen in many decades, and the men I talked to rarely had a "good month." Some were scratching by with four hundred dollars a month.

Most of the cases of wage theft constitute small amounts of money: one, two, three, or four hundred dollars being the usual amounts before people realize they are not going to get paid. These amounts, which can represent more than a week's pay, are so minor that making complaints is hard to justify to the institutions, NGOs, and lawyers that are supposed to deal with the issue. Furthermore, making such claims requires patience, time, and the ability to manage interactions and complex instructions in English, as I realized when I tried to help Francisco deal with a related problem. In fact, contesting four hundred dollars might take so much time that a person could make up the amount simply by going to the corner instead.

FRANCISCO AGAINST THE ODDS

In early November 2007, the Multicultural Institute outreach team told the Fifth Street regulars that they were dealing with the case of a Guatemalan—Francisco—who had been bitten by a dog. During their weekday visits to the corner they updated us on the case, telling us they were in contact with various NGOs and trying to find out how to take the dog owner to court. Francisco had apparently been duped out of the hospital bills the owner should have paid and was also trying to get her to pay for wages he lost due to his injury. We had heard that the bite was pretty bad and that it had taken Francisco a week to get back to the corner. These conversations went on for a few days, creating much excitement about the possibility of suing someone. However, as the MI began to realize, pursuing recourse was not so easy and the group eventually sent Francisco to the East Bay Sanctuary Covenant, which had a new community liaison who was supposed to work such cases. Knowing I had worked with the Sanctuary, people started suggesting I get involved. The men on the street believed Francisco could sue the dog owner for a lot of money. They had all seen injury cases reported on Channel 14 and looked forward to experiencing one firsthand, although there was also a lot of skepticism that anything would really happen. The difference between Francisco's problem and abuse related to wages was that proof was unequivocal: he had an injury, stitches, and hospital bills. I remained uninvolved until I bumped into Francisco on the bus one day. Three weeks had passed since his first meeting with the liaison at the Sanctuary and he was beginning to get anxious about the money.

Francisco was bitten on the sidewalk one morning as both he and the dog owner stepped out of the way of a group of young children: "I wasn't doing anything, just looking at a phone bill, when the dog suddenly jumped up and bit me in the butt!" The owner was apologetic and embarrassed. She sat him on her doorstep, gave him first aid, and promised to pay the hospital bill. "She asked me not to go to the police because it was the second time the dog did that," Francisco told me. "I could have told a policeman then, he was writing parking tickets, but she was a *gabacha,* she spoke some Spanish and seemed nice." At the hospital Francisco refused to file a police report, which in theory all dog-bite victims must do, "because it looked like she was going to pay"—*parecía que ella me iba a responder.* Francisco got a 360-dollar hospital bill and lost a week of work for which he had already been hired. Since the accident happened at the end of the month, he also had to ask someone to lend him rent money and he was not able to send his family in Guatemala their bimonthly remittance.

After several failed attempts to contact the woman by phone, he finally went to her house one afternoon—so as not to bother her in the morning, he explained—but no one came to the door. He returned early that evening, when the lights were on, and knocked. No one answered. Francisco called the woman again, only to get her answering machine. The next day, while in the shower, he got a phone call around 9:30 at night. In English, a woman he did not know left a message claiming to be the dog owner's lawyer. Although he did not understand what the woman said, he felt she made it clear he should stop calling. He shared the recording with the people at the MI, who helped him decipher it and ascertain that the lawyer was claiming Francisco was harassing her client. It was fortunate he showed the MI staff the message, he told me, because somehow it got erased from the cell phone's memory. It was the lawyer's accusation that led the MI to suggest that Francisco take the dog owner to court.

On the bus, Francisco explained that he still had not paid the hospital bill or the money he owed. His family was also complaining about the missing remittance. Francisco thought he could easily get the owner to pay more than the hospital bill and lost wages. He was beginning to believe he was entitled to greater compensation, mainly because the woman had been dishonest: "Look, at first I just wanted her to pay the hospital bill and the wages for the week. Now I am not so sure because she acted in bad faith, she took advantage of my condition [meaning that he was undocumented]." Nonetheless, Francisco also seemed apologetic about suing her and tried to explain it as civic duty, since one of the children could have been bitten: "I do it also for the children, there is a daycare center there." I gave Francisco my number and told him to call me if he needed help after talking to the Sanctuary. He called a few hours later, confused about the packet of papers they had given him and asking me to go with him to the Oakland courthouse the next day: "They say I should take an interpreter."

We met at 8:00 A.M. the next morning in the Twelfth Street BART station in Oakland. Francisco showed me the papers it had taken the Sanctuary three weeks to get. They were the basic packet for a "small claim," all in English. As we emerged onto the street, Francisco also showed me his digital camera. The pictures of his injury were in the camera, but he had no idea how to print them or get them on a CD. We walked to the courthouse in about fifteen minutes. We were lucky he knew where it was—he had been there with his *patrón* to pay a ticket—because the address on the papers was incorrect. We went into the building through a tight security checkpoint and were then directed upstairs. The place we were supposed to go was the Self-Help Center on the second floor. The center was closed, so we sat on the floor next to the door. As we waited, two men came up to Francisco and showed him a yellow paper, asking in Spanish where it was they should go. Francisco pointed at me: "Show him, he is the one who knows." I chuckled and looked at the paper. Just as lost as everyone else, I was already an expert.

At 8:30 a woman opened the door. Francisco and I went in, wrote down his name and his "business"—a small claim, apparently—and then sat down. A young *china* came up and asked how she could help. Since there was no one in the office who spoke Spanish, I explained the problem. She nodded and pulled out the same packet the Sanctuary had given Francisco the day before. She showed us a table where we could sit down to fill out our claim and went back to the front desk. Francisco looked at the papers in disbelief, annoyed that the Sanctuary had taken three weeks to get him these papers instead of just telling him to go to the courthouse. Nonetheless, we started filling out general information—Francisco's name, contact information, ethnicity, language preference, and income. Our first problem was determining how much Francisco made in an average month—a good month being two thousand dollars in his rendering. We settled for an average of about sixteen hundred. Then we came to the part where we were supposed to list the amount of money we were claiming the woman owed him. There were no instructions on how to calculate the amount or what we were entitled to claim.

Following conversations he had with *conocidos*—acquaintances—on the corner, Francisco told me he thought he was entitled to the rent money he had to borrow (350 dollars), four days of lost wages (100 dollars a day), the missed remittance (200 dollars), and the hospital bill (360 dollars). This added up to 1,310 dollars. I thought he probably could only ask for the lost wages. "Lets ask for as much as we can and then see what the judge says," he said, adding that he had also missed about four days of possible work trying to get to this point in the process, so he thought he could ask for that too. We attempted to make all these calculations but hesitated when we saw that the fee for the claim was proportional to its value, up to the limit of 7,500 dollars. Francisco was revved up with the talk about suing, crossed out our initial amounts, and said we should go for the maximum.

The Asian woman saw us arguing and asked if she could help. I asked her how to calculate the amount. She said she could not give us legal aid but that everything had to be itemized. "You decide," she said with a smile as she gave Francisco a photocopy with information on small claims in Spanish. It was the first and only document in this process that he could actually read, but it did little to clear up our doubts. In the end we wrote the initial amount Francisco had calculated, around 1,300 dollars. I gave the woman the papers and asked if Francisco should include the pictures of his injury in the claim or take them to the court. She said there was no need for them in the claim but that we should print them out for the judge.

The woman was very nice, asked us to call her by her name, Alice, and took a careful look at our papers. We were missing the form to serve the dog owner. I checked the paper she handed me and felt a little wary when I saw that the only option to "serve" someone that costs nothing is to send a friend to deliver the papers. I did not feel like serving anyone. I liked the idea of mailing the documents, but Francisco thought it would be better if I went to the dog owner's house. Either way we were at a loss, since legally we needed the woman's full name and address in order to serve her. Francisco only had her first name and cell phone number. We showed Alice what we had and, shaking her head, she explained, "It is essential that you have this information." She ushered us to a computer where we could look the dog owner up. We tried various phone and address listings to no avail, so an hour later Alice came over and helped us for about half an hour, with the same result. We were only able to determine that the phone number Francisco had was cellular and that the landline for that address was under somebody else's name. Trying to be helpful, Alice insisted we could find the information and continued making the same search over and over. To show her how useless this was, I tried to find my full name and address using my cell phone number. Nothing.

Desperate, Francisco suggested I call the number and try to hear the name the woman gave on her answering service, but it was too jumbled to understand. Alice then suggested that we go and talk to the neighbors or look through the dog owner's mail. I laughed at this, trying to imagine how the neighbors would react to us sifting through mail or asking questions door to door. Once Alice realized the situation was hopeless, she gave up and went back to her desk. A few minutes later, she came over again and gave me a card with a number to call, for the Alameda County Bar Association (ACBA) Lawyer Referral Service. She said we would have to pay thirty dollars to talk to a lawyer for thirty minutes. She thought the ACBA would be able to help for sure but told us it would probably be good to make a police report about the incident before talking to a lawyer. Not knowing what else to do, Francisco and I left.

On the street Francisco looked at the business card again and recognized the acronym ACBA. He had been sent there a few weeks before, but when he got there he found no one who could speak Spanish. The ACBA office was nearby, so we decided to see what they could do. As we walked Francisco said he really wanted to get this done, so the dog owner would learn "that even though they see us in the way they see us, they cannot treat us like this." A few minutes later we were at the ACBA, on the second floor of a building on Jack London Square. Inside there was a small waiting room with a sofa and a door with a little window in it. I stuck my head in and saw people shuffling about, but no one seemed to notice me. I turned to Francisco, who pointed to a phone on the coffee table. I looked at the list and called the volunteer services liaison. She came out and explained they did not take walk-ins, gave me the same card we already had, and said we should call. I told her Francisco's story anyway. She opened her eyes in surprise when she heard that someone claiming to be a lawyer had called and implied Francisco was harassing the dog owner. Hesitating for an instant, she went back into the office for a few moments.

When she returned she told us we were in luck, because the Spanish interpreter was there; they would make an exception and talk to Francisco now. As she made us promise not to tell anyone about this favor, an older woman with a strange accent came out. She sounded like an eastern European who had learned Spanish in Argentina; her accent was so obscure and confusing that Francisco and I did not recognize our mother tongue initially, which eventually resulted in me having to translate into Spanish what the interpreter said in English.

The explanation was elaborate and unclear, but we gathered that the legal service consisted of a thirty-minute phone appointment with a lawyer who would call us after we mailed thirty dollars and a brief explanation of the case. The interpreter explained that the lawyer would tell us if he would take the case and how much he would charge. I told her we just wanted to know how to write in the amount in the small-claims case. She said no lawyers were allowed in the small-claims court but we could ask about the amount. Both women thought our problem sounded like a personal-injury case, but at no point did any of us agree about what we were actually trying to do. To this day I think none of us really understood the other, but I get the impression that I tacitly inquired about a civil lawsuit. The exchange was so obviously confusing to us that the well-intentioned interpreter brought out more information about other places that might help Francisco. She insisted we should go to the Centro Legal de la Raza in Oakland, which would help us for sure. At the same time, the liaison gave me a small yellow pad and asked me to write down the story and my phone number. She then took the thirty dollars from Francisco. I was confused. Were they going to help us or should we go to La Raza? Francisco could not figure it out either. By this time the interpreter was acting like I really could not even understand her English. She took the pad with my number and the account of the event, patted me on the shoulder, repeated slowly that we should go to La Raza, and then basically showed us the door. Behind her the liaison called out to remind us not to tell anyone that the ACBA had actually helped us in person. I feel little remorse about mentioning it, however, since they really were no help at all.

When we walked out of the building, Francisco took the information sheet and with a sardonic scoff exclaimed, "Hey! The Centro Legal de la Raza was the one who sent me here in the first place." Francisco said he paid the thirty dollars because I was there and he thought it was right, but he was having second thoughts about the whole thing. He was not sure what the money was for and seemed aware of the fact that he had been given the runaround. Fluent in English and half a PhD myself, I did not understand the situation any better, but at least I knew the rest of his story. After the bite, Francisco had gone to one NGO (the Multicultural Institute) to ask for help. The people there sent him to La Raza, the most well-known center of its kind, who in turn sent him to the ACBA. There, the language barrier sent him back to the first NGO, which then sent him to a different NGO (the Sanctuary) that rally did not know what to do but promised to find out. It took them three weeks to get some documents Francisco could have received the day of the injury had he known to go to the courthouse. Excited that the claim was starting to take shape, Francisco had drafted me into the process, only to find himself once again at the ACBA, thirty dollars poorer, being told to go back to La Raza. Almost a month had passed.

The next day Francisco and I bumped into each other on *la parada.* He seemed even more convinced that we were going to get help and was asking the MI to take him to the doctor so he could have further proof of his injury. In a businesslike tone, he told me to call the Emeryville Police Department and make the report that Alice, *la chinita* at small claims, had suggested. Somewhat annoyed, I called the police and was told to contact Animal Control and leave a message with my phone number. Animal Control called back in the afternoon. The woman was very nice but said she spoke no Spanish so she would rather talk with me. She explained that Francisco should have made the report within forty-eight hours of the bite so they could quarantine the dog. There could thus be no report, but she promised to look into the dog's history anyway. I gave her the information I had (address and first name) and asked about how to get the woman's full name. The answer was that we should get the dog owner's license plate number and go to the DMV, since the registration—she thought—must be part of the public record. I called Francisco to see if he could get the woman's license plate number. He later called me and said with great excitement that he had the number of a car he *thought* must be the woman's. He remembered she told him she had been in an accident, so he picked the dented car parked on the curb near her house and wrote down the number.

Five days after our courthouse visit, I got a call from Francisco inquiring about his case. His tone was different; he was anxious but also seemed to expect that I should be on top of things. I told him I was waiting to hear from Animal Control. I also called the ACBA that afternoon. I was again given a small runaround, asked for information I had already given, and so on until the woman I was speaking to hung up after promising to find out about our case. Desperate, I had asked if they had Spanish speakers so Francisco could do this himself, and they again told me I should do the talking. About ten minutes later she called back and asked how much the medical bill had been. When I said 360 dollars, she became condescending and told me with exasperation, "That's a small-claims case, not one for our lawyers; they only take cases larger than 7,500 dollars and charge 200 to 300 dollars an hour." She said we must have misunderstood. Angry, I told her we had explained all this to the liaison at the ACBA and were under the impression that we could talk to a lawyer for thirty minutes. She insisted that I was misinformed. She was really nasty about us getting the card from the Self-Help Center at the courthouse and blamed them for the waste of time. I insisted that the other woman at the ACBA had repeated the same information. In the end, the woman on the phone gave me an address and told me to write in and request the thirty dollars. When I told Francisco, he just shrugged his shoulders and said, "That money is gone, Tomás."

Like many jornaleros had warned after Francisco started giving me instructions, I was beginning to regret my involvement, because I had turned into the main motor of a process that seemed unending, and Francisco expected me to follow up on everything so he could go back to work. A week after calling Animal Control, the woman I spoke to called me back. She had talked to the dog owner, who admitted that Francisco had done nothing and offered to pay the hospital bill. The owner also said that there was no previous report that the dog had bitten someone else. I was surprised at how much information Animal Control actually got. The owner admitted that the woman who called Francisco was a lawyer friend and insisted that Francisco had never tried to contact her. The Animal Control woman suggested that I try to speak to the dog owner before we did anything else, since she seemed nice and willing to compromise. Francisco decided to forgo our attempts to sue her and asked me to set up a meeting. He explained apologetically that he had not been able to send a second remittance home and his family really needed the money. He was also about to have his cell phone disconnected. I called the dog owner and left a message.

As I waited for the bus later that day, the dog owner called me back. She said her name was Silvia. She sounded young and very *gabacha.* She claimed that Francisco (she remembered his name) had never called back. "Francisco was just walking down the street looking at a paper, he did nothing. I don't know why my dog did that, but it was not Francisco's fault and I told the police that." She was annoyed that he had gone to the police and claimed he had lied by telling them she had asked him not to go: "I never said don't go. Sure I don't want the police at my door, but I never said don't go." When I told her I had called the police she became defensive, uncomfortable with the implication that she had acted in bad faith.

To prove to me that Francisco was not telling the truth, she told me there had been another man with him that day. "[The man] was drinking a forty [a beer] and said 'Fuck the police,'" did Francisco tell you that? I wasn't going to pay so they could go drinking, I mean, I am not going to pay for these guys to go on a heyday, I'm not going to pay for someone to party." She said she offered to pay Francisco's medical bills but not his lost wages: "He's a gardener for God's sake, what does he mean he can't go to work?" She did not seem to believe me when I said Francisco actually had a semiregular job in construction, adding, "Four days is ridiculous, I won't pay for that." In her opinion the bite was minor and she thought it was absurd when I told her Francisco was still stiff. "I even tried to take him to the Berkeley Free Clinic," she added, "so he wouldn't have to pay anything, but he said no so I gave him first aid myself for God's sake, with alcohol and a Band-Aid." She could not believe the hospital had cost 360 dollars. I tried to argue briefly that the Free Clinic would have referred him to a hospital anyway, but she started rambling on about Francisco taking advantage of her. She came up short when I asked about her lawyer's threat. Her voice changed immediately.

The woman who called Francisco, Silvia explained, was in fact her lawyer, although she had no idea why the message had not included a name and number. She became apologetic about not answering the phone or the door and said she was in the hospital herself. She even offered to show us her hospital bills. In a soft tone, she said wanted to explain all this to Francisco, and she asked me to translate for her. She agreed to pay his hospital bill and to consider paying for three days of lost work, but then again became irate and added loudly, "I gave him a hundred bucks that day, a hundred, did he tell you that? So whatever we agree it will be minus those hundred." By this time I did not know what to think. The woman sounded authentic enough in her excuses but also made stupid and racist remarks about Francisco and how he would spend the money. I nonetheless called him and set up the meeting, warning him that the woman was being defensive. I also asked about the hundred dollars and the second man. Francisco told me Silvia had given him the money and said the other man was simply a guy who lives in the neighborhood who sometimes works on *la parada:* "He is an acquaintance that saw me and came up to me, but I am not his friend."

Once it was clear that we were going to confront Silvia, Francisco again began to think he could get a significant sum of money. But Silvia was busy and took some time to answer my calls about setting up a meeting. As the days went by, Francisco became more and more frustrated. He called me nonstop to see if I had heard anything and finally I simply stopped answering his calls. Then he turned to the Multicultural Institute, asking the staff to check up on me and telling them to push me to find out about his money. Although I understood his distress, I was loosing my patience. Friends on the corner had begun to chide me about having a *patrón* and were beginning to advise me to send Francisco to hell; clearly, they argued, he was "taking advantage"—*esta abusando*—of the fact that I had tried to help. I needed to save face and not appear so easy to boss around.

Finally Francisco and I met on the street with the MI people, who advised him on how much money to ask of the dog owner. They thought he should ask for a lump sum, like fifteen hundred dollars, but the issue of how to justify this was, again, the main problem. We decided if Silvia did not go for the lowest number Francisco was willing to accept, namely twelve hundred dollars, we would take her to court. He was nervous, since he had already paid the hospital bill and was now considering moving to a cheaper place. The back and forth was annoying, and Francisco even scolded me for not having everything set up, suggesting I had made him miss yet another day of work. Someone added that he might be able to include "interpreter's wages" in an itemized list, and I lost my patience, said "No way," and left them to decide whatever they wanted—and I told Francisco not to take any more days off work. My friends on Fifth Street greeted my actions with a "Well done, Tomás, let the *guatemala* solve the problem on his own." After a week and a half we managed to arrange the meeting with Silvia. By this time Francisco was telling me he could not afford to fight and would take anything she gave him.

Short of two months after the dog bite, Francisco, Silvia, and I sat down to talk. Silvia, a twenty-seven-year-old bartender from Maryland, broke down in tears when we told her Francisco made about 100 dollars a day at the job he lost. She meekly shook her head in disbelief when I added up the 360 dollars for medical bills and the days of lost work. Nervous about her reaction, Francisco became apologetic and explained over and over that he was only asking for what was fair. Silvia sobbed and said under her breath that she could not produce 1,000 dollars, repeating, "What do you want me to do, sell my car?" She became aggressive and, once again, said she could not believe he had lost four days of work, noting that the medical report only said he would have limited mobility for three days. I explained that missing the first day meant he missed the whole job. She seemed to understand and then not understand intermittently. Francisco was calm, nice, and apologetic, telling her he was not trying to get more than was fair. She insisted that she could not cover the amount and finally offered him 450 dollars, 200 then and there "and I will have to give you my tips for tonight in the morning." Francisco thus settled for 350 dollars (plus the 100 he got when he had the accident). After the whole ordeal he lamely said to me that his conscience was clear and that he got what he wanted.

THE ABSURDITY OF SMALL-TIME BUREAUCRACY

There is nothing unique about Francisco's story, except that had this occurred in any place other than the Bay Area, the scene of mutual pleading between him and the dog owner would have never occurred. What differentiates Francisco from most jornaleros, in fact, is that he was willing to deal with the system and that he possessed a sense of entitlement to legal redress that many people do not believe in. After all, "We are all wetbacks here *[todos somos mojados]*, we have no rights." But the fact that Francisco pursued the issue is also grounded in the woman's ethnicity. Had she been anything other than a *gabacha* it would have been obvious from the beginning that getting recompense was a lost cause. Furthermore, I doubt he would have gone through to the end without my help, and there are few people on the street with the capacity, time, and interest to do this. I, for one, never let myself get involved in such an issue again, simply because it put me in a position of trying to meet impossible expectations.

This event reflects the common problem of redressing abuse that is minor in economic terms and the absurdity of bureaucratic dealings, especially for migrants whose cultural and social capital puts them at a great disadvantage in relation to everyday proceedings. It always amazes me how often language is the essential barrier—that is, beyond the ability to deal with bureaucracy. In multiethnic California, the most common complaint I hear from both documented and undocumented migrants is that the people they are supposed to ask for help do not speak their language. My friend Santiago, for example, called me repeatedly after obtaining asylum and then legal residency to help him deal with the Social Security office and other institutions. On one occasion I even had to translate between him and his social worker over the phone.

In terms of the bureaucratic machinery, one reason for the absence of Spanish speakers might be the state's ethnic diversity itself—state offices are staffed by African Americans, African migrants, Asians, and others who often have little working knowledge of Spanish. Francisco had a singular advantage because his interpreter (me) could manage these interactions. Getting a full-time interpreter to help as I did would have entailed more money than the dog owner owed him or a very close friend with a lot of time. As for the NGOs, volunteers, and yes, anthropologists, Francisco's tale might help explain the disenchantment that arises when times are hard for jornaleros, who never ceased to remind me that the Multicultural Institute and people like me make a living from their *situación*. The runaround is a common occurrence that leaves migrants frustrated and at odds with the very people and institutions that have made names for themselves by helping disenfranchised populations. Yet what I experienced with Francisco involved people who did not know what needed to be done, could not understand the particularities of Francisco's case, and were unable to explain these issues in a way he could understand.

To wit, the most absurd part of Francisco's saga is that it was deemed a success on the street. After word got around that I had managed to actually get somebody money, I received a barrage of phone calls and visits on my corner from people looking for advice; jornaleros I did not know who walked up to me with crumpled pieces of paper full of notations of hours worked or the names and numbers of *patrones,* asking if I knew how to get them to pay. In a few cases I was not the first person they consulted, and many came out of frustration after several failed or confusing attempts at redress. In other cases, word got around that I did this for a living, and six months later I was still getting calls and messages. My friends on Fifth Street had so much fun with the constant harassment that they would call out, "Here's another one that needs your help," every time someone new came up and said hello. But the harsh truth is that jornaleros have little recourse when the amount disputed is so small that seeking legal aid is not economically "worth it," even though the amount might represent between one-fourth and half of what a jornalero makes in a given month. This futility reinforces the belief that the only way to deal with outright exploitation is to avoid *patrones* who are suspicious and the certainty that once someone has been a victim of abuse, the best and most economically reasonable course of action is inaction.

STRUCTURAL CONSTRAINTS AND THE NATURE OF MIGRANT VULNERABILITY

In rethinking the theoretical implications of structural violence, Quesada, Hart, and Bourgois (2011: 341) have tried to go beyond the structural constraints that different types of oppression and marginalization force on individuals. People's individual agency, culture—whatever it may entail—and worldview, they argue, tend to be bypassed by the urgency of taking marginalization as a form of socially sanctioned violence. These authors response is to incorporate individuals' positionality within the social structure and open their analysis to the elements of personal history, which play a key role in operating the mechanisms of exclusion. This perspective is not new and plays into much of the work the authors themselves have undertaken—most notably Bourgois—along with perspectives that have been put forth since the 1970s.

In an attempt to set inequality into the framework of capitalism, but also to reincorporate individual agency in the study of its reproduction, Willis (1981), for example, combined both cultural and structural elements in his analysis . He argued that Marxist perspectives had established clear-cut relationships between class structure and oppression and had missed how class reproduction actually occurred. Studying the 1970s education system in England, Willis concluded that working-class students got working-class jobs but not through the expected structures of class reproduction, which a Marxist analysis would assume. Rather, a student's development of a culture of resistance is what ended up locking him or her into a position in the class hierarchy. Bourgois's (2003: 9) encounter with Puerto Rican drug dealers in Harlem takes a similar perspective. Here, the street culture that arises as a response to racism and marginalization, as a search for "respect," results in the inevitable destruction of the participants themselves. This search furthermore becomes directly involved in the ruin of the communities from which these individuals come. Bourgois thus frames inequality within the political economy of exclusion inherent in the inner city while simultaneously allowing for an ethnographic approach to how people make decisions and affect their own destiny.

Similarly, in the now-classic ethnography *Death without Weeping,* Scheper-Hughes (1992) goes beyond a simple analysis of the structural effects of inequality on the lives of people in a particular place and time. Instead, she centers on how suffering, violence, and oppression are internalized and become part of everyday experience. Her informants are conscious of the social silence they are condemned to; they understand the hunger and suffering inherent in their lives and seek improvement of their lot through personal strategies and political participation. One of the main contributions of Scheper-Hughes's analysis is to call attention to the cultural and social nature of emotions. Emotions constitute social discourse and are particular to historical processes, which construct a framework that normalizes and reifies what "feelings" should be (Scheper-Hughes 1992: 431).

For the jornaleros in Berkeley, the internalized structures of marginality come together in attitudes toward injustice that cannot be construed as ignorance or apathy but are rather pragmatic acceptance of the men's position within US society. The outcomes of legally sanctioned redress are not necessarily beyond their reach but more realistically are out of the question. Eduardo was lucky to get a third of his pay; Francisco's endeavor to obtain a measly amount of money, heroic. Their own understanding of the events, the internalized perplexity they felt—did employers and dog owners not understand how hard their travails were, or the righteousness of their claims?—illustrate these men's inability to understand themselves as rights-bearing subjects. Their *situación* furthermore points to a reality where the pace is set by the "runaround" or the outright certainty that all is in the hands of others. And herein lies the caveat that speaks to the racial hierarchy that has emerged in the previous pages and that regiments most of the labor relations at the site. For others become "the other" in a society whose own stratification is articulated in the language and structure of racial classification, a divide that is politicized and played out in practice through the hierarchization of worth that jornaleros must learn to understand while standing on the corner.

Betwixt and Between

Life itself seems to be left, in a fantastically intensified purity, when man has cut himself off from all ordinary social ties, family, regular occupation, a definite goal, ambitions, and the guarded place in a community to which he belongs by birth.

Hannah Arendt, *The Origins of Totalitarianism*

Jornaleros, in a way, are always in the gray zone between social inclusion and marginalization, which ultimately affects every aspect of their life. In the following section I explore the social and physical space that day laborers inhabit, from their rented ramshackle apartments and houses to the racial/ethnic and even gender apartheid in which they inevitably end up inscribed and that they help perpetuate. Overcrowding, isolation, separation, and estrangement from families back home are the order of the day. Two elements are at the heart of these effects of migration. The first is part of the process of racialization the men go through when they migrate. In the United States, their own conceptions of race and ethnicity must be rearranged to fit the racial geography that shapes US society. Inevitably, this process sets day-to-day life into a racially informed social structure from which the men emerge highly biased.

The second element is that amid problematic relationships with housemates, neighbors, and the urban landscape in general, living and working in the United States also establishes new and awkward ties to family members back home. The men's role as providers takes center stage in their interactions with loved ones far away and contributes to a disarticulation of male identity that threatens jornaleros' social and physical integrity. For while day laborers can provide for their family with the money they make, wives and children come to depend on their absence. Thus, the men in these pages felt unappreciated and talked about their families underestimating their sacrifices and misconstruing their *situación*. Living by the day wage for many of my close acquaintances and friends was a bittersweet *compromiso*—commitment—embodied in the impossibility of reconciling the "here and there" (Coutin 2005).

RACE AND INNER-CITY VIOLENCE

For most migrants from the global south, coming to the United States implies an encounter with US racial politics that is confusing and disconcerting, at best, but that can also be violent and highly problematic. Founded on the contradiction of democracy and slavery, the country has defined its population in terms of racial citizenship and exclusion since its inception, its Constitution initially declaring all citizens equal but only in reference to "white," male, and landowning subjects (Rosaldo 1994; De Genova 2006). This process established a clear-cut racial line based on notions of biological purity and cultural superiority. The system was built on the principal of hypodescent, which erased the diversity and internal variation of various populations through an absolute categorization of black as everything not exclusively white (Harrison 1995: 60). The bipolar black/white racial line has influenced how the nation has come to understand itself and has determined the racialization of other populations (De Genova 2005). Irish, Italian, Jewish, and Puerto Rican migrants have all at some point been classified as inferior to the dominant "white" population (Bourgois 1989: 122; Sacks 1994; Bourgois 2003; Lee and Bean 2004: 224–225). The racial divide thus has shaped notions of belonging and alienation in the national polity, the inside/outside distinction that has marked certain foreigners as "incorrigible outsiders who could never be incorporated into white civilization" (De Genova 2006: 2–7).

As an example, De Genova (2005) has illustrated the tensions and contradictions inherent in Mexican factory workers' insertion into the racial politics of Chicago. Here, the subordination of migrants and their labor is articulated through racialized structures of exclusion in which they are caught between the "white" and "black" categories (De Genova 2005: 211). Particular groups are set in positions of subordination vis-à-vis white "America" and distanced in relation to the "black," in terms of their socially constructed and perceived worth. This not only entails a superimposed structure of meaning but also a particular positionality for migrants themselves, as they interact with institutions, labor hierarchies, and the city itself. Rather than an identity carried over the border, being Mexican in Chicago or Latino/Hispanic in the Bay Area are subjective experiences shaped in those places. In this sense, through their participation in the US informal labor market and all this entails, jornaleros become entangled in a world where race is the name of the game and where their own notions of social distinction—racial, ethnic, and even class based—become rearranged and rearticulated in their new setting.

Racialization is, in essence, a process of distinction along "racial" lines, where migrants must learn to navigate racially informed structures of understanding and governing populations that are particular to the country's history and politics. These structures shape the social relations jornaleros establish and color the geography they inhabit—especially in cities—but they are not necessarily scripted onto everyday notions about race that the migrants understand when they arrive. Race in the US sense, in other words, is something the jornaleros learn through experience and embody on and off the corner, as life in the Bay Area rearranges their own notions of social distinction. Similarly, when day laborers enter the country, they also enter racial categories, "Hispanic" or "Latino," that are absent from their own representations of identity until they cross the border. Thus, people from radically different places, social classes, ethnicities, and nationalities, who identify as categorically dissimilar "kinds" of people from one another, are collapsed into all-encompassing racial classifications. This, for even the most liberal, "color-blind" people I encountered in the United States, was hard to understand because racial distinction for them has typically been reified, taken for granted. My own discomfort with categories like Hispanic was thus many times taken as snobbishness. Yet even my wife—the least snobbish of people to walk this Earth—received dumbfounded looks of incomprehension when she jokingly said at a party that she had been "white" her entire life until she migrated to the United States.

Whatever the case, observers looking up or down *la parada* can mistakenly assume they are seeing a discrete and specific group of people that come from the "same place" and think and act following the same logic. Nothing is further from the truth. Quesada (1999: 172), for example, has called attention to the complex process of accommodation that Salvadoran migrants—previously combatants on different sides of the war in the 1980s—must go through on the streets of San Francisco when they find themselves suddenly part of the same group; that is, as "Latino" day laborers on the corner. He also discusses the enmity between Mexican and other Latin American migrants who must come to terms with each other and take advantage of the political clout and visibility one or the other has achieved. On the street, people of different national origins may come together and joke around; they may become friends and work on communal jobs and ultimately start to talk about peers from different countries as a cohesive group. But as is clear from the previous section, this can be turned upside-down during disagreements and outright confrontations, as with Clemente claiming everyone hated him because he was Salvadoran, or Guatemalans accusing the Multicultural Institute of being pro-Mexican.

Jornaleros in Berkeley thus find themselves in a racialized world of exclusion, sharing and vying for the urban spaces they inhabit with other racially scripted minorities, especially African Americans, who have come to embody the archetypical antithesis of everything jornaleros identify with. In a discussion of the production and manipulation of labor extraction and discrimination of the African American population, Wacquant (2002) argues that after slavery ended, the southern states developed new institutions through which to control black labor and maintain the black/white distinction. This realignment of social institutions was the origin of Jim Crow legal and social codes. The ghetto similarly served to regain control of the black labor force after the civil rights movement but failed to channel labor effectively, in part because of the influx of even cheaper labor from Mexico (Wacquant 2002: 48). Labor and competition for work, at least for the Latin American day laborers, follows these lines, for the men see themselves as sharing a structural position with *morenos*, whom they consider lazy and unresponsive to the social recognition the state offers.

It is in this sense that radically distinguishing themselves from African Americans becomes discursively salient. Thus, until I came to the corner, the term *moreno,* for me, spoke to a fluid array of loosely racialized skin tones that most of the population in much of Latin America would identify with, although not all in the same way. But like the Mexican migrants in De Genova's study (2005: 198), jornaleros seem to have displaced the category from themselves onto African Americans, becoming complicit in the production of hegemonic and rigid racial classifications. A little more distant from the jornaleros own experience, *tongas, chinos, árabes,* and other such categories also establish clearly distinct populations that, in reality, encompass a wide variety of people of multiple nationalities and ethnicities. That racial stereotypes regiment many of the decisions the day laborers make speaks to the compartmentalized nature of their exclusion, where the social topography they inhabit seems constructed by clear-cut and distinct racial blocks.

Throughout the years I spent working with Latin American migrants from all walks of life, I heard innumerable conversations in which people argued that they would probably all be entrepreneurs and well off if they had the support that African Americans can get from the government. They were usually talking about welfare and education (see Quesada 2011). For day laborers, notions of laziness and abuse of the welfare system confirmed their own work experience—riddled with tales of stingy and unscrupulous *moreno* employers—and the stories every man has about inner-city violence perpetrated by black youth. Notions about nationality, race, and ethnicity that jornaleros bring from their countries of origin thus enter the social sphere of US racial production and become articulated in these men's experience of marginality.

Particular takes on what characterizes *morenos, chinos,* and *árabes* show the effects of urban segregation, where migrants must live in dangerous neighborhoods and are separated into ethnic niches. This also helps explain why the men tend to see *gabachos* as ideal employers, for they have no counterparts—especially negative ones—in the inner-city neighborhoods the men inhabit. Strangely, however, older *gabachos* also come to represent a threat to the masculinity and physical integrity of day laborers through a latent fear of homosexual propositions and the threat of rape. Again, this may be a product of the distance between the jornaleros—who after all are caught up with *morenos, chinos,* and others in the same neighborhoods—and white males. But it is also clearly tied to the racial structure itself, which from these men's perspective has everyone pitted against each other in a system where they are all subordinate to white supremacy. Jornaleros' own tacit understanding of their structural position of marginality seems to translate the terms of their subordination into notions of threat to the body itself. After all, they are standing passively in plain sight, waiting for uncertain, often abusive employment in a system where they have no rights. It is not the conditions of labor and life themselves that constitute these men's vulnerability but rather their potentiality in a system where the men have little sense of control.

UNDERSTANDING VULNERABILITY

The harsh working conditions that characterize undocumented day labor in the United States, coupled with the realities of social and economic marginalization, have led academics and social workers alike to construct jornaleros as a particularly vulnerable and high-risk group of migrant workers. The nature of their vulnerability is usually taken as the product of dangerous and unregulated working conditions (Esbenshade 2000; Valenzuela 2003; Rhodes et al. 2009), substance abuse (Worby 2007), and high-risk sex practices (Organista 2007). Thus, much has been published on drug and alcohol abuse, along with HIV and other sexual risks (Organista and Kubo 2005; Worby and Organista 2007; Organista et al. 2012). Studies that underline the feelings of desperation—*desesperación*—that day laborers develop on the street have also looked at jornalero mental health (Organista 2007; Walter et al. 2002). Isolation and harsh working conditions can thus trigger issues like stress, depression, anxiety, and further risky behaviors such as alcohol abuse. While pointing to the very nature of day labor, these perspectives do not necessarily cover the ways in which labor contingencies function in the discursive realm of everyday interaction among peers standing on the corner.

In truth, everyday life on *la parada* is shaped more in the verbal articulation of these risks than in actual events themselves. What is most unsettling to me is not that a day laborer undertakes dangerous work, for example, but rather that he does so with the certainty that if something happens to him there will, most likely, be nowhere to turn. Vulnerability, in the epidemiological sense presented above, is not only a function of unregulated labor practices but also a product of attitudes toward the notions of aid, redress, and fair treatment. Lorenzo once called me to say that his neighbor, another jornalero, had fallen off the balcony after a few drinks and hit his head. The man's roommates were trying to avoid taking him to the hospital because they were unsure what would happen to them if they showed up with a dazed *compañero* who was bleeding and drunk. Who would pay? What would happen if the police came? What if they asked for documents? Lorenzo thought that if they spoke to his friend from the university (me) they would realize they were risking the man's life.

Ethnographic accounts of day labor sites in the United States have described jornalero vulnerability as a function of the problems involved in unregulated work and the structures of exclusion the men inhabit. Ethnicity and masculinity, again, appear in analyses of how the men organize in labor sites, their relationships to each other, and their perspectives of the benefits or faults of labor centers. Purser (2009) studied how gender shapes the self-image—"self-worth"—of day laborers, as an effect of the oppositional relations between those working on the street and those who frequent a formal labor center in Oakland. Unlike Malpica (2002), who looked at the activities men participate in as a gendered cohort—for example, catcalling and harassing female passersby—Purser addresses the ways in which moral standards of worth are linked to the cultural construction of gender. Men working on the street "feminize" those in the labor center, and vice versa, in order to position themselves at a higher echelon of social and moral value, which ultimately gives meaning to their condition as migrant jornaleros. Purser illustrates the complexity of solidarity among workers, since the oppositional nature of identification with the corner or the center hinders the production of an effective cohesiveness that could proactively improve their situation.

Other perspectives look at the social practices that characterize the corner, where men come together to deal with the contingencies of everyday life and to socialize. For Pinedo Turnovsky (2006), *las paradas* emerge as meaningful social spaces in jornaleros' lives, where they build a sense of belonging and offer support to each other. In Quesada's (2011: 389) analysis, however, vulnerability is a structural position of marginality that sets migrants within relations of power that force them into attitudes and practices that end up placing them at risk, both socially and physically, which points to the contradictions throughout this book regarding friendship and the management and dissemination of information.

Being a jornalero, especially for men with wives and children left behind, entails coming to terms with the fact that their family gets used to and depends on their absence. And while many day laborers' commitment to loved ones is strong, they can never completely resolve the contradictions of their absence. They feel their families do not understand their sacrifice, and they resent comments and complaints that imply they are living it up abroad. For the jornaleros I got to know well, the good life that people in their home countries sometimes attribute to them is clearly beyond their grasp. They live in crowded spaces under conditions they would mostly be embarrassed to have people back home see. Many consider the work they do undignified and humiliating and spend their days either waiting on the corner for better things to materialize or hiding behind closed doors amid people to whom they cannot always relate.

MASCULINITY

The precarious conditions these particular migrants encounter collude against them, curtail their ability to establish support networks in the United States, and make it impossible to maintain their position within the family structures back home. Day laborers' experience is thus riddled with tensions surrounding their notions of masculinity. Health risks and the threat to the family, and to the intimate realms of jornaleros' lives, are also at the forefront of the work of Walter and colleagues (2004), who tackle the social implications of work injuries among day laborers in San Francisco. These authors see "constructions of patriarchal masculinity" as the guiding force in a tenuous balance of self-worth and purpose that falls apart when injured day laborers are unable to work. Thus, the tension between being good providers—by migrating—and these men's absence from the role of "patriarch" becomes paramount in their experience of anxiety, fear, and depression (see also Walter et al. 2002).

Masculinity in Berkeley was an evident preoccupation for the men on the corner, mostly addressed in jokes about cuckolding, in complaints about people back home, and in discussions about sex and family. Jornaleros deployed different versions of what masculinity entails, ranging from traditional "macho" attitudes of male supremacy and patriarchy to eclectic compromises that reflect contemporary and cosmopolitan images of gender roles and relations. In the same conversation, a jornalero might use hierarchical representations of gender difference, such as keeping a woman in her place through physical violence, and then turn to a younger man and explain that all relationships are based on negotiation and that partners in a marriage must have equal say for it to work. Similarly, the Sancho emerges as a trope that represents the anxieties about what happens during a man's absence, both in terms of his "replacement"—the Sancho moves in on his wife and family and enjoys the fruits of his labor far away—but also as a problematic alter ego that must take care of those left behind. Thus, a common theme in many Latin American countries is restructured by estrangement from family and points to the various mechanisms by which poverty and exclusion become embodied in experience (Farmer 2002: 424).

This complexity of gender representations is characteristic of contemporary configurations of masculinity in Latin America (Gutmann 2006, 2007) and is furthermore affected by migration, where traditional gender roles became redefined for both men and women. Studies have shown how among first-generation Mexican migrants, for example, many women feel greater freedom and autonomy as they enter the labor force and gain independence from the household, while men take up traditionally feminine activities like cooking and childcare (Hondagneu-Sotelo 1994). For some people, migration contributes to a reformulation of relationships, with greater equality between partners, while others try to reinforce more traditional structures (Smith 2005: 97). These changes not only occur in relation to the greater society migrants are inscribed in but also within migrant communities and across national boundaries (González-López 2005). As a particular male version of these processes, however, the rearticulation that jornaleros undergo appears incomplete and fractured, since there are few, if any, female counterparts to the men and because the social referents upon which a gendered identity is built are absent from immediate experience. The chapters that follow articulate the elements of isolation, estrangement, overcrowding, and masculinity into the experience of day laborers caught up in a racialized world that they must manage effectively to survive.

4 The "Other" among Others

Whatever the degree of social interaction on the street corner, much of a day laborer's everyday experience is tied to what I can only describe as a constant and intimate state of siege. This is an effect of the conjunction of day laborers' structural position within the Bay Area and their separation from family. In the United States, most of the men I met lived in crowded dwellings where they did not know their roommates well and where they many times dealt with the rowdiness and drinking that ensued by resorting to self-imposed isolation. Those with family members nearby seemed less lonely and desperate. Although on the street the men shared most of the realities of day labor, those with family in the area usually had more stable living arrangements supported by kinship networks that helped cover expenses in a bad month. Those who did not live with family had more volatile living arrangements and depended on personal relations among roommates and the economic tolerance the household might have for one or more of its members not paying rent on time. For both groups, overcrowding was pervasive, with three or four men sharing a room, each sleeping on the floor, a cot, or an old mattress. Most of the homes I visited looked shabby, mainly because the men rented apartments or houses in run-down areas but also because jornaleros tended to see these dwellings as temporary, always subject to *la situación* or *la migra,* either of which could change day-to-day life without warning.

During the economic downturn in 2008, a man could end up living on the street after a bad month or be forced to find more men to share the burden of rent. Immigration control was also on the rise, and several jornaleros changed their residence from one day to the next when they felt the threat of *la migra.* Either way, jornaleros spent little money on furniture and appliances; beds, chairs, tables, sheets, blankets, and the like were usually inherited from roommates who left or were acquired on the street or through charity. Televisions were one notorious exception, because they were usually the men's main source of entertainment and played a central role in how they accessed information about the world around them.

CROWDED SOLITUDE

In 2008 Luis lived in an apartment complex with three brothers, a brother-in-law, and two uncles. He was the only one of the six who worked as a jornalero, although his uncle, in his early sixties, sometimes went to the *esquina* when his usual job as a plumber was slow. Luis's housing situation was more stable than other jornaleros'; his rent contract had not been interrupted in the last fifteen years—which also made his rent fairly cheap—because there was always a male member of his immediate family living there, even though Luis had gone back to Mexico and returned several times since he had started living in the complex. Three to five people shared each of the two one-bedroom apartments the family rented, depending on how many men were in the United States at the time. Aside from the discomfort of overcrowding, which they dealt with by keeping everything tidy and using the beds in the living rooms as sofas, Luis lived in a reasonably safe part of Fruitvale in Oakland and had a landlord who, for the most part, maintained the building. The family members shared a strong work ethic and a sense of responsibility toward those in Mexico, so they did not party often, hardly drank, shared chores, and cooked for one another. Luis and his uncle were especially proud of their culinary abilities. They also spent most of their free time watching television. Because of the number of people pooling resources, they had cable TV and, during my fieldwork, one of the men even got DSL Internet service.

In general, however, Luis, my closest friend, was an exception. Of the people I interacted with, only Eduardo and the *trillizos* had family members in the area. Lorenzo's older brother and niece lived in Oakland, but his drinking led to estrangement from them when he had just arrived. None of their living arrangements were as structured as Luis's household. And yet because Luis always gave priority to his wife and three children in Mexico, sending almost everything he made home, he was often forced to borrow money to pay his rent. Although his brothers could always lend him money, Luis looked to others first, because he already owed his family so much that he could not return home before paying them back. Two years after I left the corner, Luis, who managed to get a regular job in San Francisco in late 2011, was still not sure when he would be able to repay the debts incurred during the years *la situación* forced him to be a jornalero.

The rest of the day laborers lived in small and overcrowded apartments or ramshackle houses, sometimes with more than five people sharing a single room. Such setups reduced rent and usually started with three or four men renting the place and then one or more of the main renters inviting someone else to sleep in his quarters to reduce monthly payments. A man who pays 400 dollars a month can bring his rent down to 100 dollars if he gets three other people to live in his allotted space. When he could not get enough work to pay for food, for example, Sindi was able to cut his rent from 230 to 130 dollars by letting his *paisa*—a person usually from the same country but also used to indicate someone from the same town or region—sleep on the floor of his room. At first Sindi was excited about the arrangement and jokingly boasted about his newfound ability to afford a beer every once in a while. The downside was that late-night TV and privacy were out of the question. Also a downside, if any such "subletters" cannot produce his share at the end of the month, it is usually the first jornalero's responsibility to cover the full rent. This is a significant source of conflict that inevitably leads to disagreements and temporary homelessness for many men.

A typical jornalero dwelling I visited was a run-down house in "the bad part" of Fruitvale in Oakland. The place seemed to be right in the middle of the ghetto, surrounded by dilapidated cars, parked or abandoned on the street, and discarded furniture on the sidewalks. Lorenzo asked me to go see the house, since he was considering moving in with friends because his Mexican housemates were trying to get him kicked out of his current room: "You know how it is, Tomás, we Hispanics"—he was the only jornalero who ever used the term—"are also racists. They [his current roommates] prefer having someone—*un paisano*—from their own country." Lorenzo and I entered the house and were received by his drunken "friend"—a man he had met twice before—lying on a queen-sized mattress with no sheets. He was watching children's morning programs on an ancient Sony TV with a dial. At the foot of his mattress was another, smaller mattress with crumpled sheets and clothes on it. There were clothes on the floor and in boxes all over the room. Next to the TV was a lopsided, wooden round table, covered with plates, glasses, papers, and a toy robot. I sat by the door in an old office chair, while Lorenzo and another man who lived there sat on makeshift benches. From my vantage point I could see the only other room in the house (they only rented the first story). It was smaller, with a wooden bed on one side and a mattress on the other. That room had a bigger and newer TV and a big mirror on the wall. The mattress had sheets but was covered with things. The floor of the main room was wood while the other had an old blue carpet.

The walls in the house were in disrepair, the paint and plaster were falling off or had been ripped off, and posters of football teams and naked women were haphazardly taped to the walls. One of the walls in the main room was severely damaged, apparently when a mounted shelf had been ripped out. You could still see where each of the drawers had been. The wood finish on the doorframes was also scratched and damaged. At the entrance to the house a naked woman was drawn on the wall, with a plastic vagina attached in the appropriate place. Next to this were three small plaques reading "God is love" and "Protect this home," which I was told someone had put up for *protección*. The guys offered us lunch, so I saw the kitchen, which was tidy and had dishes drying on the rack. A coin-operated washing machine sat next to the stove, and signs reminded people to turn things off. The bathroom was through a little door to the right, next to the fridge, down a tiny hall and through a doorway that looked like it had been cut out of the wall. I could not fit through it without turning sideways. There was no door, but the bathroom was clean, with the exception of a used condom lying next to the toilet. All the windows in the house had makeshift curtains that looked like they were primarily composed of dirty sheets. When I asked Lorenzo how many people he would be sharing the house, he said probably six or seven.

People living in these circumstances inevitably have problems with their roommates. The most common tensions, besides living with someone who cannot pay his part, have to do with alcohol consumption and rowdiness. Adolfo, for example, once lived in a house with eleven other jornaleros who always had two cases of beer on the floor when he got home on Fridays. During the week some of them also drank and stayed up talking or listening to music. His roommates always invited him to join them, but Adolfo, ever conscious of work, preferred to watch TV and rest. He left the place, tired of the drunkenness that sometimes lasted several days. He also tried to share a room with Lorenzo but could not deal with his monthly drinking binges. Although they were close friends, Adolfo kept his distance to avoid Lorenzo's drunken bouts, which also included multiple and incomprehensible phone calls that I myself fell victim to. The last time we spoke, Adolfo was living with three other men he did not know well but who mostly kept to themselves. Many of the day laborers I met had similar problems. Jaime, the Honduran in his midfifties who constantly repeated "I am no machine" on the street, wanted desperately to move but felt obligated to his friend (the main renter), whose share would almost double if he left. His problem was that his roommates drank every night and the temptation was so strong that he feared he would not be able to keep his newly found evangelical abstinence.

Most of these arrangements last no more than a couple of months, because people either get tired of their roommates, get scared of the neighborhood, or have to leave because they cannot make the rent. My friend Chucho moved four times during the time I was on the corner. He started out subletting space in a room for 130 dollars a month but had a falling-out with one of the other renters who constantly nagged him to pick up his things. He then moved in with some friends and paid 200 dollars a month, until *la migra* knocked on the door early one morning, allegedly looking for someone the men did not know. Although his roommates knew not to open the door—the people on the other side had no warrant—

they all left permanently before the day was over. Chucho then found a run-down house in Berkeley, which cost him and four friends 260 dollars a month each. This arrangement, however, was well beyond his means, and two months later he went back to living in an overcrowded apartment with strangers he met on the street.

Conflicts often translate into animosity between people. A few weeks after getting his new roommate, Sindi complained nonstop that the "kid"—fifteen years his junior—played loud music all evening. The arrangement lasted only a few weeks. Ramiro, an indigenous Guatemalan, called me several times in terror of his housemates, who threatened to beat him (Ordóñez 2014). He wanted to know if calling the police would affect his asylum case, since he had not yet received his work permit in the mail. He was also worried he would get the others deported but was beginning to take their drunken threats seriously, explaining the source of their enmity as envy—*envidia*—of his papers. The roommates, all indigenous Guatemalans like Ramiro, had decided the asylum application was too dangerous and had advised him to forget about getting papers. Now they resented him because, not having taken their advice, he got asylum and could petition for his wife and son to join him. The situation escalated to the point that Ramiro only went to the house to sleep a few hours a night.

Less common arrangements are strikingly reminiscent of indentured servitude, like in my friend Leonel's case; he worked, in part, in exchange for living quarters. I met two other men who lived with their *patrones*—other Latin Americans with papers who worked as subcontractors in construction. These jornaleros worked for their landlords, who charged rent in terms of their labor. When work was good, the employers considered the rent paid, but since things were slow during my fieldwork, the *patrones* started to charge the men extra. Both of these jornaleros spent part of their time on the street trying to make extra money to send home and support themselves and complained that they were not sure how their landlords were calculating what they owed.

Despite complaints about overcrowded dwellings, solitude is the usual experience for most of the men on the Fifth Street corner. Contact with other people is limited to a small group—usually men who live together and hang out on the street—all of whom compete for resources and crowd each other's existence. And although some jornaleros get along with their roommates, nostalgia for family back home, desire for women, and complaints about housing arrangements color the conversations on the corner every day. Furthermore, day laborers have little access to leisure activities because of their economic precariousness and fear of being out in public when not at work. Money is always lacking, even when work is good, because the priority is to keep up with weekly or bimonthly remittances, and many times this means that the men do not keep enough for themselves to make ends meet. Ramiro, for example, only ate once a day during the time he was having trouble with his roommates, because his son in Guatemala was sick and needed medicine.

The contradictory nature of day labor is that a jornalero spends a great deal of time making himself visible on the corner, only to spend the rest of the day keeping a self-imposed low profile. The only exceptions are places in Fruitvale or San Francisco where everyone is a migrant and where most day laborers buy their food and clothing. It is in these neighborhoods that those who do socialize go out. Most of the young, single men I met, like Eduardo, tried to get out of the house to socialize and meet women. The middle-aged men, however, considered this foolish because of the risk of immigration raids or fights that result in police intervention. As in Chucho's case, *la migra* is an ever-present threat dealt with, mainly, by avoiding public places. Even so, most jornaleros, young and old, consider the *morenos* in their neighborhoods a more immediate threat. After dark, it is the threat of violence from *moreno* gangs or individuals that keeps the men behind closed doors.

THE ARTICULATION OF RACE IN EVERYDAY LIFE

Oakland, where most of the day laborers in Berkeley live, is one of the most segregated urban areas in the United States. Segregation between black and white populations, in fact, has risen in the last decades. The growth of the Latin American migrant population has caused the working-class ethnic niches to somewhat encroach upon and become part of the black neighborhoods, where poverty is concentrated, leading to high unemployment, lack of access to services and education, and inner-city violence (Massey 2007). In this urban landscape shared by different ethnic groups, undocumented day laborers—many with little or no support networks in the United States and limited English skills, who furthermore carry their day's or week's pay in cash—make easy targets for theft and gang violence. Jornaleros are also vulnerable because, in general, they avoid contact with the police. The combination makes day laborers ideal victims, for as one *New York Times* article put it, they are seen as "walking ATMs" (see Nossiter 2009).

To hear of being robbed by *morenos* was a daily occurrence on the Fifth Street corner, to the point that the men "swapped" stories about theft and violence perpetrated by black youth in the same offhand manner they compared food recipes from their hometowns. Clemente was once attacked by three *morenos,* who beat him and then partially undressed him until they found the three hundred dollars he was carrying. Adolfo quit smoking after two *moreno* teenagers attacked him on his doorstep one evening. Lorenzo always chose bars near the San Francisco BART station in the Mission District because he had been robbed several times on the street. Twice I missed asylum interviews for Guatemalan jornaleros because the person I was going to translate for was mugged and had his phone stolen. Animosity, in other words, runs high, and day laborers tend to consider any African American, especially young male adults, a potential attacker. Day laborers thus make great efforts to avoid *morenos,* even just in passing, going as far as getting off the bus when a rowdy group of teenagers boards. This distrust flows into other spheres of social interaction, and the men do not trust *morenos* working at NGOs and other institutions. The few asylum seekers I know who managed to get state-funded aid, for example, tended to drop out of the programs when their social workers were black.

The violence jornaleros suffer is both banal and spectacular. Sometimes it is limited to intimidation; other times they are attacked with bats, knives, and guns. Among Clemente's many scars, two on his face are not from the shell wound he suffered during the war in El Salvador but from fighting off attackers on the streets of Oakland. The most spectacular story I heard was from Ramiro, the man whose roommates threatened him. Waiting long hours for his interview in the asylum office, Ramiro and I sat behind some African women. Keeping an eye on them throughout our conversation, he finally whispered, "The *morenos* all look like they were taken from a mold," making a sign with his hands to indicate a massive mold. "They all look alike." I nodded and let him continue. "But there are good ones and bad ones, lots of bad ones." I asked if he had ever had any trouble, since he had been in the United States only eleven months.

"One morning," he told me quietly, "I left for work around six; it was October and the sun wasn't up yet. I went out with a hammer because a friend told me you have to be very careful with the *morenos*. I was walking down the street when I felt someone coming up behind me, I could hear the jacket. I managed to turn around and I saw him, I saw the *moreno* like this [he imitated pulling out a gun]. He was pulling out the gun when I hit him on the arm with the hammer. I heard the gun fall on the ground and saw it go underneath a car. Then I jumped on the *moreno*, holding him hard, I don't know if I screamed or what, but I didn't let go because I was afraid he would get the gun. Then people started looking out the windows and another *moreno* opened his window and asked in Spanish, *"¿Qué pasa ahí?"*—What's going on down there? Afterward he told me his father was Mexican and his mother was from Jamaica or something, but he didn't look like a Mexican. Anyway, the *moreno* who attacked me told him I was attacking him, and I screamed in Spanish that it was the other way around. The guy in the window disappeared for a moment and then came back with another gun and pointed it at the *moreno* who attacked me. He told me to release him. I let my attacker go, but then I noticed there was a *morena* behind the car and she came at me with a knife, so I dove under the car and pulled out the gun and managed to turn around before she reached me. I grabbed her by the arm and pointed the gun at her, shaking. She and the guy then ran away. The Mexican *moreno* invited me into his house. We could hear the police was coming and he wanted to hide the gun I took. He said, 'That's a good gun, we can get five hundred for that!' He repeated that we shouldn't tell the police we had it."

Several policemen arrived before Ramiro could run away, and he ended up explaining the event to the only officer who spoke Spanish. He lied when they asked for his address, saying he didn't know it because the street address was in English. The police reassured him that they were not *la migra* and that they helped people like him, eventually getting his phone number. Ramiro then described how the policeman picked the gun up with a pen and bagged it—*"como en television"*—adding that it was not every day that people in this situation would relinquish the firearm. The police said they would call Ramiro if they got any information, but he never heard from them or the Mexican guy who helped him. He was so freaked out that he went home and locked himself in his house for two days.

Hiding behind closed doors, Ramiro explained, was the only time he ever felt safe. Like him, most of the men I knew on Fifth Street spent their free time at home, isolated from the world around them. The men talked about going out as if *morenos* and *la migra* loomed around every corner, and mostly referred to their *situación* as being alone. Living in the United States is a lonely endeavor, where the only companions are other lonely men, many of whom the jornaleros I knew would rather not be with. For most of the day laborers in Berkeley, other men on the street and their roommates are the only people they have extended social interactions with. Isolation, coupled with the inability to go out and feel safe, is at the heart of the men's experience. Worby (2007) has looked at some of the effects of this issue, mainly an increase in drinking due both to the isolation and the influence of others. Adolfo, who moved because of his roommates' drinking habits, also talked about the danger inherent in drinking alone, just to pass the time: "Look, I'll get home soon, tired, no family, I don't want to go out for fear of being caught [by *la migra*], so I'll drink some beers; and before I realize it I will have drunk a six-pack while watching TV."

Sometimes the vicissitudes of jornalero wages and heavy drinking collude against the men, as one can see in the afternoons at *las vías*. Here, a few of the onetime day laborers gather to drink beer and other alcoholic beverages in paper bags. They wear ragged clothes and have a stink that the others describe as "what the homeless *gabachos* smell like." Of the men on Fifth Street, only Eduardo ever drank down there, sometimes late in the afternoon with Bicho, the guy who eventually stole his iPod and disappeared. The *borrachitos* epitomize failure for active jornaleros, who express compassion for their lot but disdain and revulsion toward the drunks themselves. The *borrachitos* also appear at Friday lunch and take *mercados*—groceries—and clothes, sometimes trying to sell them to others later. For the most part, they have also lost contact with their family and no longer support themselves through work, although every once in a while an unsuspecting *patrón* lets one jump in his or her car, only to kick the person out once the smell of alcohol becomes obvious. Isolation in these cases has become absolute, since many of the drunks live under the freeway overpass or sleep in empty lots on San Pablo Avenue.

The jornaleros I met in Berkeley thus belong to a precariously situated subgroup of Latin American migrants in the United States; they are especially isolated from strong social support and live in highly segregated areas where they are at odds with members of other ethnic groups. Everyday life takes on a specific form of what Bourgois (2003) has called "inner-city Apartheid" that is both socially articulated in space (the men are isolated in the city) but turned inward toward their own spheres of intimacy (Bourgois and Schonberg 2009). US racial categories thus become central to the ways the jornaleros understand their life and position in society. And while violence from *morenos* is the main reason most men dislike African Americans, racism among Latin American day laborers is much more complex and a favorite topic of street-corner conversations.

RACE ON THE CORNER AND BEYOND

Much of what jornaleros think and hold to be true within the context they inhabit in the United States is the product of long conversations with peers. The men swap stories about things they have lived or heard about; they propose theories about social conditions that affect them and shape their understanding of the world around them through the consensus that seems to arise from many of these conversations. As I was taping Eduardo singing his songs one afternoon, the conversation suddenly turned to talk of race when William noticed a few African American teenagers sitting across the street and chatting in rowdy and excited voices. As he shook his head in disbelief, I heard William mumble the word *perezosos*—lazy—and I inadvertently registered his own theory on race in the United States by asking, "So why do you say the *morenos* are lazy?"

"You want to know why [I think they're lazy]?" said William. "My point of view is that it [racial problems] is a monster the whites created." Eduardo was curious and asked him to explain. William continued, "Because in past years, decades ago they [the whites] made them [the *morenos*] work really hard, by force . . . and those ancestors made the modern *morenos* feel that they don't need to work anymore because their ancestors worked in their stead." Eduardo nodded emphatically, "Yeah, it's what I think also."

William seemed to have thought this through, since his answer to whether *morenos* would agree with him was, "Well if they don't say it, they have internalized it," before continuing: "The whites bought them, because the *morenos* were bought. They [the whites] brought the slaves, they went to buy them to bring people here to work . . . really strong blacks, good for labor . . . they built everything. These were deserted countries, these were empty lands, so they brought those people and they built [the country] by force."

For William, laziness had become part of black ideology—he used the term as I do here—and this explained why they were bad at school as opposed to more racist explanations about racial inferiority: "They're just as capable as we are. It's that they prefer to be playing around and all that." Both William's and Eduardo's comments followed similar rationales and led them to talk about misplaced black resistance. William thought laziness was the main way most African Americans got back at the whites instead of organizing politically. Eduardo chimed in, noting that Barack Obama was running for president, to which William concluded, "[That's] the way to get revenge and take the power [of the whites], and they can take the power, they can, one of them is running [for office] to take power."

Both men, like most jornaleros on the street, had little experience with people of African descent in their countries of origin. Having had only negative contact with African Americans in the United States—both unscrupulous employers and through street violence—they expressed their ideas about *morenos* in opposition to what they considered themselves to be. Eduardo and William acknowledged later that there was racism toward black people in their home countries, but their point of view was mainly articulated in relation to how African Americans and Latin American migrants compete for the same resources in the United States.

Like Eduardo and William, many jornaleros think *morenos* have access to services and work that migrants need and want but cannot have because they are undocumented. African Americans are said to come to depend on welfare, which makes them lazy, while jornaleros kill themselves to work and would never abuse such help. The conception that African Americans abuse the system and depend on social services also illustrates how day laborers enter a sphere of racialized stigma and how they end up replicating it by counterposing themselves as different, something Quesada (2011: 394) has shown for street corners just across the bay from where we stood and talked into the recorder. The brief mention of Barack Obama also points to a preoccupation on *la parada* in the pre-election months of my fieldwork. Most of the jornaleros I spoke to did not like Obama, and discussions about the upcoming elections always revolved around the effects that a *moreno* president would have on their lives. The general consensus was that Obama would be the revenge of African Americans on the *gabachos* and that Latin Americans would continue to be ignored and mistreated. Other men expected more violent effects on their lives, since they saw a *moreno* president as posing an inherent danger to undocumented migrants, who would find their greatest threat suddenly empowered. The candidate's more liberal outlook on immigration was utterly lost on all the men I spoke to, since they assumed that being *moreno* would come before being liberal.

Other racial/ethnic groups get mapped onto jornaleros' worldviews less violently, following the men's experiences of the Bay Area's racial enclaves. In a strange twist of imagery, Beto, for example argued that the *árabes,* who own many corner stores and gas stations, sold expired food products because only *"los morenos y nosotros les compramos,"* that is, "only the *morenos* and we [undocumented immigrants] buy from them." Again, this comment underlines the tacit understanding that African Americans and Latin Americans share the bottom rung of the hierarchy. The *chinos* are also reportedly in collusion against Latin Americans with whom they too interact in corner stores and businesses. But their actions stem from the assumed internal cohesiveness of the group, as jornaleros perceive the *chinos* to be more supportive of their compatriots. "They came like we did, but now look where they are," Clemente told us one morning, meaning the *chinos* were more affluent than Latin Americans. Laughing, Ivan added, *"Aunque viven como veinte en una misma casa"*—Even though they are about twenty to a single house. I facetiously asked how many people each of the men lived with, and Iván answered defensively, "But they help their own kind, they help those who are their own kind *[a los que son raza].*"

Latin Americans, the theory goes, *"no ayudan a su propia raza, mas bien se chingan entre ellos, son bien culeros"*—don't help their own people, instead they screw them, they are real misers. This assertion usually goes hand in hand with stories of unscrupulous *patrones* (themselves Latin Americans), who have no problem firing people or abusing employees that come from their own countries. *La raza*—used to describe compatriots, close friends, and Latin Americans in general—is infamous for not taking care of its own.

Racial segregation is thus structurally imposed by the conditions of relative marginality of the various groups, who internalize the difference and develop a high degree of self-segregation. There were a few African American day laborers on the corner but nobody ever spoke to them. On Fifth Street we had a young *moreno* who appeared every couple of months and sat next to us, sometimes smoking marijuana, and who claimed to be a day laborer on the only occasion we exchanged words. When he was about, my friends would turn their back on him and shake their heads when he asked for cigarettes. Even more stark was a barbecue at Luis's apartment building held by the landlord (a *filipino)* for his tenants. I was surprised to find all the *morenos* in one corner of the patio (most were Jamaican migrants), the Mexicans in the middle, and others—Asians and Russians—on the opposite side. On a long line of tables in the middle of the patio, the tenants had set out the food they contributed, following the same distribution. During the party the only person who interacted with all the groups was the landlord, who got drunk and tried everyone's food. Everyone else kept strictly to their own kind.

Among jornaleros in Berkeley, perceptions about race and ethnicity order the men's relations with the world around them and, in conjunction with their own feelings of national and regional identity, mark their relationships to other men who share the corner. US racial/ethnic categories that group these men together erase the fact that on the street they often understand each other to be markedly different. I always wonder at the use of categories like "Hispanic" or "Latino" that many indigenous Guatemalan asylum seekers must mark on their Social Security application and other documents, after getting asylum on the grounds that they are singularly different from what most people in this country would consider to be Hispanic. In fact, the only jornalero I ever heard use the terms

"Hispanic" or "Latino" was Lorenzo, who had been in the country for twelve years and used the words in the US sense when referring to news he had read or heard about.

For nonindigenous jornaleros, distinctions on the street start with national origin and then subdivide into regional or state provenance. On Fifth Street there were the *chilangos* (people from Mexico City), *los de Veracruz, los de Guadalajara,* and Campeche who was the only one from this state and hence inherited its name. Other Mexicans on the corner came from different parts of the country but did not have *paisas*—regional compatriots—and so did not make up a subgroup. There were also the *pochos,* US-born Mexicans who usually were employers and who were always suspect, not considered completely trustworthy. Non-Mexicans included Clemente, a Salvadoran; Lorenzo, a ladino Guatemalan; and for a few months Mariano, who was indigenous (a native Mam speaker) but who spoke Spanish fluently, dressed in the "inner-city" Oakland youth style, and was just treated as a Guatemalan. My friends referred to the people I spoke to whom they did not socialize with as "that Honduran guy," "the Salvadoran who came to talk to you," and in the case of Lorenzo who they disliked, "your *guatemala.*"

Among the Mexican, Salvadoran, Honduran, and nonindigenous Guatemalans there is a common understanding of where each man comes from. People of these nationalities come together on the corner and discuss the differences and similarities in their particular versions of Spanish, food, alcoholic beverages, the size of their hometowns, and so on. When I was on the street, these discussions were an everyday occurrence and aided my own relations to some of the groups I studied, since people were always interested in comparing notes with someone from a country not represented on the street. And yet the seeming fluidity of these conversations becomes violently reversed when conflict arises and people revert to their nationality or regional identification. "They hate me because I'm Salvadoran," Clemente concluded after explaining his problems, even though no one had publicly or privately said anything negative about his nationality. Lorenzo also had to move when his Mexican roommates colluded to kick him out of the house, on the grounds, as he understood it, that they preferred someone from their own country. Eduardo, who was from Mexico City, had a similar problem when an employer, who had already hired the *trillizos,* picked him up on the corner. Eduardo claimed he found himself among hostile men who kept telling him he did not look strong enough to work. "There are times when the people, instead of saying hey cousin *[hola primo]* or something [like that], they look down on you, their same people *[su misma raza],*" he explained. In many cases, as with Clemente, the men explained this type of discrimination as a form of racism, where this term gets conflated with nationality or regional provenance.

One slow July morning on the corner, I sat on the wall with Beto, Fernando, Iván, Clemente, and two other men I did not know well. As we were chatting, Beto came along and, shaking his head, told us a *patrón* had offered him seven dollars an hour. We all scoffed, and he continued, *"El problema es que hay mucho guatemalita"*—The problem is there are too many *little* Guatemalans. Everyone nodded at Beto's condescending use of the diminutive and, encouraged, he added for emphasis, "The little ones work for nothing"—*Los chiquitos trabajan por nada.* Fernando, who had lost his job as a baker and was returning to the corner after months of absence, joked that Guatemalans advertised themselves as *tres por diez*—three laborers for the price of one (i.e., ten dollars).

While the men used the term *guatemala* to refer to different kinds of Guatemalans, in most cases they meant it pejoratively because most of the Guatemalans were in fact indigenous men the others looked down on or viewed with suspicion. Most corners had people of mixed provenance, both national and regional, but indigenous *guatemalas* usually hung out with members from their own communities, speaking in indigenous languages or Spanish with heavy accents. Indigenous jornaleros were usually less educated than the rest of the men and in many cases seemed more clueless and less street savvy. More importantly, coming from rural backgrounds and discriminated against in both Guatemala and Mexico, indigenous *guatemalas* tended to work for less money, taking on jobs that no one else would even consider. My friend Fabio, for example, started his time in the United States undertaking full days of heavy labor for sixty dollars a day until his Mexican workmates told him not to be stupid. Fabio and other indigenous Guatemalans I met all agreed that *patrones* who frequented the Oakland labor site chose it because they knew there were more indigenous men there and they could get away with wages no one in Berkeley would agree to.

Many nonindigenous jornaleros also referred to the physical appearance of their indigenous counterparts, calling them *los chiquitos* or *aceitunas*—olives—pointing to their short stature and dark skin. Although indigenous men constituted almost half of the day laborers in Berkeley (Worby 2007), they were isolated in many ways from the rest of the men. On the street this difference was translated into geographical segregation, as when several indigenous men from Guatemala slowly colonized the three blocks north of Sixth Street, drawing unwanted attention from neighbors who complained to the city. As tensions rose, the *guatemalas* were branded by other day laborers as troublemakers who would end up hurting everyone's chances of getting work. For most of my friends, the central issue was that the *guatemalas* were doing this out of ignorance. "*Those people* do not understand and they are going to harm us all," my friends repeated constantly. Clemente complained that the *guatemalas* had "invaded" the site, noting accurately that they were relatively new in Berkeley.

Access to legal status is also a source of friction linked to nationality, the Mexicans being at a disadvantage in relation to Guatemalans and Salvadorans, who are sometimes eligible for asylum, Temporary Protected Status, and other forms of legal immigration status. Many Mexican men feel it is unfair that they cannot get papers while others on the corner can, although few know the inherent difficulties and risks involved (Ordóñez 2008, 2014). Guatemalan indigenous jornaleros are usually the main objects of these recriminations, even though few of those at the Berkeley site actually had legal status. Jorge, the only Mexican I met who was in the process of applying for asylum, told us one morning that his case was getting complicated and that the asylum officer did not seem to believe his story. He was purposefully vague about his case, which opened the door for jokes about what he should have told the officer. Laughing, Luis concluded that he should have made up a language: "You should have talked like this," he said, imitating an indigenous language and asking me to corroborate its authentic *guatemala* ring.

Whether in jokes or serious complaints, the association of papers with ethnicity reinforces mestizo jornaleros disdain for indigenous *guatemalas* who, in contrast to assumptions about their intellect, are accused of putting on airs and treating others condescendingly when they have legal status. In a typical street-corner turn in semantics, however, Luis also liked to use a play on words, replacing the first two syllables in the term "undocumented"—*indocumentado*—with the word *indio,* meaning "Indian," to refer to himself, thus rendering the political construction of his own immigration status in the United States into the pejorative term *indiocumentado,* which only a fellow Latin American would find funny. Luis used an ethnic slur that in much of Latin America has been scripted onto class difference to jokingly refer to his social status—caught between the political economies of representation of both the United States and Mexico—in a self-deprecating way.

Both the street corner and the neighborhoods where jornaleros live are spaces where notions about race and ethnicity emerge from a conjunction of racial/ethnic, national/regional hierarchies that the men bring from home meshed with US racial hierarchies as they are encountered in everyday life. This mixture leads to latent contradictions in these distinctions, where jornaleros who have been discussing the absurdity of Chinese-speaking communities in Mexico or Guatemala, for example, accuse the DMV, or a particular *patrón,* of racism because the said institution or employer wants them to be able to speak English.

BOASTING

Assumptions about race, ethnicity, and regional and national origin are not the only considerations that the men on the street make when they measure each other in order to align themselves with particular cohorts. Among acquaintances *humildad*—humility—plays an important part. A person's treatment of others and his own behavior are tied to the moral economy of perception. Most complaints about problematic characters on and off the street refer back to "racism" and treating others as if they were lesser men—*tratar de menos.* Sometimes the issues of humility and race coincide, but in many cases men are simply weary of others who talk too much about their own economic gains.

Men complain about jornaleros who talk about the houses they have built back home or all the money they make. In truth, after a few months on the street, when I realized that people talking to each other avidly did not know one another well, I simply took everything I heard about affluence with a grain of salt. Boasting is so ingrained in life on the street that everyone counts on it in one way or another. One character even earned the nickname *el mil vacas*—a thousand cows—because he told outrageous stories about the cattle and land he bought in El Salvador. Everyone on the corner "knew" this was lie, and most just laughed at the stories. Others, however, became tired of this person putting on airs, trumpeting his success, and *el mil vacas* was not welcome on every corner.

Boasting for day laborers is a way of dealing with the hard circumstances that affect their lives, by making the men narratively exempt from the most common problems. Either in jest or through snobbery, exaggerating wealth, sexual prowess, or social networks, the men separate themselves from the reality on the street. Boasts are a way of presenting oneself as an exception that incarnates some aspect of the imagined figure of a successful migrant, the macho man, and so on. This issue points to the very shaky ground upon which jornaleros' identities as bread earners and men stand. But in terms of how boasting affects the way that day laborers relate to one another, it is clear that not all men are willing to openly accept how dire *la situación* really is and thus opt to set themselves apart.

Standing near the drunks down by the railroad tracks, there was a small group of men whom Eduardo, William, and Bicho joined. Among these were two brothers who were considered snobs and were distrusted on the corner because they tended to look down on other day laborers. For starters, they owned a small pickup truck and talked constantly about their "business" while chiding others for not proactively bettering themselves and learning English. This notwithstanding, they seemed just as bad off as the others and spoke very broken English to the employers I saw them interact with. This conflictive imagery led many jornaleros to hate them and talk poorly of them. Eduardo even composed a song that mocked their pretentious attitude. "El Jornalero Rucanrolero" in many ways encapsulates boasting from the perspective of the street.

"So what is the background of this song?" I asked Eduardo one afternoon when he and William had co-opted my recorder.

"Well, [I wrote it] because that guy is constantly bothering me, calls me a whole bunch of names, no?" He nodded to William, who agreed with glee and anticipation—whether he wanted to hear the words or see Eduardo make a fool of himself was hard to determine.

Eduardo continued, "He bothers me and bothers me *[chíngueme y chíngueme],* until [one day] this guy," he slapped William on the shoulder, "came up with that word and started telling him he was *ruco,* and it hurt him, it hurt, *ruco* means he is old."

William laughed again, repeating the word over and over, "I call him old man, 'Listen, Grandpa!'"

"So I said to myself," Eduardo interrupted, "ja! If he doesn't like being called *ruco,* I'll write him a song about a *rucanrolero.* It's a parody. Instead of *rocanrolero* [i.e., a rocker] it says *rucanrolero.*"[1]

"Meaning old man, geezer," William interjected.

Holding a finger to his temple like a singer in a recording studio, Eduardo lowered his head an instant and then raised it, eyes half closed, and started singing in the out-of-tune, high-pitched voice that contributed to his self-imposed but warranted exile from the Fifth Street corner. For once, however, I saw his peers react to his exaggerated facial expressions and sappy demeanor with genuine pleasure rather than contempt.

I am a *jornalero,* even though they call me a *culero* [a miser]
They call me *farolito* [the little lantern] maybe because I am so short
Some [women] call me *la combi* [a small bus] and I don't know if it's a custom,
But one thing I promise you, that is I barely reach a meter [high]
My name is Pablito, and of all those here I am the ugliest

Because I am, the *jornalero rucanrolero*
and of all of us I am the best *[soy el mero mero]*
I wish I was whiter and to drink a coffee
With Britney [Spears] or with [Paris] Hilton
Or at least with Milton [another guy on the corner].

I walk the streets, searching for a thousand details
Dreaming about my *güera* [white woman] always waiting on Fourth Street

1. Eduardo was using a play on words, taking the term *rocanrolero,* as in a "rocker" or "rock and roller" (that is, someone hip), and turning it into something closer to "old man" with the term *ruco,* which was clear when he sang and spoke because he said *rucanrolero.* When he wrote the lyrics down, however, his spelling inverted the middle *r* and *l,* rendering the word hard to pronounce: *rucanlorero.*

My chocolate heart and my peanut nose
I can do any job [*todos lo jales me la pelan*]

Because I am, the *jornalero rucanrolero*
and of all of us I am the best [*soy el mero mero*]

Here I spend my days, watching the girls
And even though I know they are bitches
My heart palpitates for them
And even though they pay no attention to me
I am here until dusk
I stay until five
You should already know what I want
[speaking in English] Money, money, more money

Sometimes I get hungry and run to the food truck
For I have only a dollar left
Eating, I return to the corner
Watching the sky
And thinking of that moment
Another day here, another day of my life
I don't know what will become of me
For I am no longer young
Because I am, the *jornalero rucanrolero*
and of all of us I am the *mero mero* [Eduardo and William laughed]

Eduardo, sensing that some of the laughter was directed at his singing and not at the lyrics, finished with an explanation: "I sang it to you to explain it, because it is written in *chilango* and you are not a *chilango* [a person from Mexico City]." We then discussed the phrase *todos lo jales me la pelan*, which Eduardo and William explained meant the speaker could do any job. "According to him [the man being made fun of], he is the king of construction," Eduardo emphasized. To which William added, "A know-it-all."

The men's resentment became more serious, however, when I asked about the line *"a él le gustan las morras y no le hacen caso"*—and even though they (the girls) pay no attention to me. For Eduardo, the man's boasting about women was the worst. He said this line meant that although the *combi* was always looking at women on the corner, "he always is saying they are bitches and I don't know what else . . . "

"He just likes to destroy people," William interjected, finishing Eduardo's thought. "Like for example, he comes here and starts talking

El Jornalero Rucanrolero

Yo soy un jornalero
y auaces ma dicen qua soy un colero.

Ma dicen al farolito
Taluez porque soy tan chaparrito.

Algunos ma dicen la combi
y yo no se si sara so costumbre.
Paro yo una cosa te prometo.
Puas sera que sólo llayo al metro.

Mi nombra as fernandito y da todos
soy al mas feito.

Poi qoa yo soy al jornalero rucanlorero
y da todos soy el mero mero 2v.

yo quisiera ser yuerito
y tomarme un cafesito
con la britney o
con la Hilton o ya
de aperdis con el
milton.

Eduardo holds up the lyrics to “El Jornalero Rucanrolero.”

about things from his country, I mean, with his accent, so [people say] 'Look how he talks,' or maybe he tries to say something in English but can't pronounce a word. They think they are better and say, 'Hey, we didn't understand you, what did you say?'" Putting on airs about speaking English, like in Luis's case discussed earlier, was a great source of conflict and recrimination. "They don't allow others to grow," continued William, with Eduardo adding bits of information to complete the picture.

William finally came to a close, proudly stating that he stood for none of this ill treatment and treated the two brothers with disdain, which all of a sudden shifted the conversation toward a discussion about race. With his hand on William's shoulder, Eduardo pointed to the other man's face: "And at least this guy they don't pick on you so much because you are white man, a little white, but they jump on those that are darker. Man! Those guys are racists! . . . You just don't know [how it is]. They are racists!"

Eduardo often complained about people calling him names on account of his looks, but that afternoon he was particularly mad because the two brothers from the railroad tracks had recently made fun because he was "really dark." I asked if Eduardo considered the other two particularly white.

"Nah man, but they think they are, like if they were white. They look down upon our . . . countrymen . . . like if they were embarrassed." The group went on to complain about the brothers boasting of having five houses in Mexico and about all the money they made in rent. Apparently the brothers talked about their wealth a lot, which made their peers suspect they were lying. After all—Eduardo, William, and I agreed—we would stay home if we had such work-free income. "I wouldn't stay here," Eduardo concluded, "I'd go back to my country."

"El Jornalero Rucanrolero" was Eduardo's attempt at making fun of someone who constantly bullied him. The song has a racial undertone that suggests that putting on airs, for the men he hates, also entails putting him down for his dark complexion. But the greater issue is that Eduardo's tormentors set themselves apart as successful entrepreneurs who "had made it" while sharing their lot with men who are destitute. The brothers managed to intimidate other jornaleros with their ability to learn English, even though their own proficiency was almost nil, which for William, who was new in the United States but avidly attending English classes at the adult school, became a favorite way to challenge them.

Although they complained about others boasting, men like Eduardo, William, and Lorenzo were prone to boasting in their own right. Eduardo bragged about his sexual exploits with women. William talked about having overcome spectacular obstacles to make it to the United States. And Lorenzo, who was usually grounded in reality, tended to give himself high social status after a few drinks. Since I knew from our "sober" conversations about his family back home, I was always surprised to hear him say, "My sister might be elected minister of education soon," or that his ex-wife's nephew was the most important engineer in the country. Lorenzo tended to turn all his acquaintances into important and powerful figures: soldiers in the army became generals, lawyers turned into Supreme Court magistrates, and so on. Lorenzo never remembered having told me these stories. He also made me party to them without my knowing. One night at the San Francisco bar we frequented, the bartender, a Honduran woman we chatted with several times, asked if I had really been sent to Europe for work. I was not sure what she meant, but Lorenzo patted me on the back and told her I had just returned. As she turned away to serve some drinks, Lorenzo smiled shyly and said, "Sometimes one says things to have a little fun. Vah, Tomás?" Apparently, since I had not been to the bar with him for a few weeks, he had told the bartender "our" company had sent me abroad, and he also seemed to have mentioned that we might get sent away together in a few months.

While boasting can be taken as playful joking, as in Lorenzo's case, or as antipathy toward others, it has strange effects on the men on the corner. Even though the two brothers whom Eduardo lampooned with his song seemed to be exaggerating about themselves, other men obsessed about whether the brothers were actually making more money than they were. When Lorenzo and Adolfo tried to convince me to buy a truck with them and make a webpage to advertise their gardening business, they justified the investment by pointing to other men who seemed to be doing well. After Francisco—whom I helped get paid for the dog bite—returned to the corner, his tale of our efforts became spectacular, involving threats that intimidated the woman and much more money exchanged. This in turn led Sindi and others to exaggerate winning arguments and confrontations with employers, which created uncertainty among other men about how effective challenging abuse could actually be. Everyone thus acknowledged boasting as such, but the men's tall tales sometimes changed—if only momentarily—jornaleros' perceptions about the world that surrounded them. While I take boasting as a product of jornaleros' coping mechanisms, it must also be understood within the complex dynamics through which erroneous, incomplete, and warped information is exchanged on the street. Facts and fiction on *la parada* are not distinguishable.

On the street, personal relationships with peers and organizations are structured around competition and distrust, but they contribute to a worldview where everything is possible and simultaneously doubted. This is not to say that every interaction among jornaleros is hostile, for as should be clear by now the nature of the street corner is always contradictory; friendship and competition go hand in hand, while humor, comradeship, and ostracism are aspects of the same contingencies. And these contingencies in fact relate back to the state of siege that characterizes these men's experience in the United States. Racialized in a highly segregated world, they find themselves alone, in danger, and among peers who hardly ever become anything more than passing acquaintances who are all out to maximize their own earnings. Among the men in Berkeley, there was a great sense of frustration with this *situación,* which many felt was clearly not what they had come to the United States for (cf. Mahler 1995) and was something their families could never understand or imagine.

5 Bittersweet Nostalgia, Sexuality, and the Body at Risk

As with other aspects of socialization, jornaleros in Berkeley deal with family tensions back home and the effects of separation through humor, often quite cruel, and conversations that depend on saving face on the street and not appearing week. All jokes taunt and at the same time address real sources of anxiety and desire that sometimes turn tongue-in-cheek banter into serious and heartfelt exchanges. What follows is an account of the preoccupations that jornaleros have as men, fathers, and providers, which accordingly deals with notions of masculinity and gender on multiple levels. I will not try to disentangle these notions, put them in context, historicize them, and so on, because I think it more pertinent to illustrate how they are expressed in everyday life. I am also not particularly interested here in addressing the sexual lives of the day laborers I knew. My intent is to illustrate how the men's gendered self-conceptions play out on the street and the multiple ways they become salient in the production of meaning among the jornaleros in Berkeley.

I first address the anxieties and recriminations about family members who remain in the countries of origin and who depend on the money the men send home. I then turn to the more banal interactions on the street, in which the absence of women plays out in the hypersexualization of the corner. It is difficult to write about these issues without resorting to accounts of horny, macho, working-class Latin American men. For the most part, how the men watch women and speak about them is not entirely foreign to me, since I remember similar behavior from high school. The difference is mainly the context, the intensity and frequency with which the issues discussed here appear, along with the multiple age cohorts that participate. The street corner, as many jornaleros would say, is a place with little else to do than to talk and joke around, and humor is only funny when it is relevant to the issues that mark the pace of our lives.

BOOTS FOR MY SANCHO

The first time I took a camera to the street I made a joke of it. Initially nervous about pictures—most jornaleros normally shy away from a stranger with a camera—I felt I had made friends on Fifth Street, and I took advantage of their constant bickering about me not bringing them food or drink. With a six-pack of Coke, I appeared on the corner to the great delight of Luis, Clemente, Sindi, and Don Raúl. They commended me on the drinks repeatedly, sneering and scoffing that I had finally complied, until I mimicked their offhand manner and said, "Don't be smart asses—nothing in life is free and I'm taking pictures today."[1] Everyone laughed and complained about how I "used" them, but the photo session was a great success. We played around with the camera for a while, taking pictures of one another. Clemente stood next to a little electric car parked in the driveway next to us and said, "Take one with me next to my car, Tomás."

He was mocking a common trope on the street, wherein men take pictures next to fancy cars and send them home claiming the have bought them. This eco-car was ridiculous to us in a sense that no liberal-minded Californian could ever understand. In high spirits, they all wanted a picture with it. Clemente and Sindi posed stoically, their bodies rigid and

1. Reviewers of an earlier version of this text thought that I seemed to be forcing the camera on the men. While always conscious of power relations in the field, on the street and in most of the conversations I participated in, I was usually the one at a disadvantage. This was me trying to "talk the talk" and keep up with the men.

One of the jornaleros next to "his" car.

their expressions serious, but when it was Don Raúl's turn he extended his arms, threw his chest outward, and said, laughing, "Take it like this, Tomás, I want to look big to scare off that *cabrón*." The picture is somewhat out of focus, and Don Raúl's eyes are closed, but this became one of the most memorable and discussed events of my time on the Fifth Street corner. The other three men and I bent over laughing and later sat on the wall looking at the picture over and over again. We all knew Don Raúl was going home soon; we had heard about buying the plane ticket and his desire to go back to Guadalajara in time for the Christmas season. The picture became a running gag on the corner, and for the next few months—even after Don Raúl left for Mexico—people came by to ask about *la foto del Sancho* and find out if he had really sent it home to scare off his *compadrito*.

It is not easy to explain who the *cabrón*—roughly, "bastard"—is that Don Raúl wanted to scare. This figure only arises as a joke men use to pass the time while they wait for work. The Sancho is a ubiquitous and yet elusive character on the street, the man who has hypothetically moved in on a day laborer's family, sleeps with his wife while he is away in the United States, and, in general, reaps the benefits of the money he sends home. Although distinctly Mexican, the Sancho has counterparts among Guatemalans and Salvadorans, who call him *el lechero*—the milkman—and other names that refer to trades that bring strange men to one's house in one's absence. He is also sometimes called *el compadre,* a quintessential Latin American term of fictive kinship that links the day laborer to his Sancho through ties of reciprocity.

The Sancho is so elusive that one can only catch sight of him in jokes set off by someone sneezing or in jibes that make fun of friends during talk about home. In the same way that other people say "bless you" when someone sneezes, jornaleros scream "Sancho!" prompting a back-and-forth about what the *compadre* must be doing to their women or what he needs. "He's taking her clothes off," someone remarks. "No, he wants you to send him some new boots," corrects another. Or when asked if he was speaking to his Sancho, one man who was trying to call Mexico answered, "I just want to know if he got the money I sent him. I just want to make sure he is taking care of her and that he is taking my kids out. Maybe I'll tell him to take them to the movies."

The jokes are not always cheerful. Sindi, for example, clasped his hands one morning and begged his Sancho, "Don't mistreat her. I'll send you the money as soon as I can."

"Is your Sancho thinking of you?" I asked.

"Not thinking of me," he corrected, "beating my wife!"

"We say the Sancho is thinking about us when we sneeze," explained Don Raúl, enjoying my bewilderment the first time I heard this kind of exchange. "We do it to joke around, *para no agüitarnos* [to keep our spirits up]." But the Sancho is both a joke and a reality for these men. "We all have Sanchos, although not everyone likes to admit it," Don Raúl said more seriously the day before he went home to a family he had not seen in five years. "We all know they are roaming about, taking advantage of the women we leave behind."

The Sancho trope reveals the fears and anxieties about separation from wives and family that characterize the experience of most of the jornaleros

I worked with. The figure is by no means an effect of migration, for tales about women running off with the milkman and other such characters are prevalent in Latin America and elsewhere.[2] What is particular to the street corner is the tension between the Sancho as a cultural representation of the fear of cuckoldry (cf. Brandes 1980) and the reality of family disarticulation that pervades the labor site. Jokes become weapons of the weak (Scott 1985; Goldstein 2003) turned inwards, a space of resistance where absence from the family and its dangers turns into a personal relationship to the fear of loss itself. To "care" for the Sancho—to keep him happy, well fed and clothed—allows men to vent their anxieties about what happens in their absence and to make light of the their families' expectations. But through the ties of kinship entailed in the term *compadre,* the men can feel present and represented—the cuckold notwithstanding—in a sphere of relations that is otherwise mediated solely by telephone calls.

The *compadrito*'s playful character also points to how the men deal with these fears, that is, through camaraderie with acquaintances who share the same lot. Men never act jealous when talking about their Sancho; they address the issue with dark humor that touches on the Sancho's ever-pressing need for their money, his quasi-marital status to their wives, and, to a lesser degree, his role as parent to their children. The Sancho exemplifies the complex configurations of meaning embedded in the migrant experience; he is a threat to a jornalero's masculinity (he takes men's wives, children, money, and position in society) and yet embodies him in absentia; he makes light of dire realities but also represents and personifies them.

There is a great sense of loss on a day labor site where jornaleros hang around for hours with little prospect of work. Men like to have conversations about how life was back home, comparing neighborhoods, food, and people. Pictures of wives and children emerge from wallets and cell phones, the men's personalities and tastes adding to the character of the noisy sidewalk. Jornaleros discuss the right way to raise a family, how to keep their spouses happy, and what their children think and do—always positioning themselves as if they were still at home. Inevitably, children

2. In Colombia, for example, a child who does not look like his father can be jokingly referred to as *el hijo del lechero.*

appear frozen in time, and for people like Luis, away for five years when I knew him, it sometimes suddenly registers that the little girl they are talking about is almost fifteen or, in Don Raúl's case, a woman of twenty with two children of her own. Nostalgia, however, is coupled with the ever-increasing demands from the people the men miss so much. After a long session on fatherhood, for example, Luis told me one afternoon that the daughter he talked so lovingly about had called him the day before. "They always call to say they need something. I understand; she is already going to high school." Similarly, Adolfo once finished a tale of his family with a sorrowful smile, telling me his wife had asked for 600 dollars for last year's Christmas celebrations: "The first years I sent 50 dollars, afterward they asked for 200, now they want 600." Getting a DVD recording of the party he subsidized—filmed with a camera he sent back—was bittersweet.

Such tensions mark almost every conversation about family I heard on the street. No matter how nostalgic or loving a man appears when he talks about his wife and children, the issue of their increasing demands always comes up. Like the Sancho, families back home always seem to need more money and to enjoy the fruit of a jornalero's labor at his expense. The men feel their loved ones doubt the hardships they suffer. "Back there they think we have a lot of work; they don't know that we spend most of the time sitting in the street, dirty, trying not to get depressed, and talking about the Sancho we are supporting . . . They don't understand that we often go without work, or that we don't have enough money for food; they don't understand our reality," Don Raúl explained one morning. Sindi added, "If we don't call every day, they ask if we found another woman," and, having an imaginary conversation with his wife, he continued, "Look, the thing is I don't have money for the phone card, that's why I haven't called." Don Raúl nodded: "I made forty dollars last week, but it costs four to get to the corner and back whether I work or not; plus you buy a chocolate or a coffee, plus the phone cards, and then you have to pay rent, buy food, and send money home. It would be better if we worked every day, but we don't. Nobody here does."

For many, there is little dignity in the work people hire them to do. "I never used *pantalones de mezclilla* [work pants] every day in Mexico," Luis told me, referring to his jeans. He had worked in factories and at construction sites, but he had carried his work clothes with him, not on him. "In Mexico they don't realize we hang around on the street dirty, that we sometimes get paid to pick up the excrement of people's pets," said Eduardo. So when their children or wives call to ask for more money, as if they had regular jobs, it is somewhat difficult to swallow whole. They must answer for—*responder*—their familial responsibilities, but at the same time they resent the explicit petitions for money.

Walter and colleagues (2002: 225) address the disarticulation of male identity among migrant men as a central aspect of their lives. When these men are abroad and on their own, the roles of "patriarch" (a man at home guiding his family) and provider (a man who works hard in order to make ends meet) are at odds because of the distance involved. The authors understand this double bind as a tenuous balance that disintegrates when a day laborer can no longer provide for his loved ones, as in the case of injury. "Can you talk to my wife and tell her why you're here?" pled a jornalero to an *SF Weekly* reporter after being injured on the job. "She doesn't believe me. . . . She thinks I'm not working because I'm messing around" (Smith 2008).

In truth, the double bind shatters the possibility of balance as the years pass. A man's role as provider becomes his strongest and most essential link to those left behind. But ultimately it is impossible to be a full member of a family via timed phone calls, and the men feel compelled to satisfy their loved ones' needs at the expense of their own. Remittances, computers, music players, cameras, and other items sent back with "travelers"—*viajeros*—become essential for the family's sustenance (see Landolt, Autler, and Baires 1999: 297).[3] Yet the people at home who benefit from these "sacrifices" seem to constantly doubt the day laborer, who feels they unjustly wonder how much money he must be keeping and misspending. This never-ending vortex of work, remittance, and recrimination in both directions reshapes family relations. As "a few months" turn into years, the men feel that life for those back home has become easier, while their hardship and loneliness only increase (cf. Mahler 1995).

Being misunderstood is not always an effect of suspicion and misconception from the home front. Stressed about not working, Luis spent a few

3. Many *viajeros* make a living going to and from their countries of origin, taking things like cameras, video games, and an assortment of gifts for a fee and bringing back documents and other items migrants might need in the United States. These travelers have regularized their immigration status and make several trips back and forth each year.

weeks telling me that the needs of his children were overwhelming. It seemed clear that his wife understood the situation, but he was desperate. On the one hand, he was trying to borrow money to send her and the children; on the other, he complained that his wife wanted him to come home as soon as possible, as if she did not understand what would happen if he returned. As the months went by, the US economic crisis got worse and Luis's objective of buying a van and having me drive it home to Mexico dissolved into simply getting enough money to survive.

In another heart-wrenching conversation, Adolfo, one of the oldest jornaleros, wistfully exclaimed, "I'm married to a great woman." We had been talking about other people's Sanchos and misfortunes and he wanted to separate his wife from accounts of betrayal. "She raised my daughters because I was never there," he said. "I left when they were little and when I returned they were all grown up. Then I left again and now I have been here six years. I have three grandchildren I have never seen; she educated them, she taught them right from wrong, I just sent them money." Commenting on common sources of disagreement between couples separated by such distance, he added, "Sometimes when she gets mad at me because I am not there, I talk to her like this, 'Do you remember when I met you?' And she laughs. 'What do you mean?' she says. 'I mean when I saw you the first time, the day I found you,' I tell her. 'I said good-bye to you,' I tell her, and then she can't stay mad. 'I said good-bye and you turned around and looked at me, and you smiled at me,' that's what I tell her. 'Since then I have been your slave,' I tell her, 'and now look at me, look where you have me working.'"

It was during this conversation that Adolfo was also most candid about betrayal. For tied to love and nostalgia are jornaleros' growing suspicions that their families have become accustomed to their absence. In a sense, a jornalero's experience is riddled with the scars of abandonment and mistrust—his own in relation to his family's and vice versa. For men working toward saving some income or building a house, or for those who send back trucks and tools for use when they return, fear also entails losing the fruits of their labor. Adolfo leaned against a bus sign and with a small tremor explained to me how the Sancho was a reality to them.

"That happens here all the time," he told me. "Look, Tomás, for example, I lived with a Salvadoran who had been here seven years. He was the type who never spent a penny, everything he made he sent home. In the morning he had just a coffee and a doughnut, those that only cost forty cents. If he was working at lunch he wouldn't eat anything, only drink a soda. At night he never bought chicken or meat, he only ate that if we treated him. He spent nothing; he was, like we say, stingy. Look, Tomás, he slept in one of those cots—so do I—but he slept there with no mattress, only a blanket. Well, before he just slept on the floor, but someone left and gave him his cot. After that someone left and gave him the sheets—he never bought anything. With the money he sent home, his wife built a house, but since he wasn't around she just put it in her name. When he went home he went to see her at the market where she worked, but at the market he found she had another man. They started fighting and she finally said, 'Leave, but leave alone, the house is in my name.'"

Permanent estrangement from family is a common subject of conversation on the street. Everyone knows someone who has lost it all. Everything a jornalero works for can disappear in an instant. The Sancho looms at every corner because most men do not have bank accounts in the United States—a possibility precluded by the ever-present threat of deportation—so those at home manage a man's savings and things he sends back. When a jornalero loses his family, he also loses everything else he saved, built, and bought with his effort. The ascetic lives of most of the men can ultimately lead nowhere.

The tenuous balance that defines a day laborer's relationship to his family while simultaneously eroding their ties of trust and faith in one another forces the rearticulation of many of the ways the men see their own masculinity. The overdetermined provider finds himself amid destitution and marginalization in a cohort of men whom he usually only knows in passing. Masculinity thus must reconstitute itself at a distance from its traditional frames of reference (women, family, social networks) (cf. Hondagneu-Sotelo 1994; Purser 2009; Stephen 2007).

MEN, WOMEN, AND DESIRE

Rethinking the image of the Mexican macho, Gutmann (2006) suggests that masculinity among working-class people in Mexico City is a fluid social construct in which "traditional" stereotypes of what it means to be a man interrelate with historically specific economic, political, and cultural changes. Age, ethnicity, class, experience, and personality color the ideas that men put forth when understanding themselves as providers, partners, lovers, fathers, and workers. Ideas about gender, for Gutmann (2006: 243), develop into a contradictory consciousness where traditional notions about maleness from the past interact with practical transformations of the social and political body to produce ambiguity, confusion, and contradictions in male identities. Jornaleros are distanced from the complex dialectic through which masculinity emerges as a function of male/female and family relations within a particular historical and cultural milieu (González-Lopez 2005; Smith 2005). Men on the corner are isolated and their engagement in life back home becomes limited to phone conversations.

Masculinity thus rearranges itself in a contradictory set of representations where family members deploy certain traditional expectations—man as provider, man as potential womanizer or drunk—while the men must redefine themselves in terms of their experience of isolation. Thus jornaleros find themselves inexorably tied to the stereotypical image of the macho who can be easily tempted by women and alcohol. The men can happily engage this persona in daily performance on the street (cf. Pena 1991), but in truth it does not reflect their very real commitment to family, which among the day laborers I knew was central to their understanding of their *sacrificio*. As Sindi tried to explain to his wife, it is not supposed dalliances with women that hamper remittance but lack of money.

Few of the men I met had sexual or affective contact with women, in part because they were committed to their families at home, but also because they had little access to women in general. Male subjectivity thus became tied, not only to the absence of face-to-face relationships with family, but also to an almost complete lack of interactions with women in the United States. While absorbing traditional female roles into their daily lives—cooking and cleaning, mainly[4]—and dealing with the tensions

4. Gutmann (2006) identifies degendering transformations in Mexico, whereby traditionally male and female activities become reconfigured and their gender specificity de-emphasized. For example, women and men drink together or men play more intimate roles in child-rearing and household chores. A jornalero's life is not degendered by the absence of women but rather hypergendered in that he must undertake all activities necessary for his sustenance, regardless of their imputed gender association.

inherent in their isolation, the men also had to come to terms with an experience devoid of significant interactions with women. Not surprisingly, the issue of sex emerged as a central trope through which the men related to their social environment (see González-López 2005; Pena 1991).

On my corner, the *trillizos* had a female cousin living with them, Luis's younger brother and his wife lived upstairs from him (although she went back to Mexico with their newborn baby), and a couple of young guys had local girlfriends and no counterparts back home, but in general a jornalero's world was almost uniquely male. So what happens to men living among men, dealing with men, working with men for extended periods of time? On my predominantly Mexican corner on Fifth Street, conversations about sex and sexuality, like the Sancho, are initiated and sometimes solely held through *albures,* a genre of joking where the aim is to beat your interlocutor with a double entendre. If not *albures,* humor is nonetheless the main vehicle for expression, similar to what Brandes (1980: 98) describes in Andalucía, where humor seems "to provide the main fabric by which men are bound to each other on a daily basis."

Jokes express the wax and wane of sexual tensions or allude to people's sexuality. Past sexual exploits mix in with descriptions of the latest *triple equis* (i.e., XXX porn film) bought *en la pulga*—at the Oakland flea market—and, along with theatrical representations of both heterosexual and homosexual intercourse, produce a rowdy revelry among different groups of men. Cell phones invariably become a great source of fun, because many men have snippets of pornographic movies or animated cartoons of "Scooby Do Doing Wilma," Mickey and Minnie Mouse "doggy style," and so on. The same phones also have pictures of children and wives that are shared at other times, when the conversations flow back into talk about family life.

The street corner itself is scripted in conversations about sex. Standing for hours in the same place every day, the men inevitably cross paths with a number of different people who inadvertently become the source of much gossip. Men and women who walk by often are "known" characters, and small mythologies arise about what these people are like in bed or what their sexual orientation is. Women, especially, become the object of speculation, their beauty and dress style assessed and compared to others. During the time I spent on the corner, almost every woman who came in contact with us—passersby, saleswomen, NGO workers, students, and even nuns—were sexualized in one way or another. Each was assessed in terms of her relative beauty, her imagined sexual prowess or lack thereof, and her hypothetical willingness to engage jornaleros sexually. This does not mean that women were the objects of lewd comments but rather that they became tropes through which sexuality was discussed. Eduardo's predilection for older women, for example, led us to nickname one "regular" *la charpei*—a reference to the wrinkled Shar-Pei dog breed. Her daily appearance usually led to heated debates over Eduardo's exaggerated accounts of his past love affairs with married, older *veteranas*. Some men also told of horny *patronas*—female employers—who hired them to work on their house and then appeared naked in the doorway, but few believed these stories.

Early one morning, I sat drinking my coffee and leafing through a fashion magazine Eduardo had found on the bus. Luis sat next to me, naming all the celebrities he knew and commenting on their low-cut shirts. I said that in my grandfather's time everyone wore a suit, tie, and hat and carried an umbrella. Luis said that was better than what you see today, everyone wearing less clothing each week: *"¡Un día vamos a terminar todos con el títere por fuera!"*—One day we'll all end up with our puppet on the outside![5] And then he stood up, striking an exaggerated pose. Eduardo, whom we had been making fun of because he was drawing, looked up and laughed. Luis turned to him and, striking the same pose, said, "I'm going to have to take my clothes off so you can paint me with my puppet in the air."

"What? We wouldn't see a thing!" Eduardo answered. "I'd have to get a magnifying glass to see that, it's nothing!" Everyone started laughing and going on about the size of Luis's *títere,* some saying we would need tweezers and magnifying glasses, others just repeating that it was tiny. Luis took this good-naturedly, laughing and answering back without a hint of spite. Each answer he gave, in turn, challenged the other person's penis size.

As we joked around, a woman walked by on the other side of the street. "In Mexico [City] I'd say, I'd like to eat your *empanada!*" Luis told me. Following his cue, Beto—another of the Mexicans—gave the Salvadoran

5. *Títere* literally means "puppet" but refers here to his penis.

version he had learned on the corner: *"Me gustaría comerte la popusa."* We all laughed and I gave them the Colombian equivalent, *arepa,* a sort of flatbread made with corn flour akin to a *popusa.* Although this was all done quietly so the woman could not hear, we started discussing whether women actually liked it when men call out such things.

"Of course not," Luis scolded us in disbelief, "it shows lack of respect." An older man sitting quietly beside us interjected and said that some women did like to be talked to that way. Everyone was laughing and started talking in *albures* or having conversations with imaginary women on the street. Finally the conversation shifted and Luis said he had bought ten movies *en la pulga.* "¿Porno?" asked someone. He said no, adding that he sometimes watched porn but only for ten minutes or so because he got bored. They laughed and chided him about falling asleep while masturbating. We got into a contest about who had seen the longest porn movie, and Iván finally asked each of us to show him our hands: "Lets see who has more hair on their hands." When I tried to turn the joke back around to him, he shook his head and said he never watched porn movies, "because they make me hungry." There was laughter and jokes about masturbation for quite some time.

I got tired of sitting, so I stood and leaned against the bus sign. A young student type rode by on a bicycle. Beto nudged me and said, "Mira, Tomás, eso es un puñal," meaning the guy was homosexual. The group laughed and talked about my initial blunder with this term—*puñal*—, which to me simply meant dagger. Beto again added the equivalent from a different country: "En Guatemala les dices *huecos*"—literally, "holes." Everyone laughed. None of them were Guatemalan.

While we were joking around, Eduardo got bored and put his earphones on. Suddenly the corner grew quiet; he was singing. The silence caught his attention and, looking up from his music player, he asked, *"¿Qué pasa?"*

"Nothing," Luis cooed, "you sing beautifully." The men all laughed. Eduardo ignored them and started singing a sappy love song out of tune.

"¡Ay! ¡Ay! ¡Ay!" everyone started laughing and making cooing sounds.

"I am not singing it to you," Eduardo said defensively, never sure if this behavior was directed at him personally or was just general revelry. We laughed harder.

Luis then returned the magazine to Eduardo with mocking carefulness and said, "Take this my love"—*Toma mi amor*—, in a very sweet and feminine way. The pair exchanged brief words as if they were lovers. The other guys laughed. When Eduardo finally got tired of the jokes, he stood up and left. As he walked down the street, somebody called out, "*¡Ay! ¡Qué nalguitas tienes!*," something to the effect of, "What beautiful buttocks you have!"

It is clear that this joking is a product of behavior not unique to the migrant experience but ingrained in male interaction as it is learned and practiced throughout one's life. Mexican men on my corner were much more likely to engage in such conversations. In fact, *albures* are sometimes referred to as uniquely *chilango*—from Mexico City—and when I had difficulty understanding the double meanings, people told me not to worry, referring to others present who, coming from other regions of Mexico, had had to learn how to *alburear* on the streets of Berkeley. That said, although *albures* might be construed as a Mexican phenomenon, joking about sex is generalized on the street.

Day-to-day interactions among jornaleros are riddled with offhand comments about masturbation and pornography, and even older and more "serious" men participate actively by adding to the barrage of comments or passively by laughing. Gutmann (2006: 142) found that a common way to refer to a single man in Mexico City working-class neighborhoods was to refer to a masturbating man, but on the corner this is extrapolated to almost everyone. When joking and talking about women, the conclusion of the conversation many times leads to allusions of the need to masturbate or masturbating too much. Every once in a while the latent sexual tension on the corner emerges with a loud "I can't take it any longer, I am desperate!"—*¡Ya no aguanto mas, ya estoy desesperado!*—to which people answer, laughing, something to the effect that it is time to masturbate: "*Ya es hora de echarte una chaqueta.*" Jokes notwithstanding, on some occasions such comments were made quite seriously, not in the context of humorous exchange.

These conversations point to sexuality in the absence of women, both in terms of sexual access and, on a deeper level, the absence of relations with the opposite sex and thus to the issue of masculinity itself. Feminizing oneself in order to make a joke also recalls Gutmann's (2006) argument about the contradictions inherent in the "macho" image and serves to overdetermine the absence of females with whom to interact. It also reveals the deployment of notions surrounding homosexuality, which, through humor, position the speaker in either a passive, feminine role vis-à-vis the interlocutor or vice versa, like calling out to Eduardo as if he were a woman.

Another favorite conversation topic is past sexual exploits. This usually comes up with people you are more familiar with and is not always humorous but can be simply conversational. For about two weeks, for example, the same three or four guys kept going back to the issue of sexual positions, and some told intimate details of their married life and past sexual partners. A lot of the talk was about finding positions your woman would also enjoy, which inadvertently turned into conversations about the *Kama Sutra* and other books about sex. Most of the men knew about the book from television programs and had seen it in bookstores, but Sindi, who said he really had a hard time reading, wanted to buy a video version he had seen in *la pulga.* The humor of the conversations climaxed when Sindi confessed he had not bought it because he would much rather buy Disney cartoons, which were more entertaining. In the end, it turned out that one of the men had a modern version of the *Kama Sutra,* with photographs (not pornographic ones), that he brought and lent to Luis, who liked reading.

It was during conversations like this that Eduardo showed his inability to understand social cues, as he went too far in his descriptions, telling us he always hydrated during sex by keeping a bottle of water near the bedside table. Intimacy can be serious, it can be humorous, but there is also a guarded threshold jornaleros avoid crossing. Eduardo's transgressions made it seem to us that he was boasting and thus either exaggerating his exploits or lying outright. This threshold was made clear to me only after Luis and I became good friends. One afternoon in his house, he was talking about wanting to go home, telling me his wife was complaining a lot about his absence. We were alone, his brothers and brother-in-law having gone next door to drink and watch TV. He was telling me his wife was not as *güera* as her brother and suddenly said, "Now that no one is around I am going to show you a picture, because the guys here they don't know how to show respect." He stood up, went to the closet, and, after rummaging through it for a while, came back with a grainy picture that might have been printed at home. "These guys *[estos güeyes]* don't know how to look at a woman with respect," he told me, "and they make fun of me." He handed me the picture. His wife was lying on a sofa in jeans, holding a stuffed animal and a finger to her lips. It was sensual and private in a way that put me off a bit, and I fumbled with words about her being quite fair as I handed it back. Luis showed the vulnerability of the act by worrying about what the others, all members of his family, would say. Luis, for me, was the master of *albures* on our corner, a smart and witty joker, a good friend, but also someone who picked on everybody else. That he was so nervous about the picture shows the importance of intimacy within its public, representational context.

Lack of female contact transects the age cohorts on the street, and a wide variety of men discuss the possibility of sex and dating. Chucho, a bachelor in his early twenties, once met me on the UC Berkeley campus to check out some online job applications. When I greeted him, he was beside himself with joy. Wide-eyed and rubbing his hands, he exclaimed, "Wow! This is great, there are *some* girls walking around! look how hot they look!." His giddy excitement and stares made him appear quite deranged, and people on the street started avoiding us. Finally we managed to sit down and start browsing the Web in relative calm. After a few minutes in which we failed to find him a job, he asked, in more of a pleading tone, if I thought any of these women would ever consider dating him. Lorenzo also spent a week seriously considering the possibility that a *patrona* he met would date him after she expressed mild interest in his accounts of going out with his "friend from the university" for beers. "Do you think she would go out with me? I wouldn't believe it," he concluded with flushed cheeks. He never called her. In twelve years in the United States, he has had one girlfriend, who left him because she got a well-paying job.[6]

For a few of the younger jornaleros, the search for women turns into drinking binges in the bars of Oakland and San Francisco—nightly

6. Although one could argue that the cases described here involve potential relationships with women in a different structural position than the jornaleros, that is, that desire is somehow scripted onto class and ethnic hierarchies—here embodied in white college students and employers—in truth, it is these types of women whom the jornaleros are more likely to have contact with.

outings that put them at risk of getting caught by *la migra* or, more likely, getting mugged or arrested for rowdiness or fighting. These stories are inevitably tragic in that they never end well for the teller. As Chucho complained one morning, "I always end up at *las cuaras,* but not even that helps." *Cuaras* is a latinized version of "quarters" (twenty-five-cent coins), which refers to cheap peep shows in the area.

Along with joking about women, a great deal of time is spent on the corner making fun of others' sexuality. Jokes can have homosexual connotations, where the speaker bullies his interlocutor with offhand remarks that directly or indirectly threaten anal penetration. As stated above, in other instances the joke lies in how the speaker feminizes himself or engages his audience in mock homosexual propositions (see Prieur 1998). Masculinity is, in these cases, an issue of how you behave with others and the tenuous line between asserting your manliness through feminizing others and not appearing truly effeminate in the process (cf. Brandes 1980).

Yet for most men, talk about homosexuality oscillates between a humorous exchange and a threat. Eduardo, in fact, lost face with the group as the months went by and became known and referred to as a *maricón*—pejorative for "homosexual"—mainly because of his habit of singing love songs out loud while listening to his MP3 player. Eduardo's lack of social ability probably contributed to this perception, since he "shared" too much information with us and set himself up to be the brunt of many jokes. For example, he told us—quite innocently—he had made a male friend on the corner who, after beers in San Francisco, had tried to kiss him. A couple of men wondered aloud why he had not beaten the guy up. Defensively Eduardo said the man had hit him and threatened to kill him if he told anyone. It had been months since anybody had seen his attacker, so he felt it was all right to tell us, but this seemed to confirm all of Luis and Clemente's suspicions about Eduardo, and they scolded him for being so stupid. "It must be that you really wanted something," they concluded.

Day laborers' precarious living conditions and the absence of women from their lives have led to interventions from epidemiologists, researchers in public health, and social workers, who consider the men to be at high risk for HIV and other sexually transmitted diseases (e.g., Organista and Kubo 2005). While Chucho loved to tell us how he got "that sickness that sounds like the name of a woman"—chlamydia—from a prostitute in

Los Angeles, most of the men I hung out with were not likely to visit prostitutes, either because they thought it was a breach of the *confianza*—trust—necessary to survive separation from their wives or because "good" prostitutes were really expensive. More relevant for day laborers is the stark contrast between the friendly revelry and joking involved in *albures*, the scripted machismo mixed in with intimate conversations that indicate strong commitment—but also reproach—toward their families, and how these men feel their work threatens their physical integrity. Talk about sex, homosexuality, and prostitution brings conversations back to the very real vulnerability that these men experience.

THE MALE BODY AT RISK

In many ways, day labor looks a lot like prostitution. On the cold foggy Berkeley mornings, the dark figures standing out on the curb waving down passing cars are eerily reminiscent of other corners I have seen, where women lean against the street signs or sit on the steps of buildings, laughing and waiting for men to stop and make a deal. Day labor sets men up on the curb in a "feminine" role (Purser 2009), passively waiting to be chosen by a *patrón*. This is not lost on jornaleros, who, like Luis, refer to standing on the street as *pirujear*—slang for selling yourself sexually. Somewhat like the Sancho, this analogy is a metaphor that melts into reality.

I first heard of men selling their bodies in reference to jornaleros who had ceased to work and had become *borrachitos*, the alcoholics living by the train tracks nearby. These were well-known characters on the street, people we all saw defecating in vacant lots early in the mornings, begging for hot water at the coffee shop, and sometimes walking into Friday lunches at the nearby church, stinking of liquor, calling out obscenities, or quietly hording food. The lumpenized image of the failed jornalero reaffirms the worth of those who remain able and serves as a referent to delineate the "true" man who works for his family and future. People told me that these *borrachitos* became so dependent on alcohol that they would even sell their bodies for a couple of dollars in order to buy booze. Chucho, who before we met spent a week under the bridge because he could not pay his rent, said that he saw firsthand how *puñales* drove by at night and took them away. When I started bringing this up in conversations, I discovered that almost everyone had a story about being propositioned by men. Talking into my recorder one day, Jaime offered the most direct account I heard.

"Even gays come to pick you up," he told me as we were talking about the street corner and its problems.

"Gays, here?" I asked in mock disbelief, wondering aloud if they also needed work around the house.

Jaime's pitch became louder, "Yes, yes, they come, [they pick you up] for work, but when you get there . . . " he hesitated, "they offer you . . . " He was uncomfortable and at a loss for the right words. Finally he simply said, "They ask if you want to have sex with them." Jaime then told me his experience, which had started on the very corner where we were speaking.

"Once this bastard *[fregado]* picked me up. He says, 'You want to work?' 'Sure, how much are you paying?' 'Look,' he says, 'I'll pay eight [dollars an hour].' 'Listen,' I tell him, 'eight is too little, at least pay me nine.' 'I don't know; it's a really easy job," he says . . . Bah! 'I'll go,' I said. 'Friend, what is it we're going to do?' He says, 'You are going to clean a birdcage.' But when we were [driving] he said, 'What's your name?' 'My name is Jaime.' 'And where are you from, do you have family here?' 'My children are in Honduras.' 'And a wife?' he asked. 'No, I'm divorced.' 'I,' he says, 'don't care about women.' 'Why?' I ask him 'I do, they're the most beautiful thing God made,' I say. 'I don't think so,' he says. 'My family doesn't accept me because I'm gay.'"

I asked if this bizarre exchange really happened in the car. A bit exasperated, Jaime retorted, "Yes, [in the car] in English." Jaime continued: "'Fine,' I said, and we got to his house. I cleaned the birdcage, fed the birds. And then he suggested we go to the store. He bought turkey, prepared it, we ate, and he says, 'Rest,' and says, 'Do you like porn movies?' 'Well,' I said, 'sometimes, not always though.' 'Do you want to watch one?' he asked. 'I don't know,' I said. Then he played this porno . . . horrible things with two men. No, no, no!" Jaime's agitation increased and he started flailing his hand violently. I tried to laugh and asked, "Really, man on man?" And he continued in disgust, "Yes, man on man. 'No, no, no!' I told him. 'Turn that off,' I said. 'No. If you like I'll do a good job on you.' He said that to me and started masturbating, 'No, no, no!' I said, 'I don't want that . . . turn that off, pay me, and then I'm gone. I'm going to call the police,' I said this all in English because the man spoke no Spanish. 'No, no,' he said, 'I'll pay you.' And he put his pants on, and we went in his car, and [near the corner] he paid me."

Jaime's horror at this proposition affected his narrative and probably jumbled the facts. His conversation with the man was complicated by a very limited knowledge of English. His weird reaction to the whole episode, asking the man to take him back to the corner, probably meant that he had no idea where he was in relation to the labor site or his home. Jaime's anxiety, however, was clear. Like him, many day laborers I spoke to said they had felt sexually intimidated and claimed to have been propositioned by men who hired them for jobs around the house. Toño, one of the younger men on our corner, for example, disappeared for a day after he was stranded in the suburbs and claimed he had been propositioned by the *patrón* and locked in a basement for a while. When he managed to escape he ran away and, not knowing where he was, ended up spending the night by the freeway.

There were some characters who drove by frequently whom everyone claimed were homosexuals looking for cheap sex. The most well-known of these men was the *camarón* —literally, "shrimp," a reference to the man's red hair—who drove by almost every week and propositioned middle-aged men sitting alone, including Lorenzo and Don Raúl. He was so infamous that the first time I was offered work I refused, thinking the red-haired *gabacho* who wanted to hire me was the shrimp. "We wouldn't have let you go, Tomás," Eduardo said, patting me on the back as the rest of the men laughed.

Accounts of homosexual propositions clearly convey the men's understanding of their own vulnerability. Estranged from their families and supporting their Sanchos, they are left only as passive observers of the opposite sex, their masculinity expressed through their role as providers and a stereotypical, rehearsed, "macho" bravado that is nonetheless precarious. Faced with the realities of day labor, they are at the mercy of chance and open to violation. There is latent danger every time a jornalero gets into a *patrón*'s car. In every suspicious glance and question directed at the potential employer lies, not only the fear of being exploited in economic terms, but the realization of the hidden and yet obvious nature of their subjectivities as migrants: the body for sale, the body for abuse. Significantly, homosexual propositions, which challenge an already shaky masculinity, are most often perpetrated by white men, usually older *gabachos.*

Later on, Jaime mentioned being offered fifty dollars to let a *gabacho* driver's wife, recently graduated from some sort of dental hygiene program, practice on his teeth. "*No señor,* not that! I'm not going to open my mouth," Jaime said into my recorder.

"What was it they wanted?" I asked in disbelief.

"I don't know, maybe they were going to take an organ, take my teeth, and afterward who's going to pay me? For fifty dollars I am not doing that job, nor would I do it for more," he told me in a panic. "I don't know what they are going to do with my teeth, I don't know what they are going to do with my mouth."

THE FRACTURED *LEIBOR*

Life and work on the labor site manifest the political economy of US society, its thirst for the undocumented, "rightless" body and the personal tragedies and desires of the commodified laborer—*un leibor,* as jornaleros refer to themselves. This articulation fractures the men's social reality in space—they are neither here nor there (Coutin 2005)—and threatens their personal and social representations of masculinity. The structural vulnerability on the street corner endangers economic stability, family unity, identity, and ultimately, bodily integrity. Jokes become referents to latent fears shared by most jornaleros; they are funny because they make light of what is on everyone's mind. Hand in hand with these jokes comes talk about the sexual prowess of strangers, good fun to "pass the time" that nonetheless makes visible the men's lack of affective and social contact with women. The Sancho looms at every corner; families become estranged as the men's economic stability and well-being erode. Meaningful relationships dissolve and contact with women is limited to passing interactions on the street, while those back home suspect every silence, every penny not sent to support them. Labor is scarce, abuse prevalent, the sojourn abroad indefinite, and the body at constant risk.

This risk, for the jornaleros, seems most evident in how their fears shape reality. Marginalization takes the form of the abandoned provider, whose sense of self is torn asunder by the experience of migration that leaves him at the mercy of powers out of his control. This perception is by no means only relevant to the day laborers themselves. People like the *camarón* come looking for cheap sexual encounters guaranteed to be without consequence because of the ease of exploiting desperate men who will not turn to the authorities for help. There are also those who need the body itself, not only for its labor but also for sex, teeth to practice on, or, in another case, Spanish-speaking men to color a themed drinking binge for a senile parent who remembered living in Mexico. The degree to which these events actually occur is beside the point, since they are prevalent in the subjective experience of jornaleros. The Sancho, misunderstanding, isolation, and exploitation are inscribed in the body—they are all embodied referents of the same experience.

Citizenship and Other Such Vagaries

¡Cómo que señor! Pedro. Por qué señor, si lo único que me queda de la burguesía son mis papeles al día.

Alfredo Bryce Echenique, *Tantas Veces Pedro*

Sometimes legends make reality, and become more useful than the facts.

Salman Rushdie, *Midnight's Children*

But these things might have happened, they had certainly happened in other circumstances, and they belonged to the realm of real experience.

Claude Lévi-Strauss, *Structural Anthropology*

Common assumptions about "illegal" immigration in the United States usually overemphasize people's reasons for crossing the border—they are escaping poverty, looking to find better jobs, more money, and so on—and in a time of economic crisis, attribute dark intentions to migrants who, in truth, embody some of the moral premises the country is built on. A strong work ethic, individualism, and the search for opportunities open to people of all walks of life get turned into "taking American jobs," abusing or cheating the system, refusing to embrace English, and the like. However, few people wonder about how living "illegally," in practice, is actually possible. It is easy enough, after all, to forget how many everyday events in our lives are shaped or made possible by the state through its practices of inscription. Driver's licenses, institutional IDs, health-insurance cards, bank cards, and other such documents all play central roles in the practices that allow members of a contemporary nation state to move, consume, work, play, pay taxes, and in general, function as social actors. For most jornaleros in Berkeley, these documents are out of reach. How is it, then, that the undocumented manage to get by?

De Genova (2005) sees the governance of undocumented migrants as the production of illegality itself, where the deportability of people like the jornaleros shapes the "outsider" nature of their social position within the United States. The deportable nature of this labor force, in other words, makes it "an eminently disposable commodity" (De Genova 2005: 216). This ties the work of jornaleros to the distribution of labor and production in general because their disposability makes them easy to displace, move, and replace in a system where the low cost of their wages is tied to economic growth (Sassen 1988: 57, 145). Zlolniski (2006) has addressed the nature of this relationship by tracing the survival strategies and social mobilization of migrant workers tied to Silicon Valley's technological industry. But while these authors have underlined the articulation of legality and illegality in the labor market (see also Heyman 1990; Ngai 2004), I address the mechanisms through which tolerance and persecution become essential to the forms of governance that ensure that disposability is maintained. Jornaleros' experience in the United States contains a violent contradiction, because while "deportability" is essential to the nature of the work they provide, their marginalization seems coupled with the relative freedom to move and act as members of sorts in US society. In a sense, governing the undocumented both entails producing their "illegality," in De Genova's sense, and creating fluctuating exceptions to its implementation that nonetheless ensure the absence of social mobilization that could challenge the status quo. At heart here is the essential quality of citizenship for these men.

Taking citizenship as a broad category of belonging, a multifaceted relation of rights, representation, and responsibilities between people and the social order, I want to disentangle the ways in which the contours of citizenship emerge as a particular form of social status that bequeaths rights (Sassen 2006: 291). By following some of the practices that enable "undocumented" migrants to live and work in the Bay Area, I argue that substantive forms of citizenship (Holston and Appadurai 1999)—elements of citizenship that are exercised at local levels and are not necessarily enacted through state institutions—have specific effects on the experience of migration for these men. Such effects shape everyday life for jornaleros and imbue it at times with a semblance of state and socially recognized belonging that is, nonetheless, impossible to realize.

I came to see this two-faced relationship to US society as a parallel citizenship, or *para-citizenship*, where the everyday life of undocumented jornaleros seems at times to mimic "legally" sanctioned forms of belonging but never transects them. In other words, this particular form of citizenship looks and feels like belonging at certain times, but it can never be truly realized. Parallel citizenship is produced through substantive access to NGOs and other institutions that, along with the men's own nation states, produce a wide array of documentation. Although not "of the state" in the United States, such documentation follows its logics and thus enables and reproduces some of its effects. Day laborers are thus able to own cars, access housing, and work; some even pay taxes and use services such as cell phones, the Internet, and cable TV and, in general, participate in the everyday goings-on of the areas they live in. They are citizens, of sorts, and become enmeshed in the places they inhabit; as migrants in a foreign country, they also cultivate cosmopolitan tastes and preoccupations. However, these activities are also informed by fear of state persecution embodied in *la migra,* a sometimes real but also highly mythologized institution that has the power to appear violently and unsettle every aspect of belonging, turning the drudgery of waiting long hours for work into a spectacular game of cat and mouse where reality is built upon rumor and hearsay. Deportability is thus reinforced to maintain the elements of social inclusion at the margins, where belonging remains a mockery of formal citizenship.

COSMOPOLITANISM

Reality here refers to how jornaleros understand the world around them, something addressed somewhat in previous sections. On the corner, "reality" is a problematic construction of "fact" and "fiction" that both sets the men up as cosmopolitan subjects in a globalized world and makes them prone to taking action based on distorted and convoluted anecdotes and truisms they hear on the street. Cosmopolitanism, understood vaguely as some sort of universal citizenship (Ferguson 1999; Sassen 2006), has emerged from studies of globalization, usually to address the rise of transnational elites whose "groundedness" extends beyond the reach of the state (Ong 1999). Based on Kant's essay "Perpetual Peace" (1983), Derrida (2001) also posits a cosmopolitanism with which, he suggests, we should return sovereignty to the city (as opposed to the state) and reestablish a humanistically informed sense of hospitality in the face of the vast migrations (forced and economic) of the second half of the twentieth century. These two conceptualizations of cosmopolitanism are combined in the experience of jornaleros as they learn to deal with life in the Bay Area. Because they are permitted to stand on the street—that is, because the expendability of their labor makes it essential to the local economy—jornaleros can engage the world in these ways. Whether Derrida would consider this hospitality or not, I cannot say. Whatever the case, on the street, jornaleros acquire cosmopolitan preoccupations through contact with people from other countries and different walks of life and through conversations with peers. Locked behind closed doors, they also access the world via the media, where information from the local to the global informs and affects their relations to others.

Many of the men I knew developed a highly informed version of what Hannerz (2007: 71) calls "consumer cosmopolitanism", where the aesthetics and cultural diversity the men encounter—through long hours at home and through contacts on the street—shape their understanding of the world around them. Their travels and travails, in a way, make jornaleros connoisseurs of the world; they meet people of other nationalities, taste or hear of their food, learn variations of common expressions they thought were unique to their hometowns, and in general, become exposed to other worldviews. Through their own experience as migrants they also become attuned to what Hannerz (2007: 71–72) calls "political cosmopolitanism" and thus racial tensions, universal health care, military interventions around the world, human rights, the rights of immigrants, immigration in Europe, passports and visas—all appear in my field notes as common topics of conversation. They reflect the men's preoccupation not only with their lot but also with its significance on a global scale. Back on *la parada,* in their relations to others, these cosmopolitan preoccupations become subjects of discussion that the men reformulate to fit their own particular understandings of the world.

Interactions on the street thus produce a great amount of information that jornaleros access for their personal enjoyment and to learn about issues that affect them. Through conversations with a wide variety of characters, information gets passed along and interpreted in ways that make *la parada* an open forum where jornaleros acquire knowledge—albeit incomplete or erroneous in many cases—about the world that surrounds them. The street-corner version of cosmopolitanism is central to how day laborers come to understand themselves, but it is also mediated, measured, and shaped by a realm of uncertainty and unreliability that inevitably informs how the men make decisions, address certain problems, and understand events. For jornaleros in the Bay Area, street-corner cosmopolitanism shapes a particularly problematic sense of belonging, one regimented by ambiguity.

CITIZENSHIP

As is clear by now, living "illegally" in the United States does not necessarily mean explicitly hiding from state and local authorities; in fact, living "undocumented" lives in many instances follows practices and rationales similar to those required by "documented" or legal forms of living. In other words, belonging is not necessarily scripted onto an officially recognized status of social and political existence. At the same time, undocumented migrants find themselves in a highly politicized social environment, where everyday life flows in and out of public debate, becoming especially stigmatized in times of economic crisis (Mountz et al. 2002; Ngai 2004). People's ability to work, move, and live in a particular area can easily become restricted; the everyday can rapidly shift from a semblance of tolerance to persecution. Examples of this shift abound and can be found in the media with only cursory searches for the effects that immigration law and policies have on undocumented and even documented migrant populations. In recent years, for example, Arizona, Utah, Alabama, and other states have created massive panics through policies that allow police to check people's immigration status, list known undocumented migrants, and the like. Being undocumented thus constitutes a social existence that is unstable at best because it is never grounded for more than an instant of political reality, a fact that De Genova (2002, 2005) has illustrated by suggesting we look at the production of illegality itself. This entails denaturalizing "illegality"—understood as the political construction of the undocumented at a given time—and framing it as a particular relationship to the state (i.e., there is no generic form of migration; it is always situated in time and space, tied to specific regimes of governance). My intent here is to reflect on the experience of undocumented day laborers in the post-9/11 United States as it takes shape in a highly liberal and migrant-tolerant urban area of Northern California.

Classical approaches to citizenship frame the concept within the notion of political participation in a particular nation state. The citizen, embodied originally in the white, literate, landowning adult male (Ryan 1992; De Genova 2006), was taken as an active member of the national polity that, in turn, was conceptualized as existing within discrete territorial boundaries (Anderson 1991; Sassen 2006). The state's ability to discriminate between categories of people sets up a dichotomy between citizens and noncitizens, which Hannah Arendt (1973) argued was central to the social and political crises of the nineteenth and twentieth centuries. In her analysis of the aftermath of the Second World War, she brought to bear the problematic nature of the nation-state able to confer rights in light of the millions of stateless people left in Europe and elsewhere. This dichotomy, for Arendt, rendered humanitarianism impotent, since there is no way to confer rights to the "stateless." Citizenship in this view is a direct relationship between the state and its nationals. Agamben (1998) has taken up this either/or dichotomy (citizen/noncitizen) by centering on the production of bare life as the cornerstone of the state's sovereignty, understood through Schmitt's (1985) notion of the sovereign exception. Rights, in this sense, are mobilized to regiment inclusion and exclusion in the increasingly complex configurations of biopolitics that regulate modern life.

However, the binary structure of belonging in both Arendt's and Agamben's perspectives does not necessarily hold true in contemporary realities. Globalization and the human rights regime have set in motion processes and practices that destabilize the hegemony of state-recognized belonging (Ong 2006: 23). A territorially grounded citizenship (nationality), or its absence, does not preclude forms of recognition and participation. New political and economic geographies have shifted social and political recognition to both transnational arenas and local settings (Appadurai 1996; Sassen 2006; Holston 2008). The city has in many cases become to some degree "denationalized" and tied to transnational configurations of power where claims to rights are not necessarily grounded in the state

(Sassen 1999: 182). The emergence of the "global city" illustrates the contradictions inherent in globalization that simultaneously center corporate power, finance capital, and a "disproportionate share of the disadvantaged" in the same locale (Sassen 2000: 92). Marginalized populations have thus found new spaces of political action in cities where the politics of inclusion and exclusion have become reconfigured into local claims of belonging (Rosaldo and Flores 1997; Caldeira 2000; Sassen 2000; Holston 2008). This process has put migration at the heart of discussions of citizenship, as migrant populations, both state sanctioned and undocumented, concentrate in cities and mobilize politically. It also points to the links between citizenship and the global market that these populations respond to in different ways (Heyman 1990; Sassen 1999; Ngai 2004).

In the United States immigration has been inexorably tied to the production of national identity. As discussed in the previous section, national narratives have articulated migrants into the complex structures of the country's political economy through processes of racialization that position different essentialized groups in a contextual relationship to an idealized "whiteness" (Sacks 1994; Ong 2003; Ngai 2004; De Genova 2005, 2006). Depending on historical context, this relationship is not static but shifts its referents under social, economic, and political forces that nonetheless maintain the racialization of emerging populations as they enter particular countries (Silverstein 2005). In the 1990s, for example, the possibility of formalizing their immigration status was available to undocumented migrants who had lived in the United States for more than seven years and could show good moral character and extreme hardship. If they proved they had paid taxes, learned English, raised "American" families, and so on, migrants could argue for a suspension of deportation on the grounds that they had become citizens of sorts (Coutin 2003b). In a pre-9/11 United States this *protocitizenship* suggested the potential realization of full citizenship for migrants who had aligned themselves with traditionally "American" ideals and practices (Coutin 2003a, 2003b). The twenty-first century and its preoccupations with homeland security and terrorism, however, have left even the most "Americanized" undocumented migrants without such possibilities.

Inda (2006) ties this shift to a departure from governing the social to governing particular subjects within a twofold strategy that counterposes technologies of citizenship—aimed at inserting subjects into "circuits of responsible self-management"—and anti-citizenship—aimed at regulating subjects considered unredeemable in the previous rationale and whose exclusion can thus not be avoided. Here, "crime and punishment have become the occasions and the institutional contexts in which we undertake to govern illegal immigration" (Inda 2006: 12–22, 46). Thus the political stigmatization of "illegal immigrants" is advanced through modern biopolitics that mobilize practices of enumeration—demographic, social, and economic statistics that produce a "problem" population to be acted upon. In the aftermath of 9/11 these practices of anti-citizenship have effectively established a "criminal" population that threatens not only jobs and culture but the body of the nation as a whole. Inda's (2006: 118, 127) analysis maintains the either/or dichotomy mentioned above by reframing it as a distinction between proper subjects—citizens—and improper ones—anti-citizens—the latter being the object of technologies that aim to "shape human conduct and achieve specific ends . . . through their incapacitation and containment." Yet multiple studies of the everyday life of migrant groups show several instances of inclusion that are not directly scripted by these technologies (see Hondagneu-Sotelo 1994; Mahler 1995; Dohan 2003; González-López 2005; Smith 2005; Gomberg-Muñoz 2011).

In the case of the Berkeley jornaleros, access to services, freedom of movement, legal representation, medical services, and other elements of inclusion are not associated directly with any form of anti-citizenship; incapacitation and containment are not the objective. Rather, day laborers find themselves in the midst of ambiguous practices that enable their constitution as productive members of society while simultaneously ensuring their social exclusion. Undocumented jornaleros are thus at the crux of two contradictory elements of modern citizenship: one based on the tension between inclusion and exclusion in forms of governmentality that go back to the dichotomy addressed by Arendt and Agamben; the other centered on new institutional and social configurations of belonging. In the first instance, practices that govern undocumented migrants are tied to the shift toward a post-social governmentality of self-actualizing and self-fulfilling citizens (Inda 2006); in the second, "belonging" and rights are redefined and relocated to the urban political and economic geographies of the area that migrants and other marginalized populations inhabit (Sassen 1999, 2000).

Thus, everyday life for undocumented day laborers constitutes a type citizenship—understood as a socially sanctioned form of belonging articulated through state and nonstate institutions—that is tied to the urban settings within which these men live and work and that both enables their incorporation and maintenance as able laborers and ensures their marginalization as undocumented migrants. While the positive aspects of jornaleros' inclusion parallel formal, state-recognized citizenship, its unstable referents to persecution and state retribution ensure that these men's social and legal legitimacy will always be in question. This parallel citizenship is the result of the possibilities and constraints offered by substantive recognition of freedom and rights, a migrant "reality" that emerges in a twofold movement where exclusion and inclusion blend into each other. This reality shapes the everyday life of men who have no formal immigration status but who move about the urban landscape, have contact with state and civil institutions (like the police, small-claims courts, the DMV, various hospitals, and NGOs), and live at times like citizens of the area. Such interactions give rise to participation and inclusion, but they are based on informal practices of documentation and legitimation. They are also a product of information that is obtained and understood through hearsay and contradictory secondhand accounts that reveal the dangers inherent in engaging the institutions necessary to guarantee certain rights and services. Para-citizenship is a form of belonging based on fear of retribution from the state. The apparent freedom and inclusion day laborers enjoy dissolves into a state of confusion where the perception of persecution becomes latent in every aspect of their lives. In essence, then, parallel citizenship is the political mechanism through which these men's "disposability" is ensured; the threat of deportation thus serves as a reminder that reinforces the social structure that shapes jornaleros' existence.

In the pages that follow, I suggest that the governance of undocumented day laborers is the product of substantive forms of recognition that replicate state-articulated belonging. Jornaleros access these elements of citizenship by way of informal practices of documentation and the relations they make possible. The institution of citizenship proper—maintained and reproduced through documentary practices of identification that make subjects legible—is what shapes the frames of reference within which undocumented migrants must operate. The state's own technologies of writing, as Das (2004: 227) has argued, open the doors to new forms of identification—imitations, forgeries, and "mimetic performances of power" that bring the margins into state purview through the logics of its practices. The state can control or shatter the fictions of inclusion that this system produces, by way of spectacular reminders of its power. Jornaleros can thus never be completely at ease with their status as members of US society. They know and expect what is coming to them—the retribution of the state, always embodied in *la migra.*

6 Belonging

Interactions with peers, organizations, and other people shape the experiences of jornaleros in Northern California and give rise to particular perspectives among the men about the world around them. This "reality" emerges in the juxtaposition of the men's personal histories—what they carry over from home and through migration—with the context in which they become inscribed when they establish themselves in the United States. On the street, the sense of reality is so distorted that the men appear worldly, well informed, and totally clueless all at once. Here I will address the elements that make up a day laborer's "worldview"—for lack of a better word—loosely understood as a set of notions and ideas about the world the jornaleros inhabit that informs how they comprehend what goes on around them.

On a typical street-corner morning, I sat with Luis, Chucho, Toño, and Hernando, chatting about this and that. Luis and I got into our standard question-and-answer pattern, where he tested my status as a student with questions to which he always knew the answer. He invariably ended each question with the expression, *"¡Ya me creías burro, o que no sabía!"*—You thought me dumb or ignorant! We had talked about evolution, the miniseries *Cosmos,* and then about overpopulation in China and the one-child policy. Chucho was interested in this and asked if there were many poor people in China. Luis and I said some cities were technologically advanced but that there were a lot of poor people. Chucho started trying to get me to quantify the amount, and Luis interrupted by asking him what part of the world had the greatest disparities between rich and poor. *"¿China?"* answered Chucho. And Luis retorted with great pomp, *"América Latina."*

This got Chucho really interested, although Luis and I had to explain what "disparity" meant. Chucho opened his eyes wide, in his particular insane way, and Hernando and Toño joked about his expression: "The faces he makes! It's like learning something hurts!" Miguel then said, "It's like when people say the Spanish brought culture and all that [to the Americas], bah! When they saw Mexico City they were dumfounded, man *[se quedaron sorprendidos, mi chavo].* [And looking at me asked] Right?" So we started talking about the Aztecs, the Mayas, the Olmecs, the Toltecs, and the Incas. Chucho wanted to know how the Spanish had managed to conquer everyone, and Luis in turn asked what killed the greatest amount of people in America—meaning, of course, South, Central, and North America as a whole. The other men seemed stumped as Luis nodded with a smile and, setting his hand on my shoulder, concluded, *"Las enfermedades que trajeron los güeyes"*—All the diseases they brought.

We then started talking about what you learn in school, and Luis and Hernando agreed you could learn as much from TV. Luis really liked educational programs and complained that they had stopped showing the ones about other civilizations lately. It would all contribute to further ignorance, he argued. "It's like people here [in the United States] who think they are so great, so superior. But do you know who the people who came from Europe were?" Luis wanted me to answer but interrupted before I got two words out: "The dregs of society, man *[la escoria, mi chavo]* the worst people they had." He then added, "What's more, they have what they have because they steal brains *[son roba cerebros].*" I was not sure if he was talking about brain drain until he explained that the United States takes all the smart people from other countries for their own benefit. He mentioned the plaque on the Golden Gate and said that some of the engineers were "Hispanos." It was the only time I ever heard him use the term.

The conversation turned to different instances where US "genius" had, in reality, hidden Latin American contributions, until Luis finally shook his head and said, "That's why I told this guy that said he was [in English] 'one hundred percent American' that the only people who were a hundred percent were the Natives in the reservations." He laughed condescendingly. "They don't even know their own history. No? Haven't you guys seen how they show the Alamo in movies?" The others did not know what he was talking about, so we got a little more Mexican history, which ended in Luis almost screaming, "They make it look like they won!" He then commented on how the Mexicans were always portrayed as bloodthirsty killers and the US soldiers as patriots and heroes. Somehow this led us to conclude that the economy was failing and things might change. Luis gave the country ten years before the European Union would be on top. We joked that it was probably more likely that *los chinos* would ascend to the pinnacle of the global economy, politics, and military might. The men all laughed, making hissing sounds and saying, "Then we'll really be screwed!" Luis said there were also lots of *chino ilegales* and started telling us about "snakeheads," the Chinese *coyotes,* or human traffickers. Chucho said he had seen several *chinos* crossing when he walked through the desert. Everybody nodded.

Luis obtained much of the information that we exchanged during that conversation from television programs. For him and most of the other men, afternoon and evening tedium translates into proactively seeking things to do in the safety of one's home. Luis and Eduardo watched endless hours of documentaries on cable TV—something they had access to and could afford because they shared living quarters with extended family. Luis was such a fanatic for nature programs that his brothers had nicknamed him *el animalitos*. Eduardo, a decade younger, also had access to a computer and a high-speed Internet connection and spent hours surfing the Web to find documentaries about science, visiting museum webpages and, about a year after we met when he got the iPod Bicho later stole, downloading music. Another great know-it-all was Lorenzo, who discovered the Berkeley public library system early on; he spent a couple of hours a week reading newspapers from Guatemala and Spain, and every once in a while said he checked out books in Spanish. William, forever in a good mood and always proactively educating himself, liked to talk to me about poetry and appeared off and on with books by Pablo Neruda, Gabriel García Márquez, and other Latin American authors. Iván, a heavy-metal fan and an avid conspiracy theorist, shared some bootleg CDs and books with many of us. In short, my cohort of friends spent a lot of time pursuing knowledge they though was "educational" and "entertaining."

There was also great deal of curiosity about other countries among day laborers, who, for the most part, were isolated from encountering foreigners until they themselves became foreign. Thus, during the long wait for work, the jornaleros would talk about places and customs they had encountered or heard about. In a group like the one on Fifth Street, with people from Mexico City, Guadalajara, Veracruz, Campeche, El Salvador, Guatemala, Honduras, and Colombia (me), general knowledge about the differences and similarities between regions and countries was sophisticated. At Thanksgiving, for example, the men discussed the traditional dinner with great anticipation—the Multicultural Institute organized the yearly "feast" for the men—by exchanging versions of the word "turkey." The men showed off their cosmopolitan stature by interchangeably using variations of the expression "turkey day," which they preferred to "Thanksgiving" because it was easier to pronounce in English: *el día del turqui, el día del guajalote, chompipe,* or *pavo.* Luis in fact scolded me for my ignorance when I asked what *chompipe,* the Guatemalan version, meant. The men also complemented information they had with knowledge of other countries and current events they obtained from television. Whatever the sound bite of the moment was, it became central to many discussions of local and international news, variety programs, and soap operas, the latter of which were a great source of inquiry about each other's countries. For the first time in my life, I found myself following Colombian *telenovelas* to keep up with the questions Sindi and Don Raúl posed about them.

The men were also curious about and brought back information from other people they met, especially employers. Beto, for example, worked several times for a Brazilian who was close to him in age and with whom he usually drank a couple of beers after a day's work. On the corner he mentioned his Brazilian friend constantly, adding to the conversations about differences between countries, not only with his own experiences, but also with those of his *patrón,* who had traveled all over the world. Like other men I met, Beto collected bills from foreign countries and competed with his cousins to see who could get the "strangest" one. I fell afoul of the "collectors" when I gave Beto a hundred-dollar bill from Zimbabwe my wife had left around the house, and I found myself having to produce many more for acquaintances who accused me of favoritism. Similarly, I spent two years rummaging through the wallets of various family members who visited from Colombia, in the hopes of finding crisp new bills to share with friends who suddenly started returning the favor with denominations that were repeated in their collections. Whenever someone got a new bill, we stood on the corner and watched everyone pull their collections out of envelopes in their backpacks in order to compare them. Beto even sent some of his collection home to his daughter, who kept it safe for his return, while Luis—not prone to keeping such things—excitedly pulled out a bag full of coins one morning, which a *patrona* had let him keep after they fell out of a box he was moving to a dumpster. We spent some time looking at these on a paper napkin somebody produced to "protect" the specimens, which included currency from Argentina, the Philippines, France, Denmark, Germany, and Canada.

Another great source of knowledge of other people and places are the free English courses many men take at the adult schools in Berkeley and Oakland. Here the men meet other migrants, mainly Latin Americans, *árabes*, and *chinos*. Lorenzo, who consistently took these courses the whole time I was on the street, had acquaintances from India, Colombia, Argentina, and a few other countries. Although he never socialized with them outside the classroom, they popped up repeatedly in his conversations. He knew, for example, about landmarks and monuments in my hometown of Bogotá, a city he had never seen, and talked about them with great authority, even describing *soroche*—altitude sickness—which some tourists suffer at our meager eighty-six hundred feet above sea level.

Finally, jornaleros also discussed and exchanged music, sharing favorite songs using small radios or CD or MP3 players they passed around. The men's different ages and nationalities made these exchanges truly eclectic, and I heard everything from ranchera, bachata, *música norteña*, cumbia, and other Mexican and Latin American music to US oldies from the 1950s and 1960s, contemporary pop and rock music, and heavy metal. Some of my friends also exchanged bootleg DVDs bought at *la pulga*. These included pornography, cartoons, action and sappy love films, and nature documentaries. The degree to which movies inform jornaleros' lives was brought home to me when Sindi and Luis, without having discussed it or made a previous agreement, both lent me different Mexican movies in which anthropology and sociology—which I had told them were my academic interests—played a role in the plot. When I expressed surprise, they both laughed and said, "That's why I thought you would like it." These films were both from the late 1970s. The first, *Picardía mexicana,* or roughly, "Mexican Wit," is about the peculiarities of Mexican humor, *albures,* in which a secondary character turns out to be an anthropologist—well, really a folklorist—writing a book on the others (Salazar 1978). The second, *Perro callejero,* or "Street Dog," is the story of a boy who grows up on the street and ends up in jail. The first lines of the introduction read, "This movie is based on sociological study undertaken in Mexico City" (Gazcón 1980).

The street corner also sees the sporadic appearance of students, outreach workers, religious organizations, immigrant advocates, and members of financial institutions—all bearers of information that jornaleros access, interpret and recirculate among their acquaintances. Through encounters on the street, with each other, and with people who come to advertise and proselytize, day laborers come to learn about rights, labor issues, immigration, banking, remittance services, and different religions. Students from the University of California, for example, came almost weekly to interview and photograph jornaleros for class projects, usually disappearing shortly thereafter without ever returning or leaving their contact information. In many cases, the day laborers worried that the students might be undercover immigration officers or the police, or the men simply complained that they were making a living off their suffering. After it became obvious I was not leaving anytime soon, my friends started asking what it was those students were doing. My response included showing them my UC Berkeley ID and explaining that they could tell the students they preferred not to be interviewed or photographed. Eventually, the jornaleros on Fifth Street made a game of interrogating students, scaring them off with requests for e-mail addresses and professors' contact information, checking their student IDs with great scrutiny and formality. This, added to contact with several researchers conducting fieldwork and pilot studies at the site, resulted in many jornaleros knowing about their rights as research subjects. Asking people for identification thus became part of certain interactions that were specific to this corner.

By the time a freelance photographer's crew from *People Magazine* appeared to do a story on a woman none of us had ever seen, but who claimed to spend a great portion of her income helping jornaleros, most of my friends knew about asking for IDs and inquiring about their rights. Late to the corner that day, I walked in on a debate about whether they should participate in the photo shoot. Luis was quite excited as he showed me the photographer's contact information, joking that she had become nervous when they demanded to know if she had consent forms, which she did not. After a few minutes of loud discussion, they decided to prove my expertise as a researcher and sent me over to corroborate that the information the photographer gave them was correct. Then a few of us stood behind the unknown do-gooder and allowed ourselves to be photographed. Our questions about release forms, along with the men's attitude, resulted in our strange positions in the photograph: a smiling slightly overweight woman, with hands folded over in a religious way, was centered in front of four or five guys in the background, all looking away from her and out of focus.

STREET-CORNER COSMOPOLITANISM

Many jornaleros develop a flavor of "the global" through their experience of migration. In a sense, their journeys set in motion processes that put them in contact with people and ideas from other countries and give them time to spend watching television, taking language courses, and reading a wide variety of books, magazines, and newspapers. This, along with the political arena of contested belonging they enter when they cross the border, also introduces them to ideas about rights and justice as minorities and colors their understanding of their own position in US society. In no way does this mean the men I knew were not, to some extent, inscribed in processes of globalization before migrating, but rather that it is through their experience in the United States that their position, on a greater scale, becomes something they think about and act upon explicitly. I use the phrase "street-corner cosmopolitanism" to point to various contradictions in how experience, decision making, representation, and ultimately self-awareness become embodied through conversations on *la parada*. Street-corner cosmopolitanism plays with the idea that, at the margins of US society, the transnational nature of these men's lives becomes explicit and conscious—they develop preoccupations and rationales usually associated with cosmopolitanism—but that in its street-corner version, cosmopolitanism is also severely flawed and can have dire repercussions on daily life. Street-corner cosmopolitanism is based on unstable referents to realities that are produced through not only access to information from media and education but also boasting, exaggeration, rumor, and hearsay.

Cosmopolitanism emerged in my field notes early on to describe many of the conversations I heard on the street. Immigration reform, socialized health care, global warming, and other subjects were as much at home on *la esquina* as jokes about sex, women, and longing for home. While I was always surprised at how many men were able to join in the discussions, offering up their own experiences, many times the information exchanged was warped or influenced by individual interpretations that were not always logical.

One example was how to manage money, a central preoccupation because of the high incidence of theft in these men's lives, together with the mystique and reality tied to their obligations to those back home. On the corner we heard of investment strategies like buying used trucks at auctions and driving them back to Mexico for resale or to establish businesses. Similarly we heard about people who had made it big in the United States by using their *troca* to collect and then resell recyclable materials. We discussed how much it cost to build houses in different countries and the relative benefits involved in doing so. That these investments were out of reach during the US financial crisis we were in seemed beside the point, and, as discussed in chapter 4, the men did not seem to recognize that the people who owned trucks and talked about their affluence were standing on the corner with everyone else.

The fear of losing savings, along with the need to manage money in the United States, produced much interest and speculation about different strategies surrounding cash. Bank accounts were a difficult subject to understand because there was a lot of contradictory information floating about. People had heard about migrants being caught at the airport with thousands of dollars in cash, their entire savings lost to the government in a second. We also heard of men who were deported suddenly without a chance to withdraw their money in the United States, and some jornaleros claimed they knew people who had been "caught" by *la migra* only a few days or weeks after stopping to ask about accounts at a local branch. From all these stories, it would appear that bank accounts were not a good idea. But on the corner there were also day laborers that had US bank accounts, like Lorenzo, an outlier who nonetheless openly used his ATM card when he was around, especially when we went out drinking. Francisco, whom I helped with the dog bite, eventually told me he had paid his hospital bill with a credit card he got in the United States.

I could never figure out how all these different versions of reality were possible but came to believe that on the corner they could all be true. Lorenzo, having been in the States continuously for twelve years—that is, longer than most men on the street—opened a bank account in the 1990s. While I was in Berkeley I was required to show a state issued ID to open accounts, something undocumented migrants could not then have but that was possible before 2005.[1] Foreign passports might be allowed, but I never met anyone on the corner who had a current passport—unless, like Don Raúl, they were preparing to return home (discussed below). Many of the more recently arrived jornaleros who asked about bank accounts were turned away because they only had IDs from their own countries or various forms of informal identification issued by NGOs, car insurance companies, or the adult schools.

Similarly, "urban legends" about immigration, which abound on the street, were taken at face value and presented to others as fact. Pablo and Carlos—the two brothers who, along with Beto, their cousin, were known as *los trillizos*—once asked me if it was true that you could get papers if you married a woman with a green card who beat you. The word on the street was that with the help of a lawyer you could get *la migra* to deport your abusive wife and give you her green card. I heard people discuss this and its more believable opposite (husband beating a wife) several times,

1. Undocumented migrants were barred from obtaining state-issued driver's licenses in California in 1993. In the conclusion, I address a new initiative to allow undocumented migrants some sort of driving permit that has yet to be clearly determined.

something I address in chapter 7 as part of the stories of righteous retribution that the men tell. I initially thought most men interpreted these rumors simply as hearsay, but I discovered that many people make important decisions based on them. One person I met, for example, married a Salvadoran with Temporary Protected Status, thinking it would get him a green card, and then divorced his spouse when a family member told him this was impossible. Through the whole process he never thought to ask a lawyer about the legal implications of his marriage.

Street-corner cosmopolitanism is a context-specific way of "being in the world" that provides information and locates jornaleros in a transnational arena of cultural and political representations, yet it also plays an important role in reproducing the structures of marginalization within which these men are trapped. On the street, day laborers learn about the vagaries of bank accounts, rights, immigration, and other such things while simultaneously reinforcing the self-regulating practices that enable migrants to remain "under the radar," even when doing so is not in their best interest. Maintaining a low profile trumps trying to verify information or the validity of someone's assertions and results in street-corner truisms that no one doubts, like the fact that all interactions with any institutions—including NGOs, hospitals, religious organizations, banks, and the police—can lead to deportation. The congeniality and rapport among jornaleros as they wait for work, the discussions of world events, nuances in language, film, and so on, contrast with the men's inability to act—or resistance to action—when it comes to solving many of their problems. And yet, in general, the lives they lead, embedded in problematic and informal relations of labor as they are—appear to be in many ways socially accepted and recognized. Jornaleros have access to doctors, dentists, lawyers, and other such professionals; they rent houses and apartments, buy cars, use cell phones, and are stopped by the police every once in a while when people complain they are littering or standing outside the allotted labor-site areas.

DOCUMENTING THE UNDOCUMENTED

On a cold and foggy November morning I stood on the corner of the Berkeley day labor site with Luis, Don Raúl, Chucho, Hernando, Toño, and a few other men. Some of us sipped coffee bought at the gas station as we chatted about the weather and the general absence of work. Taking a seat on the little wall behind us, I noticed a man in a suit and tie waving his arms and talking emphatically to the day laborers across the street. We all stared as he approached us at a very fast pace, handing each man a business card and repeating in slightly accented Spanish, "I can get you insurance without a license, or with a Mexican license." He then quickly walked away, stopping briefly to hand out cards to other men up the street. From half a block away we could hear him tell others, "I'll insure anyone's car, whatever, Osama Bin Laden, I don't care; I'll give him insurance." We chuckled at the scene, which was common on the street—people come by often offering insurance, bank accounts, and different remittance services. Most of us pulled out our wallets and inserted the card into one of the compartments where we kept such things. By now I had begun to realize that the assortment of papers the day laborers kept in their wallets were central to how they managed everyday life. The "undocumented," it turns out, actually use a wide variety of documents to navigate the multiple worlds they traverse.

Holston and Appadurai (1999) address contemporary forms of belonging as a tension between "formal" and "substantive" elements of citizenship. The first refers to inclusion in the nation-state, embodied in the idea of membership in the national polity, while the second points to "the array of civil, political, socioeconomic, and cultural rights people possess and exercise" (Holston and Appadurai 1999: 4). While in theory the substantive forms of citizenship are a function of formal citizenship, in practice they are often independent of one another. Sanctuary policies in places like Berkeley contribute to the articulation of citizenship through a "diversity of sources and institutional locations for rights," which destabilize the notion that citizenship lies within the realm of the nation-state, that is, that citizenship is tied to nationality (Sassen 2006: 281–283). The question is how the disjuncture between formal and substantive citizenship plays out on the ground.

That someone selling car insurance would appear on a corner where most of the men cannot have a California driver's license points to the recognition of a social reality (undocumented migrants have cars and need insurance) within the framework of a nonexistent "formal" status of

Car insurance company in front of the Oakland DMV, advertising insurance available *sin licencia.*

citizenship. To own a car and obtain insurance between 2007 and 2009, a jornalero did not need a driver's license, green card, or other form of legal immigration status; he needed only a form of identification accepted at the Department of Motor Vehicles (DMV) for vehicle registration. In the Bay Area, this could be a consular card,[2] a foreign driver's license, or an assortment of other identification documents. Strangely enough, not all DMV offices were the same, and car owners on the corner usually found out by word of mouth which offices were more lenient about identification. The San Francisco DMV, for example, was known to be stricter than others in the area, and many migrants preferred cities across the bay, like Richmond, where they had heard the requirements were either less stringent or simply overlooked. This meant that many people drove around with no license at all, because men who never had the money to own a car back home, like Hernando, learned to drive while they were on the corner,

2. Although some consulates issue IDs like the *matrícula consular,* an official registration of nationals living abroad regardless of immigration status, many men on the corner thought they could not obtain them because they lacked "proof" of residence in the United States (usually service bills or rent contracts in their names).

in a system where they could buy a car and register it but could not legally drive it.

When I came to the corner my notions about undocumented documentation were skewed by my relationship with the East Bay Sanctuary Covenant, where I worked with asylum seekers. After people were granted asylum, for example, I spent a great amount of time and energy trying to explain the nature of their new status (Ordóñez 2008, 2014). This usually meant explaining the difference between their new and legitimate Social Security cards and their old fake one—*el social chueco*. Although they were not sure about the difference between legal residency, a visa, a green card, and a work permit, it was the *social chueco* that posed the most problems, since it needed to be replaced with an identical piece of cardboard that did not seem different from the one they already had.

I thus assumed that the men on the corner each had a *social chueco* and used it to get by. But the truth is that with the economic downturn and the increased systematization and surveillance of employer records, it was very unlikely to land work on the corner for which such a document was useful. Things seemed to have changed recently, since all the men who had been in the country before 2007 had fake social security cards that cost between 70 and 180 dollars in San Francisco or Oakland, depending on how "good" they were. More-recent arrivals like William or Eduardo did not see the need to spend the money. For jornaleros, the *social chueco* had intrinsic problems because it was only useful to land *trabajo regular* in factories, business, and restaurants. The card itself had no photograph, address, or other important elements of identification the men needed and so was useless in other social and economic exchanges. The men who were street savvy also had many rules about when to use the fake cards, something newcomers had a hard time understanding. To sum these up, using a fake document, because it is fake, can get you into more trouble that simply not showing anything at all.

Lorenzo, Hernando, Chucho, Beto, and I were talking about the *social chueco* in relation to the last immigration amnesty (in 1986), wondering if that kind of policy would ever be repeated and if the men would have to pay taxes for all the years they had used their fake Social Security cards. The men were confused, since they all had paid taxes when they worked at regular jobs. Lorenzo had even received tax refunds when he declared his income as a janitor. Suddenly, a day laborer named Jorge, who seemed to me a bit off, even childlike, joined us. Hearing the subject of our conversation he became giddy and interrupted us: "They say *la migra* came to Oakland yesterday and took fifty workers *[trabajadores]*." None of us believed him because we had all watched the news and, in fact, had the day's newspaper with us on the corner. Yet the man did not seem to notice and continued: "A friend of mine was taken *[se lo llevaron]* because they knocked on his door and he opened!" We all shook our heads in disbelief. "And I have another acquaintance," Jorge kept on, "who showed the police his fake Social Security card and got arrested."

Lorenzo and I looked at each other; this contradicted a street-corner truism, which states that you never show a fake *social* to the police or *la migra*. "There's no reason to show that!" Lorenzo interjected. "All you need is a consular ID or any other ID." He took out his wallet and showed us an ID from an immigrant rights center in Oakland and his adult-school student card. Jorge in turn showed us some sort of transit ID that he could ride the bus with. "Where did you get that?" I asked, wondering if he had legal status and some sort of disability benefit. Lorenzo answered for him, tapping his own temple with a smile: "He has that because he is wrong in the head *[está mal de la cabeza]*," and smiling in a friendly manner addressed Jorge directly, "You have that because you are wrong in the head, vah?" Jorge nodded yes. Although I never could find out his immigration status, the men at *la parada* assumed Jorge was undocumented because he lived in a homeless shelter; they thought he had special access to the bus and other local services because he must have had an accident that disabled him. Jorge—who somehow got my phone number before he disappeared a few weeks later—called me several times in 2010 claiming he was in Vancouver.

Lorenzo's instructions that day point to the practices of informal documentation that make living as an undocumented day laborer possible. A jornalero's wallet likely holds an assortment of documents, such as his own country's ID and driver's license, NGO IDs issued to facilitate services like legal aid or free health care, library and adult-school cards, and business cards from people who, like the car insurance salesman, interact with the men on the street and at work. A few men like Luis and Chucho also have old pay stubs or certificates from courses they have taken, which they keep in their backpacks. Jornaleros use these documents in combination, depending on the situation. The amount of identification documents the men have is extensive—anything with names and addresses can be used at one time or another—but documents replicating the form and format of an "official" US ID are the most useful. One man I met had an ID that looked almost exactly like a California driver's license, except for a bold, red-lettered warning that read "this is not an official ID." He said it cost him fifty dollars, and as far as I could tell it seemed to have been issued by an insurance company. Inherent in these inscriptions are notions about local belonging and documentation, where migrants need to provide information that can validate their social existence (name, gender, age, place and date of birth) and their membership in a specific—and geographically near—locality. Jornaleros who are newcomers to the street corner realize early on that cell phone companies, county hospitals, and the police require or prefer documents with local addresses.[3] Interactions with these institutions are thus based on the use of a combination of home documents that provide "verifiable" information and alternate IDs that can locate the migrant in the Bay Area.[4]

A "health card" issued by a local free clinic, for example, can thus help a day laborer pay bills and identify him to police officers, potential employers, or even other NGOs that might provide legal aid (and sometimes also issue IDs). This kind of ID includes a picture, name, gender, date of birth, and local address, all elements essential in these interactions. Similarly, adult-school IDs can be used to show potential employers that a day laborer is "educating" himself, and Lorenzo sometimes showed his to *patrones* who asked for laborers who spoke English. The intended use for these documents is beside the point. What is important are the logics that

3. The need to identify people in the case of minor offences is one of the rationales behind issuing city IDs to the "undocumented" populations in sanctuary cities throughout the country. During the time of my fieldwork, both San Francisco and Oakland discussed this possibility, the IDs only materializing in the San Francisco case (Kuruvila 2009a, 2009b). The impact remains to be seen.

4. Many non-Mexican migrants must "recover" home-issued documents because they dispose of them on the United States–Mexico border when crossing, in case they are caught by *la migra*. It is very common for Guatemalan and Salvadoran migrants to dispose of their home documents so they can "pass themselves off" as Mexicans if caught, which means they will only be deported across the border and not to their countries of origin (Nelson 2004; Coutin 2005).

validate a documented identity and certified skills. In other cases business cards help establish or substantiate social belonging by referring to personal relationships—real and imagined—that mobilize social capital. If stopped by the police, Clemente always pulled out the business cards of the officers who had helped him with the abusive *tonga*. This, he argued, showed he had contacts. Similarly, Eduardo would offer potential employers his own business card along with those of other contractors who had hired him, in order to prove that he had been considered trustworthy by others and was stable enough to have a card with a phone number.

This use of documentation also allows migrants to establish more formal relationships to local government institutions. Small-claims courts and other such institutions also require IDs that indicate a person's legal name and locality (over which the court has jurisdiction), even if immigration status is not considered. In another instance, Guatemalan undocumented migrants who "discover" after moving to the United States that they can apply for asylum (Ordóñez 2008, 2014) sometimes use NGO IDs to get married in the Oakland courthouse so they can include their spouses in their applications. A more complex practice, which I only heard about twice, was to take advantage the US federal system that recognizes IDs from other states and to obtain official state-issued IDs or driver's licenses in parts of the country where proof of immigration status was not required. Francisco, for example, registered his friend's cable TV in his name when he went to the state of Washington, thus obtaining a bill that "located" him enough in the area to get a driver's license. He then used the license to open bank accounts in California and even managed to get a credit card.

The substantive and informal elements of citizenship thus create the possibility of establishing relationships to society and the state that are based on the mimetic powers of the state's technologies of inscription (Das 2004). IDs, service bills, and business cards can replicate relations to different institutions by validating the logics of identification and circumventing the state's regulations in practice. Substantive elements of citizenship, such as access to health and legal services or accessing housing, television, and the like, thus inscribe a jornalero into his locality, opening the doors for social inclusion that create a semblance of citizenship that mirrors the formal recognition that rights-bearing citizens enjoy. However, the circumvention of rules inherent in its mimetic nature also makes a document's usefulness unstable and highly anecdotal. What works for one man in a certain case can both be interpreted as a rule and result in problems when applied. Thus, people who had bank accounts, like Lorenzo or Francisco, suggested the practice to other jornaleros as if it were an easy thing to do and yet were never quite clear about how exactly they had managed the process. Lorenzo, for example, could not remember what he had had to show to get an account and thus was little help when his acquaintances said the documents demanded by the bank were inaccessible: "Strange, vah? I've never had a consular card or driver's license and they gave it [an account] to me." To confuse matters further, representatives of one of the local banks later appeared on the corner, like the insurance salesman, to get people to open accounts, saying they only needed a "consular ID," which most of the men thought was useless. But problems can also be more dangerous; not all police officers accept the ID combinations in all situations and on the corner there is much talk of arrests and deportations after everyday encounters with a wide array of institutions (Ordóñez 2014).

On the street, the distinctions between state institutions and NGOs are not necessarily understood. I met a young jornalero who had escaped gang violence in Guatemala after surviving a shootout and who was told he might be eligible for asylum in the United States when I took him to the East Bay Sanctuary Covenant. After visiting a San Francisco NGO that helps migrants with such issues, he told his friends, who then convinced him that all the information he had given to the organization would be remitted to *la migra* and that he would surely be deported for having sought help. His *situación* completely deteriorated over the next weeks, and when I found him living on the street he said the only thing good that had come of his loss of phone and housing was that *they* would most likely not be able to find him. Thus, jornaleros do not feel inscribed in state practices, even though they clearly are, but rather see themselves on the margins, *ilegales* always under threat of being found (Ordóñez 2014).

There is, in fact, consensus that the more you try to regularize rights and services available through substantive elements of inclusion, the more likely you are to get caught. Rumor and hearsay are central to the production of information and commonsense assumptions. This gives rise to contradictory and confusing accounts that create uncertainty regarding the real reach of migrant surveillance and access to social institutions. I met relative newcomers to Berkeley who lied to police officers about having any type of identification because they had heard of a man who, after showing such documents on the corner, was later sought out and arrested in his apartment. Even jornaleros with no firsthand knowledge of such a case and who had identified themselves to police officers with health cards nodded in agreement, for it was not uncommon to hear of people being abruptly awoken by violent knocks on doors down the hall, made by officers coming with warrants to arrest neighbors.

Most jornaleros also assume the police and *la migra* are the same institution. And in many cases they are not completely wrong. Policies implemented by the US Department of Justice since 2001 require immigration warrants to be included in criminal databases, which means that even in sanctuary cities the police must notify the warrant-issuing institution if they arrest an individual who has such a warrant (Bilke 2009: 177; Thompson and Cohen 2014). So even though the police officer in charge of the area where the Berkeley *parada* is located told me that his officers do not share information with US Immigration and Customs Enforcement, they do inform ICE when they come across someone who has a warrant of deportation in his or her name. Furthermore, ICE is not subordinate to sanctuary-city governments and regularly conducts searches, raids, and surveillance in these cities. It is thus not surprising that most of the jornaleros I met during my first weeks of fieldwork scoffed at my questions about them choosing Berkeley because it was a sanctuary city. As Beto drily said offhand, *"Es más tranquilo, pero la migra está en todas partes"*— It's better here, but *la migra* is everywhere.

No matter how safe going to a county hospital seems to be, there are rumors about people who have been deported after such a visit, or whose home was raided by undetermined "officers'—always called *la migra,* whether they are part of the police, immigration, or other enforcement agencies. Thus, jornaleros' sense of belonging to a given locality entails expectations that result from substantive elements of access to services and rights but that follow rationales independent of such elements. A jornalero knows he can take an employer to small-claims court, for example; he has "heard" of and maybe even met other men who have done it—like Francisco, whose success became legendary—but he has also heard of people getting deported after talking to lawyers or going to the courthouse. Should he decide to go through with a claim, he *knows* he is risking something, even though in theory the act itself should have no negative outcomes. This goes beyond commonsense assumptions about living "legally" or not. Legal residents, tourists, and citizens alike know their own standing vis-à-vis the state; it is not a question of exceptions but rather of the dynamics of each interaction, that is, what they are allowed to do, what they are expected to do, what is right and what is not are scripted by instructions a person need only learn. But for undocumented migrants in the United States, this all depends on vagaries and rumor. What is possible one day can become impossible another without any clear rationale.

Many of the most ambiguous stories I heard on the street dealt with car ownership. Barred from obtaining legal driver's licenses in California, the jornaleros who owned cars either used the licenses from their home country, used expired licenses issued before 2005, or simply drove the old wrecks—that were passed down, given away, or sold very cheaply—"only with the license of God." Insurance for such vehicles ran cheap and many companies cater to undocumented migrants, who pay for it in the hopes that their car will not be impounded, something that nonetheless happens often. Everyone knows that driving without a license can result in having a car impounded for thirty days. The resulting fees and fines usually exceed the price paid for an average wreck: four hundred to two thousand dollars. Because the fees to get the vehicle back are higher than its value, it is cheaper to simply start over. In a twist typical of the street, many jornaleros buy impounded cars at county or city auctions, where you bid on these unclaimed vehicles without test-driving them.

Encountering the police without a license or with a license from another country is the source of many tales on *la parada*. We all knew people whose cars were impounded, and many told of close calls where they were let off the hook. It was never quite clear why some people were lucky. Some stories ended with a reprimand, others in arrest. Hernando, for example, had been luckier than most in that both times the police had stopped him they had let him keep his car because he had insurance, even though he had no license. At twenty one, Hernando was a third-generation seasonal Mexican migrant (although seasons for him, as for many others, are now counted in years) who had been in the States for four years. His interactions with the police were all based on local identification, a health card from a local free clinic and other such documents. The first time Hernando was stopped, the officer told him he could not drive anymore and he had to call someone to pick him up. The officer seemed nice to the young jornalero, who simply called a neighbor. The second time he was stopped was during my time on the corner. Hernando, Chucho, and Toño were pulled over in Oakland and asked to get out of the car by two officers, who kept their hands on their guns and proceeded to order the jornaleros to lie on the ground, handcuffing them. The officers searched the old Ford and talked on their radios while Hernando and the two others kept still, wondering what was going to happen to them. They were terrified, but after a while the officers let them go, apologizing because they had mistaken the three men for other people who were wanted and "known to be armed."

In another case, Adolfo managed to avoid losing his second car (the first one was impounded because he had no license) through happenstance and—he was quite sure—because of his knowledge of English and the police psyche. After a highway patrol officer requested to see his papers, Adolfo—in his fifties and with a slight tremor—acted meek and subservient. He immediately admitted to having no papers and acknowledged it was wrong to be driving around, adding that he did it to work and pay for his wife's cancer treatment (a half-truth, since her cancer was in remission and he had returned to the United States to try to pay for a house they were building). At first the officer was suspicious. "I had tools with me and he saw them," said Adolfo. "He asked what I had there, and when I said tools he told me to take them out of the bag one by one." Once Adolfo proved he was who he said he was, the officer changed his tone, saying he respected a man who supported his family: "He told me he was going to do something uncommon and that he was not going to give me a ticket or take my car." Adolfo was let off with a friendly warning to fix the lights and sell the old wreck. Unlike Hernando, with whom he sometimes shared a corner, Adolfo was allowed to drive off in his own car.

A notorious absence in the jornaleros' collections of documents are passports. Because needing a passport to legally exit the United States was a new practice during my fieldwork, many men were confused as to the use of such papers. In fact, even Luis, who had been back and forth many times, used "passport" and "visa" interchangeably in day-to-day conversations when referring to entering a country. But since 2007 all "nonimmigrant aliens" from Mexico, Canada, and Bermuda, along with most US citizens, are required to have a valid passport to leave the United States via an airport (Federal Register 2006). This changed previous rules that had allowed Mexican citizens, regardless of their US immigration status, to leave the country with other valid Mexican IDs.

Thus, short of a week before he returned home, Don Raúl found himself doubly undocumented: without the right "papers" to live in the Bay Area and—suddenly—without the right "papers" to return home. A seasoned migrant who had started coming to the States as a teenager, he had trouble navigating the bureaucracy of the Mexican consulate in San Francisco and called me in a panic to see if I could find out if what he was hearing on the street was true. He had gone home without a passport several times throughout his life, he argued, and could not believe he needed one to enter his own country. His travel date looming ever closer, he was trying to work as much as he could before returning home. He explained that he had tried to call the consulate several times but always got the same message—"Our operators are busy, please call back at a later time"—after which the line went dead. In a twist to my role as go-between with US state institutions, I ended up spending quite some time speaking with airline representatives and the Mexican consulate, trying to figure out how to get Don Raúl a passport on such short notice. Also finding the Mexican state's representative too busy, I finally got the information from a man at Don Raúl's airline. Less than a week before he left, Don Raúl spent several days in long lines before he finally got the passport, the first one he had ever been issued. Bewildered and a bit excited by the whole ordeal, he brought the document to the corner and showed it to us, stating everyone else would have to spend the money it cost if they intended to return home.

DOCUMENTATION AND EXPERIENCE

In the absence of a formal relationship to state institutions, informal documents, for jornaleros, lead to an imagined political reality that takes the narrative form of a patron/client relationship. What matters is the officer's mood that day, whether he or she is racist or not, whether one knows how to look like a hardworking, honest man. This relationship also emerges in the use of NGO IDs and business cards, which jornaleros present employers as references—something to prove, in a way, legitimation by an institution or person. Das and Poole (2004: 16) address how documents "become embodied in forms of life through which ideas of subjects and citizens come to circulate among those who use [them]." In the Bay Area the substantive elements of citizenship available to migrants validate their social existence through unstable and exceptional reactions to the documents at hand. In times of generalized calm—*cuando está tranquilo*—migrants can function as citizens of sorts, but unlike formal citizens they cannot enact a cohesive set of exchanges that are clearly legible (i.e., such and such a document will produce such and such effects) but rather are at the mercy of specific reactions to local recognition. Writing about police checkpoints in rural Peru during the turmoil of past decades, Poole (2004: 36) describes such encounters as a "mysterious ritual of 'reading' . . . that carried with it not only all the ominous uncertainty of the war but also all the tangible familiarity of the fluttering, unread, arbitrary, and shifting forms of paperwork that mark the material or lived geography of a state whose form—like the paperwork itself—is never fixed nor stable." Nothing can better describe the experience of the undocumented jornaleros whom I knew.

The use of documents as I have outlined shapes everyday experience, where an illusion of inclusion emerges through the things such documents make possible. Luis, for example, had a contract for his apartment and a phone number in his name. His uncle expanded this to a DSL Internet connection and bought a fifteen-hundred-dollar computer, having never owned or used such a device before and that he used primarily to download music. Luis's day-to-day life, for the time he had the job to pay these services, resembled that of any other person in his neighborhood whose citizenship is legitimated by the state. He had a rent contract, Internet connection, cable, car, and a more or less stable job, although he had none of the necessary documents to identify himself as a legitimate citizen, whether a US national or legal resident.

This reality is the product of the substantive elements of citizenship that jornaleros can exercise, a process that produces forms of everyday life parallel to formal citizenship (they look and feel like state-recognized forms of belonging). Everyday life is thus regimented by the possibilities and constraints that substantive inclusion provides. The effects of substantive elements of citizenship endow the social existence of day laborers with an air of the "normal"—where one can act like a citizen—that nonetheless lies outside state legitimacy and can always be reverted or denied. For jornaleros this makes the nature of belonging incredibly volatile and never tied to a single practice or definition. They are cosmopolitan subjects who unravel their daily existence as active members of the social environment they inhabit, but their lives are riddled with arbitrary exceptions that inevitably keep them at arm's length from legitimate forms of inclusion.

In this unstable realm, the state—embodied in its institutions of surveillance and control—can surface suddenly and violently. Relative tranquility can easily turn into persecution under the threat of arrest, deportation, and outright disappearance. Thus enter the police and *la migra*—both real and mythologized—into the realm of cultural production and signification for jornaleros who doubt the securities they enjoy and take them as fleeting moments of calm. The governance of undocumented migrants offers the elements of inclusion I have outlined above but is nonetheless based on the fear of retribution. No matter how "quiet"—*tranquilo*—the situation might be, many jornaleros avoid leaving their homes for anything but work. They expect to be eventually detected and chased, and they send everything they make home, lest they be deported before they can get to a local bank or, more likely, retrieve any cash they have hidden away. In this realm, everything a jornalero does must be measured in relation to the risk of encountering officers in uniform—dark figures, to say the least, that are magnified in rumors and follow jornaleros constantly, from the moment they cross the border to the day they leave. These figures are ubiquitous, said to appear at your door, your workplace, and your neighborhood. *They* are everywhere. Strategically, *la migra* surfaces periodically, and does so violently, changing the everyday in a moment that alters the geography of the street corner, and everything that transects it.

While I was on the corner, we never saw them but we felt *la migra*'s presence— we waited for them, we wondered about their whereabouts, we participated in an exchange of information that came together with media reports, rumors, and phone calls that irrevocably dissolved the pretense of a sanctuary city and left only one thing clear: "*they* are here in Berkeley, *they* are in Oakland where we live, no one is safe." The illusion of freedom is always in question; anything a jornalero has one day can be gone the next. The normal goings-on of the lives of day laborers are shadowed by the certainty of risk entailed in any interaction that sets in motion substantive elements of citizenship. Every so often the stories one hears become reality and, in effervescent moments of terror, remind jornaleros—and other migrants in the area—that their apparent inclusion, always suspect but also naturalized, is only transient.

7 Terror and the May *Migra* Panic

No one on the corner except me went to the annual immigration march on May 1, 2008, but the following week seemed to promise the usual for jornaleros on the street. The day after the march, a Friday, I went to *la esquina* and talked with Beto about what was going on. Work was scarce and he was worried about paying his bills and he did not want to borrow money from his cousins again. He had no luck that morning, so around noon we walked up to join in on free lunch at the church on Ninth Street. The Multicultural Institute was offering its weekly English classes—with ten new volunteers from some other organization—and representatives announced that they would bring a truck with computers connected to the Internet the coming week. They invited everyone to come and learn how to send e-mails and surf the Web. The following week, in other words, promised more than the usual services and, at least during lunch, nothing seemed amiss. Later that afternoon we all discovered that Friday was also a day of foreboding.

By evening we all had started hearing about the raids. *La migra* raided eleven restaurants in the Bay Area, arrested sixty-three people, and made the news on every local television channel. The raids resulted in a general outcry of protest from the Latin American community and some NGOs in

Immigration march in Oakland, 2008. No jornalero from Fifth Street participated.

the region. People were nervous and angry, and the scale of the operation was beyond what we had come to expect in the Bay Area. A spokesperson for US Immigration Customs and Enforcement (ICE) was quoted in the *San Francisco Chronicle* referring to the raids as a "targeted enforcement action" and part of an ongoing criminal investigation (Knight 2008), but nobody I talked to thought this had fortuitously occurred on May 2, the day after the annual immigrant-rights march. Whatever its stated reasons,

Immigration march near downtown Oakland, 2008.

ICE had also made its presence felt during the march, and many jornaleros saw the raids as retaliation against migrants for their public demonstrations. Following a street-corner truism, the day laborers thought that migrants and their supporters had become too vocal and too visible. What was worse, it seemed that ICE had decided to make a point. *La migra* was suddenly on everyone's mind.

The panic started in earnest a few days later, on May 6. Late getting to the labor site, I bumped into a person who worked for the Multicultural Institute. As we walked down the street, we noticed there were hardly any jornaleros on the curbs. About a block from the MI's Internet truck, announced the week before, I greeted Eduardo, who had just arrived for the second shift. When I asked about the number of people around, he said there were rumors that *la migra* was on San Pablo and Ashby, a few blocks to the southwest of where we were. He assumed that most day laborers had left when news of a raid had spread through *la parada* a few hours before. I could tell he was worried, but I was also surprised at his matter-of-fact way of expressing the problem and I could not understand why he lingered if he thought the rumors were true. When I asked him, he answered that although the news made him nervous, he wanted to take advantage of the little competition and see if he could get some work quickly. After all, he reasoned, if what they were saying was true, it was just as dangerous to try to get home.

I crossed the street to where my companion from the MI was talking to two young Guatemalans. I greeted them and asked if they knew why there was no one around. They repeated what Eduardo had told me. The outreach person and I were confused and a bit doubtful of the news, and we tried to lighten the mood by talking about the speed with which *los rumores*—rumors—spread on the corner. But the two men seemed uneasy, constantly looking up and down the street and hoping, they told us, to get picked up for work before things went bad. They were rethinking the soundness of trying, like Eduardo, to take advantage of the reduced competition.

I went into the Internet truck and spent about twenty minutes there. At first I helped Adolfo learn how to find Guatemalan newspapers online, and then I taught another man how to open an e-mail account. As I was explaining how to use the computer mouse, I heard the person from the MI talking on the phone: "They're where? Berkeley High? Really?" Everyone noticed the strangeness in her voice, but she tried not to seem alarmed. She made two other calls and then whispered to me that she had just confirmed that *la migra* was at the high school, downtown—only a few minutes away from us. The first thing I thought about was running outside to warn the few people I had seen. As I gathered my things to leave, another of the MI's staff interrupted everyone's work and said, "I'd like to warn you that it seems that *la migra* is up on Shattuck [downtown]. It's better that you all know this and decide what to do." The men all murmured to one another but did not seem surprised. Some continued their work in the relative safety of the truck, while others started packing up. Almost everyone, however, took out their phone and started making calls and relaying the information.

Outside, Eduardo was already gone, so I told another jornalero that we had confirmed the rumors about *la migra.* With a mousy smile he answered that it was probably time to leave. I saw Adolfo quickly exiting the truck with his phone in his hand. "They told me that *they [la migra]* are on San Pablo, Tomás, I'd better leave," he said as he checked the bus schedule for the number 19, which would lead him away from all the trouble. William walked down the street and stood by me, calling out to several guys that a woman had just driven up to him and said *la migra* was at Mi Tierra, a landmark Latin American market only a few blocks away, much closer to us than downtown Berkeley. I walked to the store, William leading for part of the way and announcing, like a herald, that we all had to leave. He was smiling and joking as he warned people but stopped on

Ninth Street, a few blocks from the store, just in case. Once I reached the market, nothing seemed amiss, so I went in and found it full of customers. When I called the Multicultural Institute, the staff reported hearing mixed messages from many different sources. Some people they had spoken to claimed *la migra* was on San Pablo where I was standing, others that *they* were at the high school downtown. The MI had also heard reports that *they* were going into Oakland schools and that something big was apparently going on.

The Spanish-language radio stations were also mentioning unconfirmed reports about *la migra* going into schools in different localities. Since the raids on that ominous Friday had covered many different areas, we all imagined something similar was going on, but unlike the restaurant raids what we were hearing about now seemed to be targeting people on the street and children in schools. I decided to walk back down to the corner, bumping into Mario and other Guatemalan jornaleros who were still standing north of Seventh Street. When I asked them why they were still around, Mario laughed with mock bravado: "Here we are waiting for *them, they* appear everywhere." He was trying to be both funny and defiant, but his companions' snickers were halfhearted and they looked around nervously, suspicion and fear in their eyes. A few minutes later almost everyone had left. I later learned that most took roundabout routes and tried to avoid San Pablo Avenue, which is the main thoroughfare they used to get back to their neighborhoods in Oakland.

Once the site was empty and I was on my way home, I started calling all the day laborers I could think of, to see if they were all right. Of the people I was close to, Beto was the only one unaccounted for. His cousins could not reach him and were beginning to worry when he finally appeared, not having heard of the raids because he had been picked up for work before the whole thing started. Later that evening, Luis called me to see what I knew. He said that he had left the corner when a woman in a car had warned everyone that *la migra* was about. She had her car radio on and said it was all over the news. This was around the same time that several unmarked white vans drove up and down the street, he added. White vans were an everyday occurrence on the corner while I was there, since flower shops, private contractors, and moving companies commonly used them and, in fact, often hired day laborers. But that morning Luis said people really freaked out and even ran into the side streets when they saw them. He did not know if the vans had stopped or what they were, but he was sure they were not looking to hire anyone. He told me that other people saw the officers on San Pablo and that the news was reporting that a whole family had been arrested. *"Esta canijo,"* he repeated constantly, "It's really bad."

At home I went online and tried to figure out what had really happened. There was little news until the next day. According to various local news sources, ICE had conducted "routine fugitive operations" in both Oakland and Berkeley. This means they were looking for specific people who had deportation orders (Tucker and Derbeken 2008), which in the Berkeley case meant two grandparents, the mother, and aunt of two local middle-school students. The raids, in other words, were not indiscriminate, which is what we had all thought and felt on the corner. The rumors had started because in Oakland, ICE had set up organized surveillance near two elementary schools (Thompson 2008). These events set off a panic in which rumors circulated, stating that ICE was going into schools to take undocumented children. A few hours later, schools in the area were contacting parents to warn them of the presence of immigration officers in case they wanted to send someone else (with documents) to pick up their children. There were also automated messages explaining that no ICE agents would be allowed on school grounds (O'Brien 2008). I was able to confirm this with Jorge, a Mexican who had an asylum case pending. He was the only day laborer in our group who had a wife and children with him, and he said they had been contacted by the school and told that no one would take the children. A few days later he even brought me some illustrated instructions the school had sent home, explaining immigrant rights and what to do if *la migra* appeared at your doorstep.

The next day there were few people on the corner. Those who came were nervous and talked nonstop about the raids. Chucho and Hernando said that the news was that *la migra* had arrested a family in Berkeley *near* the high school but not *in* the high school. Others claimed to have heard that ICE had arrested students, like we had imagined the day before. It was not clear what had happened, but no one could remember when *they* had taken a whole family or gone into a school. Luis said there were also raids all over Oakland. As we discussed the events, people started telling each other how close they had been to the places that were raided, and everyone eyed a helicopter that was flying over West Berkeley. Like the white vans, helicopters were a common enough occurrence that suddenly seemed suspect. "I don't know what that's about but it has flown over twice," Luis noted ominously.

Although the men were obviously worried and scared, the way they spoke was also oddly calm; they all seemed to treat the threat as part of life, one they were apparently used to, even though after almost a year on the street I had never witnessed it before. Sindi came by and told me he had been on the corner the previous day and had left when the rumors started. He admitted to running a little when they had all seen the white vans, making fun of himself by flailing his hands effeminately. Sindi also made offhand remarks about *la migra* and seemed detached from the imminent threat that was beginning to take on a life of its own. He reminded us all that he was a veteran—that is, an experienced *ilegal*—who had been in New York City on 9/11 and had returned to Mexico when he became convinced that migrants would be blamed and persecuted for the attacks. "This," he said pointing up and down the empty street, "this is nothing!" As we were talking, Lorenzo called me and whispered over the phone that a friend had just told him that the *aguacates*—"avocados," a name for the border patrol, whose uniforms are green—were near *la parada* in Oakland. I hung up and relayed the message, since many of the men I was with lived near that site. To my astonishment, those present simply nodded matter-of-factly, adding simply, *"Esta canijo,"* that is, "It's bad, really bad." Luis eyed me with a smirk and slapped me on the back. "Where did you think we were, Tomás?" he scolded. "This happens all the time!" He went to the bathroom and came back with a newspaper he had found. We all looked over his shoulder to read about the raids.

All the newspapers reported that the raids had caused a panic. People had run to the schools or sent friends to get their children and had interpreted ICE's presence as part of an ongoing attack on migrants. On the corner, the cold, somewhat distant attitude to the rumors hid my friends' intense preoccupation concerning the duration of this attack. They all speculated that it would stop soon, like it always had before, but stories on the street were painting a dire picture. Francisco, for example, claimed a few days later that he had been working in an apartment complex when *la migra* suddenly raided one of the units, "where they must have arrested that family." He described the cold sweat he went into as he descended the stairs, approached his employer, and said he had to leave because he was sick. His account was detailed—he had seen officers taking away people in handcuffs, he had felt *la migra* breathing down his neck. Other close calls included Hernando, who claimed he had narrowly missed being stopped at a *migra* checkpoint in his car. Apparently he was waved through but the car behind him was stopped. As far as I know, there were no ICE checkpoints stopping people on the street during the six years I lived in Berkeley. Everyone else, however, agreed that Hernando should not push his luck and told him to leave his car at home.

Although the media referred to ICE raids having caused a panic in the past tense, anxiety on the corner seemed to be gaining momentum, taking on new forms, none of which were mentioned on the news or in the papers. Each man that appeared on *la parada* had another story, another close call that seemed to put the speaker even closer to the action. Reality and fiction became one and the same. I began to realize that even I had been complicit in the process, first by "confirming" that *la migra* was on San Pablo and at the high school and then by relaying all the rumors I heard to the men on the corner waiting for work. People told me I must have missed *them* up on San Pablo, since the MI had sent someone—me, as it turned out—there to confirm the rumors. That I had been the person in question did not seem to convince many men who had friends who—they were sure it was true—saw *la migra* at the market I had checked out. My own network of acquaintances shows how rumors of the raids spread throughout the Bay Area, for I got calls from people I had met years before as an interpreter in asylum interviews and whom I did not remember. These calls, along with calls from the men I worked closely with, covered the areas of San Francisco, South San Francisco, East Palo Alto, Oakland, Berkeley, and Richmond. I even got a call from a Guatemalan I had met on a bus once, who lived in Sonoma. I had given him my card in case he wanted to visit the Sanctuary, and somehow he had kept it for over three years. He called to ask if I thought *la migra* would eventually reach him in wine country two hours away.

Like every other person on the corner, I told the people who called what I was hearing in Berkeley, and they told me the rumors they heard about raids in their areas. The threat thus became consolidated, confirmed, and reaffirmed through a vast network of people who exchanged vague accounts, most of them second- or thirdhand, that nevertheless became shaped into verified information. Why would friends lie? Why would the MI lie? Why would the English-speaking Colombian in Berkeley lie? Everything seemed confirmed; even that I could not find any actual news about the rumors in the media seemed to reinforce the men's certainty. *"Los medios en Ingles también son racistas, Tomás, todos sabemos lo que esta poasando,"* Luis scolded. English-language newspapers, for him, were complicit and shared ICE's anti-immigrant agenda. Along with these accounts, men who had come across the police or others in uniform thought that all such official-looking people had been at the heart of the raids, which contributed to how the rumors were "verified."

And just as we all "heard" these things, other people had started "seeing" *la migra* all around us, even though the raids were supposedly past, having happened all on one day. Every van, police car, or vehicle with an official-looking insignia that cruised past the Berkeley labor site was suspect for weeks to come and caused wary glances from the men up and down the street. I was even sent to ascertain if an ICE van was really parked near the freeway when rumors that someone had seen a strange-looking police car started flooding the street a few days later.

As usual, the men dealt with the stress and panic with humor, this time centering on the awkwardness that getting deported would entail for their families. "It's like suddenly knocking on the door and have them [your family/wife/partner] say, 'Why didn't you tell us you were coming, my love?'" said Luis, imitating his family's fake happiness.

"Or like bumping into your Sancho," added Sindi.

"*Hola cabrón,* thanks for taking care of her for me," laughed Luis, pretending to take out his wallet and drily adding, "How much do I owe you?" We all laughed.

"I hope if they catch me they'll send me to Veracruz and not just to Tijuana," scoffed Sindi. "Well, if they send me to Tijuana I'll just cross over again."

"I would cross again," agreed Luis. I told them to call me from the border so I could pick them up. Sindi said he would call his *paisas* and ask them to send the money he had stashed away just in case. Chucho joined the nervous revelry: "Anyway, I'm ready to go back home."

"Yeah, but let them send us back to our town, not just across the border to Tijuana," repeated Luis. We laughed, and Chucho finished by imitating the tone and body language of NGO staff everywhere: "You have rights! You have the right to get deported back to where you live." Everyone laughed, still looking up and down the street about twice as often as usual.

A few days after the raids, Luis and I sat on the little wall on Fifth Street. We wondered about the helicopter again as it flew over and then discussed the continued absence of most other jornaleros from the corner. The few men who were at the site were intently listening to the radio in case someone reported more raids. Almost immediately after I arrived that day, Lorenzo called to say I should warn people that *la migra* was setting up checkpoints near the Richmond *parada,* just minutes north of us. He hung up after delivering an ominous and overly poetic "With the grace of God, who we must always ask to watch over us, we will see each other tomorrow, and if not, let what must happen, happen."

I relayed the news to Luis, even though I doubted it was true, since Lorenzo was calling me two or three times a day to report increasingly closer raids. But to my surprise Luis believed my *guatemala*'s report. When I commented that Luis thought everything Lorenzo told me was exaggerated or a lie, he scolded me: "Didn't you hear about Hernando and the checkpoint? That was near Richmond, Tomás." I shrugged my shoulders, trying to remember where Hernando said it had happened. Luis never believed anything Lorenzo said; he thought the Guatemalan was a charlatan and reprimanded me daily for having anything to do with him. Yet for the duration of this generalized *migra* panic, he never doubted any of the events Lorenzo told us about and was eager to hear the news when Lorenzo appeared the next morning.

The Friday after the raids I spoke to Beto again. He had tried to come to work after the panic started, but a friend called him to say *la migra* was boarding buses and was in the BART stations, so he ran back home. On Saturday afternoon I bumped into William. His comment in Spanish was a play on words: *"Vine a ver que agarro, si es que agarro algo . . . aunque el que me agarre sea la migra,"* which roughly translates to, "I came to see if I could get [lit., 'catch'] something [meaning work], that is, if I get [catch] something . . . even if it is me *la migra* catches." The same sentiment was repeated by many of the men I saw over the next couple of days. One morning I was interviewing some jornaleros on the corner, when Iván nodded toward a white unmarked van driving up the street. With tense and cruel humor, Luis slapped him on the back and said, "They're here!" We all laughed, but the men were still concerned about the helicopter and left after it flew over the first time, calling out that it reminded them too much of the helicopters on the border.

During the panic the ubiquitous presence of *la migra* disarticulated the sense of freedom that I had become accustomed to on the street. The relative tranquility that had marked the slow mornings—even in the face of encounters with the police—was gone. No man on *la parada* could have attempted to interact with any institution. Day-to-day life had taken on a new form, that of total persecution, where the illusion of safety was shattered. No one was safe; every aspect of life could result in getting caught. That the men were both tense and calm illustrates that this possibility was also commonplace to them. It was, in other words, part of their lives and an event they all expected any day. Along with the rumors, street-corner truisms were reinforced, like with Hernando's checkpoint scare, which led everyone who saw me doubt that it involved ICE and not simply the police to tell me, "The police are with immigration, Tomás, they are racists, they are the same!" The feeling was generalized on the street; *la migra* was coming to get them.

LIVING IN FEAR, LIVING IN HIDING

The May *migra* panic dissipated as the days passed but made evident the context within which most of these men live in the United States. Everyday life on *la parada* fluctuates from the drudgery of long hours waiting for work, interspersed with piecemeal jobs, to the spectacular and unstable realities of panic about one's safety and retribution from the state. Each extreme defines the other; they depend on each other for the production of meaning. Together they form a tenuous continuum that shifts from social inclusion—sustained through practices of substantive citizenship, which enable the men to get by—to the outright perception of persecution. This is, I think, a muted version of what Scheper-Hughes and Bourgois (2004) describe as a "violence continuum," where everyday life gets scripted onto institutionalized mechanisms that, in this case, articulate the contradictory effects of inclusion and exclusion into the experience of these migrants. Their social inclusion is embedded in relationships in which, at any given moment, everyday life can come crumbling down, where reality and illusion are mediated by rumors that make hearsay fact and vice versa. The imminent threat of *la migra* became visible, tangible, and apparently sentient; it followed us for weeks and seemed to answer our preoccupations and our fears with more rumors, each one closer in physical space to where we stood on the street.

Writing about violence, Michael Taussig challenges us to think through the social production of terror as it bleeds into everyday life, shifting its referents from fact to fiction, from fiction to rumor, from rumor back to fact:

> The meticulous historian might seize upon the stories and fragments of stories, such as they are, to winnow out truth from distortion, reality from illusion, fact from myth. A whole field opens out here for tabulating, typologizing, and cross-checking, but what "truth" is it that is assumed and reproduced by such procedures? Surely it is a truth that begs the question raised by history . . . wherein the intimate codependence of truth on illusion and myth on reality was what the metabolism of power, let alone "truth," was all about. To cross-check truth in this field is necessary and necessarily Sisyphean, ratifying an illusory objectivity, a power-prone objectivity which in authorizing the split between truth and fiction secures power's fabulous reach. Alternatively we can listen to these stories, neither as fiction nor as disguised signs of truth, but as real. (Taussig 1986: 75)

For the day laborers on *la parada* there is no sanctuary from the very real "fabulous reach" that *la migra* holds over their lives. Their parallel citizenship, that diffuse and volatile semblance of social belonging that allows jornaleros to exist, is easily shattered. Jornaleros' presence on the street is based on the calculated reminder that inclusion can never be, a reminder that need not be legislated or defined by any institution—the Bay Area day laborers, we are led to believe, were never the targets of immigration enforcement that spring. ICE was just conducting "targeted enforcement" (Knight 2008) directed at specific restaurants and people who had warrants issued in their name. Yet the state's fantastic power enables it to take on the shape of anything and everything; it can suddenly overdetermine every experience and regiment its "image" as a sole referent.

This image has the ability to collapse time and space. Thus, a week after the main events described above, Lorenzo told me he had heard that on the day of the raids *la migra* had also taken *la parada* in Fremont—not a sanctuary city—something that happened in March when police arrested jornaleros "trespassing" on a Home Depot parking lot. We had discussed this scandal a great deal because the Fremont police had called ICE out of professional "courtesy" (Dyer 2008) and the men were apparently deported. And although we had heard talk of this raid and seen it on the news, it now emerged in Lorenzo's experience as something closer in time that shaped the very real notion during the May panic that *they were everywhere.* Other men I interviewed mentioned arrests in Richmond, which we had also heard about weeks before, but these now seemed to be included in the long list of things that happened that day. Reality on the corner thus shifted dramatically and condensed events that happened over many months and in a wide geographical area into the immediacy of each man's life.

From this precarious reality yet another document emerged on the corner, one upon which para-citizenship's impossible nature might be guaranteed, again, in the realm of exception. The Multicultural Institute and another NGO originally handed out this instruction card a few weeks before the panic, to teach jornaleros that in the United States no "officers" can enter a home without a warrant. The card explained constitutional rights to migrants in Spanish on one side and on the other listed some sentences in English to say to the police, should they knock on a migrant's door. The card was printed in red, which gave it the catchy name *la tarjeta roja* and inevitably linked it to the image of a referee in a football—soccer—match holding out a "red card" to kick players off the field.

About a week after the panic started to dissipate, the jornaleros slowly began to return to their corners. One morning I was approached by Mario, the man whose *patrón* I almost stole, who along with a group of angry-looking men asked aggressively, "Tomás, is it true that if you have the red card *la migra* won't arrest you?" Confused I tried to figure out what they were talking about. "They say the Multicultural Institute gave out a card, that if you show it to *la migra* they won't take you, but I don't believe that." Word had spread on the street that if you had the red card, immigration could not arrest you, and those who were not around when the card was handed out were anxious to know the truth. Men on different corners were debating whether to demand that the Multicultural Institute give everyone a card so there would be no favoritism. This also played into the prepanic tensions about the *guatemalas* expanding up the street; the men who stopped me all belonged to the group who felt discriminated against by the supposedly pro-Mexican NGO staff. The *tarjeta roja,* they argued vehemently, was their right. As they spoke about it, most men mimicked a referee pulling out a card from his breast pocket when talking about its power to ward off immigration officers.

The power of the red card was short-lived, mainly because its imputed use was just too fantastic. However, for some days it acquired a highly fetishized nature (cf. Gordillo 2006), an inherent power that was never intended for it. Suárez Navaz (1999) has argued that the state's practices of immigrant regulation and juridical inscription create a fiction of possible equality and inclusion based on "document fetishism," where the document itself acquires a magical power to confer social and juridical status upon the holder. I had seen this firsthand with asylum seekers who never understood the difference between a green card, a visa, a passport, and a work permit and fixated only on the last document, *el permiso,* that came to represent the status for which they were willing to risk applying (Ordóñez 2014). Once in their hands the work permit acquired a power beyond imagination, and its holders became obsessed with losing it and thus returning to a life of fear and persecution. It was as if the document's physical existence was the right to work itself and hence could be taken away, stolen, lost, or even kidnapped by others. But on the corner, that power followed the logics of documentation a bit further and bestowed upon a plasticized set of instructions the authority to guarantee the rights of citizenship through exception; the document itself somehow could release the holder from *la migra*'s grip, stop *them* in their tracks.

Terror cannot be understood rationally because, on the margins, persecution—embodied here by *la migra*—travels the mythologized paths of rumor and hearsay. "What happened that day"—the "real" in Taussig's sense—is the effect of information that flows along the strange course of opinion built on confusion that inevitably becomes a flash flood of events threatening a person's very existence. For the jornaleros in Berkeley, *la migra* flew over the labor site on the morning that Luis worried about the helicopter, *they* cased *la parada* in unmarked vans, *they* were on San Pablo, at Mi Tierra, and in the schools that everyone made such an effort to present as safe. *La migra* was on the buses, in the BART stations, and every other place we heard about. In this context it is not so absurd that there can exist, for some, a magic card that protects you from the brunt of this terror; something that, for once, might guarantee the impossible nature of belonging; something that might turn para-citizenship into a more stable referent of social inclusion.

PARALLEL CITIZENSHIP AND THE GOVERNANCE OF ILLEGALITY

The May *migra* panic illustrates the shaky ground upon which these men must tread while living and working in the United States. The constant threat of *la migra,* once it materialized, became the sole referent in everyday life; nothing could be measured, qualified, or understood without going back to this threat. Thus, while informal documentation enables the social, economic, and legal relations necessary to make life possible for these men, the legitimacy of the forms of belonging such documentation produces is but a passing fiction. While jornaleros might appear to embody cosmopolitan subjectivities—citizens of the world who live and work as productive members of society—in truth they live in a tenuous balance that every now and then is shattered by the reminders of the state's power. Para-citizenship is based on relations we all recognize, on the exchange of information for validation, acceptance, or legitimation in a particular sphere of social interaction. But, in truth, this is just the mimetic performance of the state's power, where the reproduction of its logics creates a semblance of inclusion. *La migra* can suddenly be everywhere, everyone, and everything. And here jornaleros become complicit in their own exclusion; they play a central and highly creative role in how misinformation, rumor, and fear are produced and propagated throughout the urban geography they inhabit. Freedom and persecution are inextricably tied to one another.

Yngvesson and Coutin (2006) look at the paper trails that constitute past, present, and future to the bearers of certain documents. Documentation in this sense produces particular subjects and relations that ultimately shape or destroy personal histories or legal versions of truth. For jornaleros, however, the paper trails of their documentation practices lead nowhere—point nowhere—because there is no legitimate base upon which the process of inscription rests. The rationality behind para-citizenship dictates a truncated existence that enables people to be free, gives them access to substantive elements of social inclusion, but always with the caveat that these are not the freedoms and rights that state-recognized citizenship bequeaths. In the articulation of these relations, a body of institutions emerge that play a key role in the governance of "undocumented" migrants. NGOs and sanctuary cities help shape the self-governing subject, endow him with the tools that—although problematic and unstable—allow a jornalero to manage his life as a productive member of society. Rumors about raids thus play into De Genova's (2002) concept of "deportability," for they remind those involved that they are expendable, disposable. And while critics argue that sanctuary policies become a "pull" factor for the "undocumented," the nature of parallel citizenship suggests that, on the ground, among many of the people these policies aim to help, the sanctity of sanctuary is lost. Sanctuary and non-sanctuary cities blend into one another in the Bay Area—the police sometimes do contact ICE, and there are no boundaries that protect social belonging from this threat. The only person surprised by the May *migra* panic was me, the anthropologist who was naïve enough to think such things could not happen in Berkeley. I was also the only one not carrying these strange, unstable, and yet powerful documents everyone else used to get by.

Para-citizenship constitutes a social and intimate experience that is always in flux. There are no stable referents to local belonging, no certainties about how or when the state's retribution will be put into action. Rumor and hearsay constitute tacit and yet effective tools of migrant governance, for they allow enforcement to take on a life of its own. In the case of the *migra* panic and in other instances—like the anti-immigrant laws in Arizona (2010) and Alabama (2011)—officials seem to push aside the effects of rumor in offhand ways. In Berkeley and Oakland, immigration officials said the rumors were overblown and outright false (O'Brien 2008), while a little more than a year later, in Arizona, ICE director John Morton was quoted as saying that he was aware that the agency's activities generated "rumors and wild conjecture" but that no intimidation was intended (Archibold 2010). Yet for the day laborers on the Berkeley *parada,* intimidation was very clear. In fact, in the world of the jornaleros intimidation was the main point, since they linked the raids to the massive pro-immigrant marches that year. The raids were punishment for speaking out, proof that the surveillance machinery had been set in motion. The state—*la migra*—was suddenly everywhere, offering a reminder that whatever the elements of citizenship the jornaleros have access to are, they are always illusory.

My take on the May *migra* panic might be considered an exaggeration; the US government, one could argue, does not persecute people in this way. The point is it does not have to, because the ways that jornaleros come to live and work in the Bay Area give rise to the perception—really the certainty—that persecution works like this. Thus all the tales I heard on the corner must be taken as "real" because they speak to jornaleros' particular version of truth. When I showed my friends the pictures I took at the march, the one they all looked at the longest was of a police officer holding a video camera amid the hundreds of protesters. "You see that, Tomás? You got them getting everyone on video so they can come looking for the ones they recognize. Those poor bastards *[cabrones]* who thought you can protest in peace here must be shaking in their houses, shitting themselves," Luis quipped while the panic was still in full force. "Poor bastards," he said into my camera screen, "does your family know where they took you? Will they ever see you again?"

The US government, for these men, has the power not only to chase, capture, and deport them but also to make them disappear. In Berkeley there were rumors and firsthand accounts of people who saw *la migra* or the police take migrants who were then never heard from again. I took this as exaggeration until I was called twice by different acquaintances of my US family to ask if I knew how to find out where a migrant who had been taken by ICE might be. In both cases the people calling were helping migrants who worked in their houses and whose family members had been "caught" on the street. US-born upper middle-class professionals, it seems, were also unable to get through to any of the state institutions that came to mind. In a now familiar street-corner twist, I gave them the

Police officer filming the protesters in the 2008 immigration march in Oakland.

names of the NGOs I knew and relayed the street-corner truism I had initially doubted. Following up on the cases, which were never solved, the only answer I have is the one that everyone swore to on *la parada: La migra* hid these people in unnamed retention centers and then moved them from one place to another so friends, family, and NGOs could not find them. Ultimately, people in these cases just cease to exist, *desaparecieron*. Everyone shrugs their shoulders, so it goes.

STORIES OF RIGHTEOUS RETRIBUTION

Amid this strange alternate reality of citizenship in the United States, at least during the time I was on the corner, there were a few tales of people overcoming *la situación*. "Making it" in El Norte was as distant as the time when you could go back and forth between countries seasonally, or jump on an airplane and travel within the United States. What was left was tied to street-corner cosmopolitanism, certain dispositions produced through tall tales exchanged on the street that gave the men some sense of entitlement and of justice. Like many elements of the men's conversations on the street, tales of people who gain access to citizenship proper, or simply to fair treatment, are put on the table as fact. That the characters in these stories are faceless—these accounts are always thirdhand—reveals the distance the men see between their own reality and some sort of retribution for their suffering and abuse. This amid the frustrations they face on a daily basis, frustrations that range from the spectacular power *la migra* has over them, to the more intimate recriminations of their loved ones' expectations and the their banal accounts of employer abuse and humiliation as laborers. From these frustrations arise a genre of stories and anecdotes, all sworn to be true, where righteous retribution spectacularly materializes. On the street, when exchanged with peers, these tales seem to settle accounts. They all follow similar narrative lines: a migrant who is abused and put down by others—usually powerful *gabachos* but often other migrants—achieves some sort of recognition from the state, again faceless, which sets things right, taking from the abusers that which the migrant so justly deserves. The stories of righteous retribution I encountered always had a hint of pride in them, something that indicated that the jornaleros relating the tales saw in them proof that recognition might be within their reach too.

Having been absent from *la esquina* for a few months, I returned one morning to find strangers waiting for work on my corner. Luis, Clemente, Hernando, and the others had all been lucky that week and in their place were men I had only spoken to in passing. Not knowing one another well, we simply started talking about *la situación,* something we all had opinions about. The May *migra* panic had passed and was becoming both legendary and anecdotal, but stories about anti-immigrant policies in other states were running rampant. *La raza,* they felt, was more threatened than ever.

"But there is justice also, friend," one jornalero told me. He had heard of a Salvadoran couple who had lost their way in the desert while crossing the border. Half dead after days without food or water, they finally came to a ranch and, seeing no one, ran to the waterspout for a drink. "They were so unlucky that the owner was a head Minuteman *[el jefe de los minut].*" As they were resting by the waterspout, several men appeared. The Minuteman in charge was armed, but the rest had bats and sticks with which they beat the couple senseless: "At first the couple thought they were going to kill them, and all they could do was pray and plead, but the men just told them to *'espic inglis'* and kept going at them with the bats." The couple was spared only because there were women and children in the house, and apparently the head *minut* became nervous about what he and his men had done, so he let the couple get up, gave them some crackers, and told them to leave and never come back. Bleeding and tripping all over the road, the couple was found by *la migra,* but instead of getting deported, they were questioned about what happened, taken to a hospital, and provided with legal counsel. The lawyers sued the head Minuteman and won. Here, the men on the corner disagreed on the ending. For the man telling the story, the *minut* had to sell everything he owned to pay the couple hundreds of thousands of dollars: "He lost everything and had to give them all his money, the government had to let them stay." But two others swore they had heard that the rancher was forced to give the couple his ranch and that the Salvadorans now owned his property and worked his land.

Righteous retribution in such tales might or might not reflect contorted versions of actual events. The point is that jornaleros tell them as proof that things might get better and that the very institutions they fear and hide from might turn around and recognize their plight. In a sense, the few times I heard people refer to the US legal system in positive terms was in relation to these stories. Luis concluded one such account with, "You see my friend? Here the law is for everyone, it doesn't discriminate"—*¿Ves mi chavo? Acá la ley es para todos, no discrimnina.* He did not seem to think that this equality contradicted everything else he and the other jornaleros had said about the police and *la migra* being racists.

On another occasion, Eduardo told me about a Mexican woman who had worked in a hotel in San Francisco for over twenty years. It was a suspicious account, because Eduardo was having trouble getting paid for work he had done in a motel in the same city. He was absolutely certain it was true because he met someone who knew the woman. Whatever the case, after working overtime as a cleaning lady for two decades, with no extra payment, the woman met a lawyer who asked her about how she was paid. It seemed that for over twenty years she had never had a vacation and had been paid below minimum wage. The lawyer helped her sue the owners of the hotel, an Indian couple who were also migrants but had been in the country much longer. "They treated her like nothing for twenty years," Eduardo concluded, "but after the lawsuit they were forced to give her the hotel and *la migra* took their papers and gave them to her."

This story mirrored a common theme I heard throughout the time I was at the Berkeley site. In innumerable conversations the men told of undocumented migrants who were caught up in abusive labor or sentimental relationships with migrants who had papers. The *trillizos* asked me constantly if it was true that men who married women who abused them—took all their money, beat them, and had lovers—could eventually get their wife's papers and have her deported. Others told of employers who, having been migrants themselves, threatened jornaleros or refused to pay their hospital bills after an accident. Here the government or *la migra*—always one and the same—would inevitably intervene, take the papers from the employer or lover, and give them to the victim.

Again, it is the papers themselves that bequeath status, not an abstract concept of citizenship they represent. No matter how much these last accounts point to just redress for suffering, they also illustrate the nature of jornaleros' understanding of their own citizenship status. For para-citizenship is ultimately the absence of "papers." Citizenship proper is thus not something you aspire to be or embody but rather something you hope to have in your wallet, a set of documents that contain, in themselves, the power to make the exceptions of inclusion permanent. These documents have the power, not only to control a man's relationship to the state and society in general, but to curtail the imaginations of the disenfranchised—silencing the fear of *la migra*'s knocking on their doors, evaporating the certainty that *they* can be on every corner, in every van, helicopter, and uniformed officer the men encounter.

Conclusions

> The tradition of the oppressed teaches us that the "state of emergency" in which we live is not the exception but the rule.
>
> Walter Benjamin, "Theses on the Philosophy of History" (in *Illuminations*)

I spent a little more than a year in Berkeley after forcing myself out of the field, a fiction that was difficult to maintain because the men I had befriended continued to call and invite me out. Slowly but surely people started moving away, and even before I left the United States I lost touch with the *trillizos,* Hernado, Iván and Chucho. Lorenzo's mother died in Guatemala in 2010, and we became reacquainted for a few weeks, spending hours on the phone and in the San Francisco bars he liked so much. He was so distraught I thought he would go back to his hometown, where apparently a niece had a saving's account with all the money he had sent over the years. For the first time since I had met him, he started talking about getting himself a little room in Guatemala and living the rest of his days in peace and quiet. He had done what he came to do, he told me over beers one evening. His daughter, who he had not seen in more than a decade, had graduated from two different university programs and could maintain herself. His ex-wife seemed willing to let him back into their lives, even though she had remarried and did her own thing. He was tired of *la situación,* he kept saying; it was high time he returned home.

But Lorenzo stayed in the Bay Area in the end and continued working as a jornalero. In 2012 I returned to Berkeley, almost two years after moving back to Colombia, only to find that most of the guys I knew had disappeared. The street corner was just as full as before, but save for some passing acquaintances, everyone seemed to be new. I managed to find only two of my close friends, Luis and Clemente; the latter was the only day laborer I knew well who was still on the corner. Of all the jornaleros I have mentioned in these pages, Clemente was also the only one who eventually got papers, the product of his asylum status and many years of paperwork. He knew nothing of Luis, whom I saw several times on his days off from two regular jobs in San Francisco. Clemente, in fact, only talked about a drunken *chino* who now shared the corner of Fifth Street with him and a few others and had them wondering if the jornaleros would now have to compete with Asians on *la esquina*. Curious about this *chino*'s presence, I went over to him and asked if he spoke English, only to find that the *chino* was actually a Korean who had been in the United States twenty years, had papers, and was just down on his luck.

I asked everyone I talked to how *la situación* had changed since I had left, and they all answered in the same programmatic ways I remembered from before. There was little work, too many people to compete with, and a generalized feeling that everything was going down the drain. Employer abuse was still rampant, and Oakland sounded like a war zone in their renderings of spectacular muggings and general violence. I was told by passing acquaintances that Sindi had had an accident that disabled him slightly and that he was waiting to see if he could sue his employer. No one, however, had seen him in months, and he was rumored to have moved back to Mexico or gone to New York City again. The phone number Don Raúl had given me for his home in Mexico never worked, and no matter how much I tried to find Eduardo I never heard from him again. By 2012 even Clemente had a hard time remembering Eduardo and confused him with two other men he had known since I left.

Clemente said that Hernando had fought over money with Chucho, who apparently had met up with people he knew and went to the border to see if he could make money as a *coyote*. Nobody believed he would manage; Chucho was well known for his insane grimace but was generally held to be a sweet kid deep down, not a common trait of *coyotes*. Hernando's beloved car had been impounded after a fender bender with another migrant. Neither had a driver's license and they were trying to fix matters privately when a patrol car drove up. Both men had since disappeared and no one else on the corner seemed to know them. William I saw holding a Realtor's sign near downtown Berkeley one afternoon. He also continued to work on the street but moved to Oakland and only came to Berkeley every once in a while. Although he greeted me by name, he did not remember Eduardo and Bicho when I asked if he knew anything about them, and it was only after quite some time that he remembered how long it had been since we had shared the Fourth Street corner in the afternoons. Everything, in other words, had changed.

This was true also of the political and economic climate. While I was on the corner, *la situación* was dire; the economic crisis and its backlash on immigrants created the world I have described and the feelings of imminent doom the men had toward their future. Since then things have improved a bit, but I cannot say whether they have radically altered the men's outlook on life. Luis, as I mentioned, finally landed not one but two *trabajos regulares* yet in 2012 had still not managed to pay his debts in the United States or those incurred by his wife in Mexico. Since I met him in 2007, he has told me every year that he will return in the winter to to spend Christmas with his family. He never has. These days he seems to have become religious about his absence and shares sappy messages on Facebook, peppered with saints or children and statements about how love and distance are not incompatible. We still talk on the phone every once in a while.

The experience of the jornaleros I met was thus only a snapshot of their lives, not a totality. That the events in these pages occurred in the Bay Area should tell readers that similar situations elsewhere, in less liberal and tolerant areas of the country, are likely worse. The men's fears of the Obama administration have not come to pass as they imagined, even if the administration is reported to have deported more immigrants than during any other presidency, especially during his first term (Preston 2014). The perception I have—at a distance—is that certain elements that once negatively affected the lives of jornaleros have improved or will improve unless things get *canijo* again. As I write these final reflections in 2014, Governor Jerry Brown has announced that California will issue driver's licenses to undocumented immigrants, or something to that effect. Assembly Bill 60 will purportedly go into effect by January 2015, and the governor was quoted as saying it "was only the first step" (Hurtado and Shoiche 2013) in an ongoing process of recognition. Along with other policies aimed at reducing the barriers between citizens and noncitizens (Medina 2013), California has opened the doors of education, work, and representation for the undocumented a bit wider. I doubt, however, that this will change much of the social-political configuration I have called parallel citizenship for immigrants like the jornaleros. Belonging, after all, is not going to be legitimated; its fiction is simply going to be managed more efficiently.

From its announcement in October 2013, the promised driver's license already sounds like the stuff para-citizenship is made of, since the DMV webpage states it "will look similar to current licenses while complying with the new law by, for example, having the abbreviation 'DP' for driving privilege, rather than 'DL' for driver license" (CADMV 2013). While I think allowing undocumented immigrants to have driver's licenses, or driving privilege, or whatever, will make the freeways and streets much safer, I can only imagine the wide spaces of exception the document will create. State-issued IDs will facilitate banking and other processes that were almost impossible when I was on the street; they will sustain and consolidate belonging for many people. They will also provide the state more accurate data about the demography and whereabouts of the undocumented and, I am sure, migrants will develop a variety of theories about how this information will end up in the hands of *la migra.* Das (2004: 227) puts it well when she states, "If the written sign breaks from the context because of the contradictory aspects of its legibility and iterability, it would mean that once the state institutes forms of governance through technologies of writing, it simultaneously institutes the possibility of forgery, imitation, and mimetic performances of power."

We can only imagine, then, the possibilities a "DP" might instantiate and the ways it will work to sustain a fiction of belonging that can still fulfill the valve-like quality that allows parallel citizenship to supply the country with needed, underpaid, and rightless labor while ensuring the means to control, stigmatize, and point an accusing finger at this same labor in times of crisis. The governor's assertion that "no longer are undocumented people in the shadows" (Hurtado and Shoichet 2013) also suggests the people in charge do not necessarily realize what living on the margins entails. For as the social and political configurations of inclusion shift, so too do the shadows they cast. The silhouettes that hide the structures of marginalization do not disappear; they change shape, cover other things, obscure new realities. And within these obscured realms of inclusion and marginalization, those living in the dark can only infer how light is shed, not perceive it directly.

The power of creating meaning from misinformation and rumor has not changed during my absence. When I returned in 2012, word on the street was that there were new ways to, maybe, get papers. I heard strange tales from day laborers I had never seen, who told me that if you saw a crime, or managed to become the victim of one, the government gave you papers. Like before, everyone had heard second- and thirdhand accounts about the lucky few who had managed to "fix" their papers like this. Many of these tales set up "papers" as a consolation or as righteous retribution for the vicissitudes of living undocumented lives. It was as if these men understood the status as a legitimation of the suffering and danger they experienced, for everyone on the corner continued to talk about being mugged, robbed, or swindled constantly. Few people really knew what this "new" immigration status legally implied, and none of the men I spoke to had access to information about the conditions of what I later learned is a U Visa.

The U Visa was created through the Victims of Trafficking and Violence Protection Act in 2000 but only came into effect in 2007 (Ellison 2010). The visa took a few years to enter the realm of rumor that shapes jornalero reality, because I never heard of it while I lived in Berkeley. It is meant to give undocumented migrants who have been victims of certain crimes the ability to stay in the United States and collaborate with law enforcement and the legal system. The visa grants its recipient permission to live and work legally for four years, and a person can apply for a green card after three years. To file for the U Visa status, immigrants must include a certification from a law-enforcement agency stating that they have been victims of a crime and are willing to help (Immigrants' Rights Clinic of Stanford Law School 2012: 4). This can open the doors to a world of exceptions in an urban area like the Bay Area, where one city's attitude towards migrants can differ drastically from another's. The people I spoke to were aware of this and said the visa was easier to get if the crimes occurred in San Francisco or Oakland. In other places, they said, with more racist police officers—they meant cities that had no sanctuary policies—it might be hard to get certificates from law enforcement.

By 2012, the U Visa had acquired a familiar and mythologized form. For the men on the street, it meant that "papers" would almost magically appear if you managed to get yourself mugged, beaten, or raped, and survived. In a strange reversal of the truisms I had learned only a few years before, I heard stories on the corner of people exposing themselves to the dangerous streets of Oakland at night to see if they could get assaulted. "If you're lucky," one man said to me, "it will just be a bunch of kids trying to get money for drugs but with no guns." These stories were fed by accounts in the local media (e.g., Smiley 2011), which made it seem that any crime would qualify. But in truth the jornaleros were not quite sure how it all worked. Like with the *tarjeta roja,* the U Visa's power was not questioned, but the mechanisms through which the status it bequeathed would suddenly appear were not unpacked in the men's conversations. No one really knew how one could actually request the status or what implications it had for people working on the street. This plays into the general perspective that I have addressed, where retribution simply appears as a just conclusion to years and years of abuse. Everything, in other words, remains the same.

ON CITIZENSHIP AND BELONGING

The power of documents among the men on the street seemed strange to me when I first started pulling out my own wallet to join in the game of comparing ID pictures. I had noticed the odd notions regarding the differences between visas, green cards, and work permits when I worked with asylum seekers, but the jornaleros had so many other papers in their pockets I could not figure what was going on. Eventually I realized these informal practices of documentation mimic the state's own technologies of inscription, and I came to see them as elements of a form of belonging that is not "lived" through the notions of entitlement and responsibility, which more classical conceptions of citizenship would assume. For the jornaleros, belonging meant cardboard and plastic cards, laminated pieces of paper and writing that they could *show*. Citizenship and legitimation were not embodied in feelings of entitlement, rights, or justice but in the practices that allowed for exceptions from the fantastic reach of *la migra*.

Para-citizenship thus seems nothing but a mockery of state-recognized belonging. Whatever inclusion it creates, the practice of hiding, not looking for help, and all the well-based paranoia about *la migra* result in dispositions that are hard to be free of when things change. Jornaleros who had recently been granted asylum, for example, obsessively guarded their work permits, hiding them on their bodies and fearing their loss (Ordóñez 2014). These papers offered a status conditioned on the documents' physicality, not on what they represented. Thus there were even rumors of citizenship being kidnapped, of people inadvertently showing their papers to the wrong characters, who somehow gained access to the IDs, hid them, and then forced indentured servitude or sexual favors on their victims. Whenever I heard such stories, I came back to the motto that asylum seekers encountered in the San Francisco Asylum Office when I accompanied them as their interpreter: "Securing America's Promise." This seemed to be the message that US Citizenship and Immigration Services wanted to send people who were not sure if they had done a smart thing by applying or if they had instead made themselves available to the state's various machineries of repression. Such self-serving righteousness forgets the suffering that America's promises are usually built on.

LA VIDA DE UN LEIBOR

My father is an engineer who can see a problem, imagine various solutions or alternatives, and then sit down and put them, first on paper, and then into practice. I am always in awe when I see things he has built or designed. Whenever we speak about what I do, I feel useless when he asks me what I think would solve the problem. Those in my field are trained to critique, I tell him, solutions are for others. I do not know what should be done in the United States about the problematic configurations of being and belonging I observed and experienced on the corner. I can only repeat what most of the jornaleros said they thought would be fair: recognition and respect.

Whatever this means in the greater context of immigration—I am not qualified to talk about immigration reform—recognition and respect in the particular case of day laborers mean more than band-aid solutions. People in the United States do not seem to recognize how many elements that are central to their national imaginings are sustained and maintained by undocumented migrants. More is going on here than the disenfranchised doing everything they can to come and reap the benefits of the "American way of life." At issue is what this way of life actually costs. In most places I know, "the white picket fence"—that quintessential suburban representation that conservative pundits like to defend so much—was painted by a jornalero. For his trouble he was probably paid a lousy wage and sent on his way without much consideration given to how he came to the corner where he was hired or to the life he leads working on the street. Living by the day wage is not an aberration of economic practice that has been brought on by uncontrolled immigration; it is a rational response to the market, a system of social, political, and economic organization that enables the contradictory nature of these men's existence. Living *la vida de un leibor* is a form of inclusion that guarantees marginalization.

Maybe the street corner gave me a fatalistic view on issues that US society thinks it is dealing with, but I see much of the "good" in immigration reform as double sided. For example, the Deferred Action for Childhood Arrivals (DACA), a recently enacted status, and the Dream Act, a previous attempt at policies similar to DACA, aim to open possibilities of inclusion for undocumented immigrants brought to the United States as minors. While these policies are much hailed as offering forms of recognition for undocumented immigrants who are, in a "moral" sense, "innocent" and potentially good citizens—so goes the argument—they validate the idea that migrant children's parents have committed a crime or at least disingenuously intend to take what they can from a society that, in truth, reaps enormous benefit from their presence. Until these migrants' existence becomes legitimated, officially recognized at all legal and social levels in the United States, every person who has eaten at a restaurant, drunk coffee in a corner shop, enjoyed an afternoon in a well-kept garden, or entered a building constructed in the last few decades is complicit with the *situación* I have described in these pages.

References

Agamben, Giorgio. 1998. Homo sacer: *Sovereign Power and Bare Life,* Meridian: Crossing Aesthetics. Stanford, CA: Stanford University Press.

Aldana, Raquel E. 2008. Of Katz and Aliens: Privacy Expectations and the Immigration Raids. *UC Davis Law Review* 41 (3): 1081–1136.

Anderson, Benedict R. 1991. *Imagined Communities: Reflections on the Origin and Spread of Nationalism.* Rev. and extended ed. New York: Verso.

Anderson, Elijah. 2003 [1976]. *A Place on the Corner.* 2nd ed. Fieldwork Encounters and Discoveries. Chicago: University of Chicago Press.

Andreas, Peter. 2003. Redrawing the Line: Borders and Security in the Twenty-First Century. *International Security* 28 (2): 78–11.

Appadurai, Arjun. 1996. *Modernity at Large: Cultural Dimensions of Globalization,* Public Worlds. Minneapolis: University of Minnesota Press.

Archibold, Randal C. 2010. Immigration Raids Focus on Shuttle Vans. *New York Times,* April 15.

Arendt, Hannah. 1973. *The Origins of Totalitarianism.* New ed. San Diego: Harcourt.

Baker-Cristales, Beth. 1999. Politics and Positionality in Fieldwork with Salvadorans in Los Angeles. *PoLAR: Political and Legal Anthropology Review* 22 (2): 120–128.

———. 2004. *Salvadoran Migration to Southern California: Redefining el Hermano Lejano.* Gainesville: University Press of Florida.

Banfield, Edward C. 1958. *The Moral Basis of a Backward Society.* Glencoe, IL: Free Press.

Benjamin, Walter. 1968. Theses on the Philosophy of History. In *Illuminations,* edited by Hannah Arendt, 253–264. New York: Schocken Books.

Benson, Peter. 2008. El Campo: Faciality and Structural Violence in Farm Labor Camps. *Cultural Anthropology* 23(4): 589–629.

Bilke, Corrie. 2009. Divided We Stand, United We Fall: A Public Policy Analysis of Sanctuary Cities' Role in the "Illegal Immigration" Debate. *Indiana Law Review* 42 (1): 165–193.

Bourdieu, Pierre. 2000. *Pascalian Meditations.* Stanford, CA: Stanford University Press.

Bourdieu, Pierre, and Loïc Wacquant. 2004. Symbolic Violence. In *Violence in War and Peace: An Anthology,* edited by Nancy Scheper-Hughes and Philippe I. Bourgois. Malden, MA: Blackwell.

Bourgois, Philippe I. 1989. If You're Not Black You're White: A History of Ethnic Relations in St. Louis. *City and Society* 3 (2): 106–131.

———. 2003. *In Search of Respect: Selling Crack in El Barrio.* 2nd ed. Structural Analysis in the Social Sciences. Cambridge: Cambridge University Press.

———. 2004. The Continuum of Violence in War and Peace: Post–Cold War Lessons from El Salvador. In *Violence in War and Peace: An Anthology,* edited by Nancy Scheper-Hughes and Philippe I. Bourgois. Malden, MA: Blackwell.

Bourgois, Philippe, and Jeff Schonberg. 2009. *Righteous Dopefiend.* Berkeley: University of California Press.

Brandes, Stanley. 1980. *Metaphors of Masculinity: Sex and Status in Andalusian Folklore.* Philadelphia: University of Pennsylvania Press.

Bryce Echenique, Alfredo. 2001 [1977]. *Tantas Veces Pedro.* Lima: Peisa.

Burawoy, Michael. 1976. The Functions and Reproduction of Migrant Labor: Comparative Material from Southern Africa and the United States. *American Journal of Sociology* 81 (5): 1050–1087.

CADMV. 2013. DMV Prepares to Implement AB 60 Testing, Licensing, and Insurance Requirements for Undocumented Drivers. California Department of Motor Vehicles news release, October 13. www.dmv.ca.gov/portal/dmv/detail/pubs/newsrel/newsrel13/2013_29.

Caldeira, Teresa Pires do Rio. 2000. *City of Walls: Crime, Segregation, and Citizenship in São Paulo.* Berkeley: University of California Press.

Chavez, Leo R. 1994. The Power of the Imagined Community: The Settlement of Undocumented Mexicans and Central Americans in the United States. *American Anthropologist* 96 (1): 52–73.

———. 2001. *Covering Immigration: Popular Images and the Politics of the Nation.* Berkeley: University of California Press.

Coutin, Susan Bibler. 1993. *The Culture of Protest: Religious Activism and the U.S. Sanctuary Movement.* Conflict and Social Change Series. Boulder, CO: Westview Press.
———. 2000. *Legalizing Moves: Salvadoran Immigrants' Struggle for U.S. Residency.* Ann Arbor: University of Michigan Press.
———. 2003a. Cultural Logics of Belonging and Movement: Transnationalism, Naturalization, and U.S. Immigration Policies. *American Ethnologist* 30 (4): 508–526.
———. 2003b. Suspension of Deportation Hearings and Measures of "Americanness." *Journal of Latin American Anthropology* 8 (2): 58–94.
———. 2005. Being En Route. *American Anthropologist* 107 (2): 195–206.
Danner, Mark. 1993. *The Massacre at El Mozote.* New York: Vintage Books.
Das, Veena. 2004. The Signature of the State: The Paradox of Illegibility. In *Anthropology in the Margins of the State,* edited by Veena Das and Deborah Poole. Santa Fe, NM: School of American Research Press.
Das, Veena, and Deborah Poole. 2004. State and Its Margins: Comparative Ethnographies. In *Anthropology in the Margins of the State,* edited by Veena Das and Deborah Poole. Santa Fe, NM: School of American Research Press.
de Certeau, Michel. 1984. *The Practice of Everyday Life.* Berkeley: University of California Press.
De Genova, Nicholas. 2002. Migrant "Illegality" and Deportability in Everyday Life. *Annual Review of Anthropology* 31 (1): 419–447.
———. 2005. *Working the Boundaries: Race, Space, and "Illegality" in Mexican Chicago.* Durham, NC: Duke University Press
———. 2006. Introduction: Latino and Asian Racial Formations at the Frontiers of U.S. Nationalism. In *Racial Transformations: Latinos and Asians Remaking the United States,* edited by Nicholas De Genova, 1–20. Durham, NC: Duke University Press.
De Genova, Nicholas, and Nathaniel Peutz. 2010. *The Deportation Regime: Sovereignty, Space, and the Freedom of Movement.* Durham, NC: Duke University Press.
Derrida, Jacques. 2001. *On Cosmopolitanism and Forgiveness.* Thinking in Action. London: Routledge.
Dohan, Daniel. 2003. *The Price of Poverty: Money, Work, and Culture in the Mexican-American Barrio.* Berkeley: University of California Press.
Dyer, Roger. 2008. Bay Area Organizing against ICE Raids. *SocialistWorker.org* (669). http://socialistworker.org/2008/04/11/bay-area-ice-raids.
Ellison, Kathleen. 2010. A Special Visa Program Benefits Abused Illegal Immigrants. *New York Times,* January 8.
Esbenshade, Jill. 2000. The "Crisis" over Day Labor: The Politics of Visibility and Public Space. *WorkingUSA* 3 (6): 27–70.

Farmer, Paul. 2002. On Suffering and Structural Violence: A View from Below. In *The Anthropology of Politics,* edited by J. Vincent, 424–437. Malden, MA: Blackwell.

Federal Register. 2006. Documents Required for Travelers Departing from or Arriving in the United States at Air Ports-of-Entry from within the Western Hemisphere; Final Rule. 71 Fed. Reg. 68,412 (November 24) (codified at 8 C.F.R. pts. 212, 235; 22 C.F.R. pts. 41, 53).

Ferguson, Adam. 2003 [1767]. *An Essay on the History of Civil Society.* New York: Cambridge University Press.

Ferguson, James. 1999. *Expectations of Modernity: Myths and Meanings of Urban Life on the Zambian Copperbelt.* Berkeley: University of California Press.

Flores, William Vincent. 1997. Citizens vs. Citizenry: Undocumented Immigrants and Latino Cultural Citizenship. In *Latino Cultural Citizenship: Claiming Identity, Space, and Rights,* edited by William Vincent Flores and Rina Benmayor, 255–277. Boston: Beacon Press.

Flores, William Vincent, and Rina Benmayor. 1997. *Latino Cultural Citizenship: Claiming Identity, Space, and Rights.* Boston: Beacon Press.

Fog Olwig, Karen. 2007. *Caribbean Journeys: An Ethnography of Migration and Home in Three Family Networks.* Durham, NC: Duke University Press

García Bedolla, Lisa. 2005. *Fluid Borders : Latino Power, Identity, and Politics in Los Angeles.* Berkeley: University of California Press.

Gazcón, Gilberto. 1980. *Perro callejero.* Filmed in Mexico.

Gill, Tom. 2001. *Men of Uncertainty: The Social Organization of Day Laborers in Contemporary Japan.* Albany: State University of New York Press

Glick-Schiller, Nina, Linda Basch, and Cristina Szanton Blanc. 1995. From Immigrant to Transmigrant: Theorizing Transnational Migration. *Anthropological Quarterly* 68 (1): 48–63.

Goldstein, Donna M. 2003. *Laughter Out of Place: Race, Class, Violence, and Sexuality in a Rio Shantytown.* Berkeley: University of California Press.

Gomberg-Muñoz, Ruth. 2011. *Labor and Legality: An Ethnography of a Mexican Immigrant Network.* Issues of Globalization. New York: Oxford University Press.

González-López, Gloria. 2005. *Erotic Journeys: Mexican Immigrants and Their Sex Lives.* Berkeley: University of California Press.

Gordillo, Gastón. 2006. The Crucible of Citizenship: ID-Paper Fetishism and the Argentinean Chaco. *American Ethnologist* 33 (2): 162–176.

Grandin, Greg. 2000. *The Blood of Guatemala: A History of Race and Nation.* Durham, NC: Duke University Press.

Granovetter, Mark S. 1973. The Strength of Weak Ties. *American Journal of Sociology* 78 (6): 1360–1380.

Guarnizo, Luis Eduardo, and Luz Marina Díaz. 1999. Transnational Migration: A View from Colombia. *Ethnic and Racial Studies* 22:397–421.

Gutmann, Matthew C. 2006. *The Meanings of Macho: Being a Man in Mexico City.* Berkeley: University of California Press.

———. 2007. *Fixing Men: Sex, Birth Control, and AIDS in Mexico.* Berkeley: University of California Press.

Hannerz, Ulf. 2007. Cosmopolitanism. In *A Companion to the Anthropology of Politics,* edited by D. Nugent and J. Vincent, 69–85. Malden, MA: Blackwell.

Harrison, Faye. V. 1995. The Persistent Power of "Race" in the Cultural and Political Economy of Racism. *Annual Review of Anthropology* 24 (1): 47–74.

Heyman, Josiah McC. 1990. The Emergence of the Waged Life Course on the United States–Mexico Border. *American Ethnologist* 17(2): 348–359.

Hoefer, Michael, Nancy Rytina, and Christopher Campbell. 2006. *Estimates of the Unauthorized Immigrant Population Residing in the United States: January 2005.* Population Estimates. Washington, DC: US Department of Homeland Security, Office of Immigration Statistics.

Holston, James. 2008. *Insurgent Citizenship: Disjunctions of Democracy and Modernity in Brazil.* Princeton, NJ: Princeton University Press.

Holston, James, and Arjun Appadurai. 1999. Introduction: Cities and Citizenship. In *Cities and Citizenship,* edited by James Holston. Durham, NC: Duke University Press.

Hondagneu-Sotelo, Pierrette. 1994. *Gendered Transitions: Mexican Experiences of Immigration.* Berkeley: University of California, Berkeley.

Hurtado, Jaqueline, and Catherine E. Shoichet. 2013. New California Law Gives Undocumented Immigrants Driver's Licenses. *CNN.com,* October 4. http://edition.cnn.com/2013/10/03/us/california-undocumented-immigrant-drivers-licenses.

Immigrants' Rights Clinic of Stanford Law School. 2012. *Getting a U-Visa: Immigration Help for Victims of Crime.* Produced on behalf of the Centro Legal de la Raza, Oakland. www.law.stanford.edu/organizations/clinics/immigrants-rights-clinic/pro-se-u-visa-manual.

Inda, Jonathan Xavier. 2006. *Targeting Immigrants: Government, Technology, and Ethics.* Oxford: Blackwell.

Kant, Immanuel. 1983. *"Perpetual Peace," and Other Essays on Politics, History, and Morals.* HPC Philosophical Classics Series. Indianapolis, IN: Hackett.

Kearney, Michael. 1995. The Local and the Global: The Anthropology of Globalization and Transnationalism. *Annual Review of Anthropology* 24 (1): 547–565.

Knight, Heather. 2008. Immigration Raids at 11 El Balazo Restaurants—63 Seized. *San Francisco Chronicle,* May 5.

Kuruvila, Matthai. 2009a. Council Votes to Proceed on Planning for ID cards. *San Francisco Chronicle,* June 4.

———. 2009b. ID for Undocumented Sought. *San Francisco Chronicle,* May 27.
Larson, Brooke. 1988. *Exploitation and Moral Economy in the Southern Andes: A Critical Reconsideration.* New York: Consortium of Columbia University Institute of Latin American and Iberian Studies and New York University Center for Latin American and Caribbean Studies.
Lacey, Marc. 2009. Migrants Going North Now Risk Kidnappings. *New York Times,* October 18.
Landolt, Patricia, Lilian Autler, and Sonia Baires. 1999. From Hermano Lejano to Hermano Mayor: The Dialectics of Salvadoran Transnationalism. *Ethnic and Racial Studies* 22 (2): 290–315.
Lee, Jennifer, and Frank D. Bean. 2004. America's Changing Color Lines: Immigration, Race/Ethnicity, and Multiracial Identification. *Annual Review of Sociology* 30:221–242.
Lévi-Strauss, Claude. 1963. *Structural Anthropology.* New York: Basic Books.
Levitt, Peggy. 2001. *The Transnational Villagers.* Berkeley: University of California Press.
Levitt, Peggy, and Nina Glick-Schiller. 2004. Conceptualizing Simultaneity: A Transnational Social Field Perspective on Society. *International Migration Review* 38 (3): 1002–1039.
Lewis, Oscar. 1961. *The Children of Sánchez: Autobiography of a Mexican Family.* New York: Random House.
———. 1966. *La Vida: A Puerto Rican Family in the Culture of Poverty—San Juan and New York.* New York: Random House.
Liebow, Elliot. 2003 [1967]. *Tally's Corner: A Study of Negro Streetcorner Men.* New ed. Legacies of Social Thought. Lanham, MD: Rowman and Littlefield.
Loescher, Gil. 1993. *Beyond Charity: International Cooperation and the Global Refugee Crisis.* New York: Oxford University Press.
Mahler, Sarah J. 1995. *American Dreaming: Immigrant Life on the Margins.* Princeton, NJ: Princeton University Press.
Malpica, Daniel Melero. 2002. Making a Living in the Streets of Los Angeles: An Ethnographic Study of Day Laborers. *Migraciones Internacionales* 1 (3): 124–148.
Manz, Beatriz. 2004. *Paradise in Ashes: A Guatemalan Journey of Courage, Terror, and Hope.* California Series in Public Anthropology 8. Berkeley: University of California Press.
Massey, Douglas S. 1986. The Settlement Process among Mexican Migrants to the United States. *American Sociological Review* 51:670–685.
———. 2007. Residential Segregation and Neighborhood Conditions in U.S. Metropolitan Areas. In *Rethinking the Color Line: Readings in Race and Ethnicity,* edited by C. A. Gallagher, 224–250. New York: McGraw-Hill.

Medina, Jennifer. 2013. California Gives Expanded Rights to Noncitizens. *New York Times,* September 21. www.nytimes.com/2013/09/21/us/california-leads-in-expanding-noncitizens-rights.html.

Mountz, Alison, Richard Wright, Ines Miyares, and Adrian J. Bailey. 2002. Lives in Limbo: Temporary Protected Status and Immigrant Identities. *Global Networks* 2 (4): 335–356.

National Commission on Terrorist Attacks upon the United States. 2004. *The 9/11 Commission Report: Final Report of the National Commission on Terrorist Attacks upon the United States.* Official government ed. Washington, DC: National Commission on Terrorist Attacks upon the United States

Nelson, Diane M. 2004. Anthropologist Discovers Legendary Two-Faced Indian! Margins, the State, and Duplicity in Postwar Guatemala. In *Anthropology in the Margins of the State,* edited by Veena Das and Deborah Poole, 117–140. Santa Fe, NM: School of American Research Press.

Ngai, Mae M. 2004. *Impossible Subjects: Illegal Aliens and the Making of Modern America, Politics and Society in Twentieth-Century America.* Princeton, NJ: Princeton University Press.

Nossiter, Adam. 2009. Day Laborers Are Easy Pray in New Orleans. *New York Times,* February 16.

O'Brien, Matt. 2008. ICE Actions Spread Fear in East Bay Schools. *Contra Costa Times,* May 6.

Ong, Aihwa. 1999. *Flexible Citizenship: The Cultural Logics of Transnationality.* Durham, NC: Duke University Press.

———. 2003. *Buddha Is Hiding: Refugees, Citizenship, the New America.* California Series in Public Anthropology. Berkeley: University of California Press.

———. 2006. *Neoliberalism as Exception: Mutations in Citizenship and Sovereignty.* Durham, NC: Duke University Press.

Ordóñez, J. Thomas. 2008. The State of Confusion: Reflections on Central American Asylum Seekers in the Bay Area. *Ethnography* 9 (1): 35–60.

———. 2012. "Boots for My Sancho": Structural Vulnerability among Latin American Day Labourers in Berkeley, California. *Culture, Health and Sexuality: An International Journal for Research, Intervention and Care* 14 (6): 691–703. www.tandfonline.com/doi/full/10.1080/13691058.2012.678016.

———. 2013. Documentos e indocumentados: Antropología urbana, inmigración y ciudadanía. *Revista de Antropología Social* 22:83–101

———. 2014. Some Sort of Help for the Poor: Blurred Perspectives on Asylum. *International Migration* (August 29). doi:10.1111/imig.12175.

Organista, Kurt C. 2007. Towards a Structural-Environmental Model of Risk for HIV and Problem Drinking in Latino Labor Migrants: The Case of Day Laborers. *Journal of Ethnic and Cultural Diversity in Social Welfare* 16 (1/2): 95–125.

Organista, Kurt C., and Ai Kubo. 2005. Pilot Survey of HIV Risk and Contextual Problems and Issues in Mexican/Latino Migrant Day Laborers. *Journal of Immigrant Health* 7 (4): 269–281.

Organista, Kurt C., Paula A. Worby, James Quesada, Sonya G. Arreola, Alex H. Kral, and Sahar Khoury. 2012. Sexual Health of Latino Migrant Day Labourers under Conditions of Structural Vulnerability. *Culture, Health and Sexuality: An International Journal for Research, Intervention and Care* 15 (1): 58–72.

Parker, Seymour, and Robert J. Kleiner. 1970. The Culture of Poverty: An Adjustive Dimension. *American Anthropologist* 72 (3): 516–527.

Pena, Manuel. 1991. Class, Gender, and Machismo: The "Treacherous-Woman" Folklore of Mexican Male Workers. *Gender and Society* 5 (1): 30–46.

Pinedo Turnovsky, Carolyn. 2006. A la Parada: The Social Practices of Men on a Street Corner. *Social Text 88* 24 (3): 55–72.

Poole, Deborah. 2004. Between Threat and Guarantee: Justice and Community in the Margins of the Peruvian State. In *Anthropology in the Margins of the State,* edited by Veena Das and Deborah Poole, 35–66 Santa Fe, NM: School of American Research Press.

Preston, Julia. 2014. Deportations by Courts Drop 43% in 5 Years. *New York Times,* April 17.

Prieur, Annick. 1998. *Mema's House, Mexico City: On Transvestites, Queens, and Machos.* Chicago: University of Chicago Press.

Purser, Gretchen. 2009. The Dignity of Job-Seeking men: Boundary Work among Immigrant Day Laborers. *Journal of Contemporary Ethnography* 38 (1): 117–139.

Quesada, James. 1999. From Central American Warriors to San Francisco Latino Day Laborers: Suffering and Exhaustion in a Transnational Context. *Transforming Anthropology* 8 (1/2): 162–185.

———. 2011. *No Soy Welferero:* Undocumented Latino Laborers in the Crosshairs of Legitimation Maneuvers. *Medical Anthropology* 30 (4): 386–408.

Quesada, James, Laurie Kain Hart, and Philippe Bourgois. 2011. Structural Vulnerability and Health: Latino Migrant Laborers in the United States. *Medical Anthropology* 30 (4): 339–362.

Ramphele, Mamphela. 1993. *A Bed Called Home: Life in the Migrant Labour Hostels of Cape Town.* Athens: Ohio University Press.

Rhodes, Scott D., Kenneth C. Hergenrather, Derek M. Griffith, Leland J. Yee, Carlos S. Zometa, Jaime Montaño, and Aaron T Vissman. 2009. Sexual and Alcohol Risk Behaviours of Immigrant Latino Men in South-Eastern USA. *Culture, Health and Sexuality: An International Journal for Research, Intervention and Care* 11 (1): 17–34.

Rosaldo, Renato. 1994. Race and Other Inequalities: The Borderlands in Arturo Islas's *Migrant Souls.* In *Race,* edited by S. Gregory and R. Sanjek, 213–225. New Brunswick, NJ: Rutgers University Press.

Rosaldo, Renato, and William Vincent Flores. 1997. Identity, Conflict, and Evolving Latino Communities: Cultural Citizenship in San Jose, California. In *Latino Cultural Citizenship: Claiming Identity, Space, and Rights*, edited by William Vincent Flores and Rina Benmayor, 57–96. Boston: Beacon Press.

Rushdie, Salman. 2006 [1981]. *Midnight's Children*. New York: Random House

Ryan, Mary P. 1992. Gender and Public Access: Women's Politics in Nineteenth-Century America. In *Habermas and the Public Sphere*, edited by C. J. Calhoun. Cambridge, MA: MIT Press.

Sacks, Karen Brodkin. 1994. How Did Jews Become White Folks? In *Race*, edited by S. Gregory and R. Sanjek, 78–102 New Brunswick, NJ: Rutgers University Press.

Salazar, Abel. 1978. *Picardía mexicana*. Filmed in Mexico.

Sassen, Saskia. 1988. *The Mobility of Labor and Capital: A study in international investment and labor flow*. Cambridge: Cambridge University Press.

———. 1999. Whose City Is It? In *Cities and Citizenship*, edited by James Holston, 177–194. Durham, NC: Duke University Press.

———. 2000. The Global City. *American Studies* 42 (2/3): 79–95.

———. 2006. *Territory, Authority, Rights: From Medieval to Global Assemblages*. Princeton, NJ: Princeton University Press.

Sayad, Abdelmalek. 2004. The Suffering of the Immigrant. Cambridge: Polity Press.

Scheper-Hughes, Nancy. 1992. *Death without Weeping: The Violence of Everyday Life in Brazil*. Berkeley: University of California Press.

———. 1996. Small Wars and Invisible Genocides. *Social Science and Medicine* 43 (5): 889–900.

Scheper-Hughes, Nancy, and Philippe Bourgois. 2004. Introduction: Making Sense of Violence. In *Violence in War and Peace*, edited by Nancy Scheper-Hughes and Philippe I. Bourgois. Malden, MA: Blackwell.

Schmitt, Carl. 1985. *Political Theology: Four Chapters on the Concept of Sovereignty*. Studies in Contemporary German Social Thought. Cambridge, MA: MIT Press.

Scott, James C. 1977. *The Moral Economy of the Peasant: Rebellion and Subsistence in Southeast Asia*. New Haven, CT: Yale University Press.

———. 1985. *Weapons of the Weak: Everyday Forms of Peasant Resistance*. New Haven, CT: Yale University Press.

Silverstein, Paul A. 2005. Immigration Racialization and the New Savage Slot: Race, Migration, and Immigration in the New Europe. *Annual Review of Anthropology* 34:363–384.

Smiley, Lauren. 2011. U-Visa: Illegal Immigrants Become Legal Residents via Crime Victimization. *SF Weekly*, March 16.

Smith, Matt. 2008. Epidemic of Violence against SF Day Laborers. *SF Weekly*, January 23.

Smith, Robert. 2005. *Mexican New York: Transnational Lives of New Immigrants.* Berkeley: University of California Press.

Stack, Carol B. 1974. *All Our Kin: Strategies for Survival in a Black Community.* 1st ed. New York: Harper and Row.

Steinbeck, John. 1992 [1939]. *The Grapes of Wrath.* New York: Penguin.

Stephen, Lynn. 2007. *Transborder Lives: Indigenous Oaxacans in Mexico, California, and Oregon.* Durham, NC: Duke University Press.

Suárez Navaz, Liliana. 1999. La construccion social del "Fetichismo de los Papeles": Ley e identidaden la frontera sur de Europa. *Actas del VIII Congreso de Antropología Social* (4): 89–102.

Taussig, Michael T. 1986. *Shamanism, Colonialism, and the Wild Man: A Study in Terror and Healing.* Chicago: University of Chicago Press.

Theodore, Nik, Abel Valenzuela Jr., and Edwin Meléndez. 2006. *La Esquina* (the Corner): Day Laborers on the Margins of New York's Formal Economy. *WorkingUSA* 9 (4): 407–423.

Thompson, Chris. 2008. Immigration Raids Spark Panic. *East Bay Express,* May 7.

Thompson, E. P. 1971. The Moral Economy of the English Crowd in the Eighteenth Century. *Past and Present* (50): 76–136.

Thompson, Ginger, and Sarah Cohen. 2014. More Deportations Follow Minor Crimes, Data Shows. *New York Times,* April 7.

Townsend, Camilla. 1997. Story without Words: Women and the Creation of a Mestizo People in Guayaquil, 1820–1835. *Latin American Perspectives* 24 (4): 50–68.

Trouillot, Michel-Rolph. 2003. *Global Transformations: Anthropology and the Modern World.* New York: Palgrave Macmillan.

Tucker, Jill, and Jaxon Van Derbeken. 2008. ICE Raids on Homes Panic Schools, Politicians. *San Francisco Chronicle,* May 7.

UCBIGS. 2009. Driver's License for Undocumented Aliens. University of California, Berkeley, Institute of Governmental Studies website. http://igs.berkeley.edu/library/research/quickhelp/policy/social/immigrant_driver_licenses.html#Topic1.

Valenzuela, Abel. 2001. Day Labourers as Entrepreneurs? *Journal of Ethnic and Migration Studies* 27 (2): 335–352.

———. 2003. Day Labor Work. *Annual Review of Sociology* 29:307–33.

Valenzuela, Abel, Nik Theodore, Edwin Meléndez, and Ana Luz Gonzalez. 2006. On the Corner: Day Labor in the United States. Los Angeles: Center for the Study of Urban Poverty, University of California, Los Angeles.

Vanackere, Martine. 1988. Conditions of Agricultural Day-Labourers in Mexico. *International Labour Review* 127 (1): 91–110.

Wacquant, Loïc J. D. 2002. From Slavery to Mass Incarceration: Rethinking the "Race Question" in the US. *New Left Review* 13:41–60.

Walter, Nicholas, Philippe I. Bourgois, and H. Margarita Loinaz. 2004. Masculinity and Undocumented Labor Migration: Injured Latino Day Laborers in San Francisco. *Social Science and Medicine* 59:1159–1168.
Walter, Nicholas, Philippe Bourgois, H. Margarita Loinaz, and Dean Shillinger. 2002. Social context of work injury among undocumented day laborers in San Francisco. *Journal of General Internal Medicine* 17:221–229.
Whyte, William Foote. 1993 [1943]. *Street Corner Society: The Social Structure of an Italian Slum*. 4th ed. Chicago: University of Chicago Press.
Willis, Paul E. 1981. *Learning to Labor: How Working Class Kids Get Working Class Jobs*. New York: Columbia University Press.
Worby, Paula A. 2002. Pride and Daily Survival: Latino Migrant Day Laborers and Occupational Health. MPH thesis, University of California, Berkeley.
———. 2007. Accounting for Context: Determinants of Mexican and Central American Im/migrant Day Laborer Well-Being and Alcohol Use. PhD dissertation, University of California, Berkeley.
Worby, Paula A., and Kurt C. Organista. 2002. Pride and Daily Survival: Latino Migrant Day Laborers and Occupational Health, Public Health, University of California, Berkeley, Berkeley.
———. 2007. Alcohol Use and Problem Drinking among Male Mexican and Central American Im/migrant Laborers: A Review of the Literature. *Hispanic Journal of Behavioral Sciences* 29 (4): 413–455.
Yngvesson, Barbara, and Susan Bibler Coutin. 2006. Backed by Papers: Undoing Persons, Histories, and Return. *American Ethnologist* 33 (2): 177–190.
Zlolniski, Christian. 2006. *Janitors, Street Vendors, and Activists: The Lives of Mexican Immigrants in Silicon Valley*. Berkeley: University of California Press.

Index

CALIFORNIA SERIES IN PUBLIC ANTHROPOLOGY

1. *Twice Dead: Organ Transplants and the Reinvention of Death*, by Margaret Lock
2. *Birthing the Nation: Strategies of Palestinian Women in Israel*, by Rhoda Ann Kanaaneh (with a foreword by Hanan Ashrawi)
3. *Annihilating Difference: The Anthropology of Genocide*, edited by Alexander Laban Hinton (with a foreword by Kenneth Roth)
4. *Pathologies of Power: Health, Human Rights, and the New War on the Poor*, by Paul Farmer (with a foreword by Amartya Sen)
5. *Buddha Is Hiding: Refugees, Citizenship, the New America*, by Aihwa Ong
6. *Chechnya: Life in a War-Torn Society*, by Valery Tishkov (with a foreword by Mikhail S. Gorbachev)
7. *Total Confinement: Madness and Reason in the Maximum Security Prison*, by Lorna A. Rhodes
8. *Paradise in Ashes: A Guatemalan Journey of Courage, Terror, and Hope*, by Beatriz Manz (with a foreword by Aryeh Neier)
9. *Laughter Out of Place: Race, Class, Violence, and Sexuality in a Rio Shantytown*, by Donna M. Goldstein
10. *Shadows of War: Violence, Power, and International Profiteering in the Twenty-First Century*, by Carolyn Nordstrom
11. *Why Did They Kill? Cambodia in the Shadow of Genocide*, by Alexander Laban Hinton (with a foreword by Robert Jay Lifton)
12. *Yanomami: The Fierce Controversy and What We Can Learn from It*, by Robert Borofsky
13. *Why America's Top Pundits Are Wrong: Anthropologists Talk Back*, edited by Catherine Besteman and Hugh Gusterson
14. *Prisoners of Freedom: Human Rights and the African Poor*, by Harri Englund
15. *When Bodies Remember: Experiences and Politics of AIDS in South Africa*, by Didier Fassin
16. *Global Outlaws: Crime, Money, and Power in the Contemporary World*, by Carolyn Nordstrom
17. *Archaeology as Political Action*, by Randall H. McGuire

18. *Counting the Dead: The Culture and Politics of Human Rights Activism in Colombia,* by Winifred Tate
19. *Transforming Cape Town,* by Catherine Besteman
20. *Unimagined Community: Sex, Networks, and AIDS in Uganda and South Africa,* by Robert J. Thornton
21. *Righteous Dopefiend,* by Philippe Bourgois and Jeff Schonberg
22. *Democratic Insecurities: Violence, Trauma, and Intervention in Haiti,* by Erica Caple James
23. *Partner to the Poor: A Paul Farmer Reader,* by Paul Farmer, edited by Haun Saussy (with a foreword by Tracy Kidder)
24. *I Did It to Save My Life: Love and Survival in Sierra Leone,* by Catherine E. Bolten
25. *My Name Is Jody Williams: A Vermont Girl's Winding Path to the Nobel Peace Prize,* by Jody Williams
26. *Reimagining Global Health: An Introduction,* by Paul Farmer, Jim Yong Kim, Arthur Kleinman, and Matthew Basilico
27. *Fresh Fruit, Broken Bodies: Migrant Farmworkers in the United States,* by Seth M. Holmes, PhD, MD
28. *Illegality, Inc.: Clandestine Migration and the Business of Bordering Europe,* by Ruben Andersson
29. *To Repair the World: Paul Farmer Speaks to the Next Generation,* by Paul Farmer
30. *Blind Spot: How Neoliberalism Infiltrated Global Health,* by Salmaan Keshavjee (with a foreword by Paul Farmer)
31. *Driving after Class: Anxious Times in an American Suburb,* by Rachel Heiman
32. *The Spectacular Favela: Violence in Modern Brazil,* by Erika Robb Larkins
33. *When I Wear My Alligator Boots: Narco-Culture in the U.S. Borderlands,* by Shaylih Muehlmann
34. *Jornalero: Being a Day Laborer in the USA,* by Juan Thomas Ordóñez